John Hume

By the same author

Neil Kinnock: The Path to Leadership

Britain's Dependent Territories: A Fistful
of Islands

Kinnock

Dependent Territories Yearbook

JOHN HUME

Peacemaker

George Drower

VICTOR GOLLANCZ

LONDON

First published in Great Britain 1995
by Victor Gollancz
An imprint of the Cassell Group
Wellington House, 125 Strand, London WC2R 0BB

A catalogue record for this book is
available from the British Library.

ISBN 0 575 06217 7

Photoset in Linotron Bembo by
Rowland Phototypesetting Ltd, Bury St Edmunds, Suffolk
Printed and bound in Great Britain by
Mackays of Chatham plc
Chatham, Kent.

Contents

Abbreviations

AOH	Ancient Order of Hibernians
DUP	Democratic Unionist Party
IDB	Industrial Development Board
INLA	Irish National Liberation Army
IRA	Irish Republican Army
NPF	National Political Front
NICRA	Northern Ireland Civil Rights Association
NILP	Northern Ireland Labour Party
PUP	Progressive Unionist Party
RUC	Royal Ulster Constabulary
SDLP	Social Democratic and Labour Party
UDA	Ulster Defence Association
UDR	Ulster Defence Regiment
UFF	Ulster Freedom Fighters
UVF	Ulster Volunteer Force
UUP	Ulster Unionist Party
UUUC	United Ulster Unionist Coalition
UWC	Ulster Workers' Council

Acknowledgements

Interviews with John Hume's family, friends, associates and colleagues have been of invaluable importance during the writing of this book. I am especially grateful for the time spared in Derry by John Hume, Pat Hume, Patsy Hume, John Bradley, Michael Canavan, James Doherty, Mark Durkan, Sally Ervine, Eamonn McCann, Denis Haughey and Declan O'Hare; in Belfast by Dr John Alderdice, Joe Austin, Professor Paul Bew, Gerry Cosgrove, Paddy Devlin, Archbishop Robin Eames, David Ervine, John Fee, Dr Joe Hendron, Charles Hill, Paddy O'Hanlon, Father Gerry Reynolds, the Reverend Martin Smyth and Barry White; in Dublin by Richard Burke, Dr Garret FitzGerald, Michael Hand, Michael O'Kennedy, Brian Lenihan and Michael Lillis; and in London by Ruth Angus, Sir Rhodes Boyson, Peter Brooke, Sir John Chilcot, Kevin McNamara, David Mead, Michael Mates, Lord Merlyn Rees, Richard Needham and Peter Temple-Morris.

Institutions which have been helpful have been the *Belfast Telegraph*, Conservative Research Department, Derry Credit Union, Dublin Ilac Centre, North West International, Susan Kennedy Photography, Pacemaker, Parnell Summer School, Press Association, the Publishing Corporation and US Embassy Resource Centre. Thanks are also due to the Derry Tourist Information Centre for arranging my field trip to Derry, Belfast and Dublin in February and March 1995.

G.D.

Foreword

by Albert Reynolds

John Hume has been a central figure in Northern Ireland politics
for over twenty years, central to democratic politics and the search
for peace in the fullest sense. He has been the political leader of
the Nationalist community, and the chief proponent of civilized
compromise.

He first came to prominence as one of the leaders of the civil
rights movement, which sought in the late 1960s to end decades
of discrimination against the Nationalist community in Northern
Ireland. He was one of the founders of the Social Democratic and
Labour Party, which replaced a sterile concentration on the ending
of partition with a reformist agenda. He subsequently became its
leader. He set his face from the beginning against the reversion
to guerilla warfare by the IRA, a tactic which belonged to a different time and situation. He refused to subscribe to simplistic ana-
lyses, which were used to justify a war of liberation, and instead
addressed himself to the problems of bridging a divided society.

Sticking forthrightly to the constitutional Nationalist path
required great courage and leadership from a politician, and indeed
a party, that were at one time reviled by both Republicans and
Loyalists. There were many times when he was under extraordinary physical pressure from both sides. Every effort at compromise, every new initiative that offered some prospect of progress
found John Hume as its source of inspiration or promoter. He
played an important role in the power-sharing executive set up at
the time of Sunningdale. In the late 1970s he helped to harness
the most influential Irish-American politicians, including Senator
Edward Kennedy, to efforts to find a peaceful solution. He
pioneered and supported the development of the Anglo-Irish

framework, first by Charles Haughey and Margaret Thatcher in 1980, and later in its evolution into the Anglo-Irish Agreement of 1985 between Garret FitzGerald and Mrs Thatcher. He promoted the establishment of the New Ireland Forum, out of which came an updated Nationalist position.

From the late 1980s he engaged in open dialogue with Sinn Fein, in an effort to persuade them that their resort to armed conflict was unnecessary and counterproductive. He exercised an unrivalled influence not just with the government in Dublin, but with the US administration in Washington, within the Socialist Group in the European Parliament, and even with some British Secretaries of State, such as Peter Brooke.

When I became Taoiseach in February 1992, he and I were close allies in our shared determination to stop the bloody violence of the past twenty-five years, which had cost well over 3,000 lives. He and I worked closely together to establish a formula for peace, which would be capable of bringing Republican violence to an end. We succeeded, and in parallel he also renewed his dialogue with the Sinn Fein leader Gerry Adams. What became known as 'Hume–Adams' gave tremendous heart to the entire Nationalist community in the North, and was one of the foundations of peace. With the British Prime Minister John Major, and with the help of Northern Protestant clergymen, I worked to broaden out the initiative so that it would address Unionist and Nationalist concerns at the same time and in an even-handed fashion. Our efforts culminated in the Downing Street Declaration, which attempted to address the root causes of violence and the stated reasons for it, and which indeed acted as a catalyst for peace.

In the months that followed the Declaration, John Hume and I were sometimes nearly alone in showing confidence in the prospect and possibility of peace. He endured much savagely unfair criticism for his efforts to draw Sinn Fein away from the futility of violence and into the democratic domain. John Hume's whole life's work was vindicated when the IRA ceasefire was announced on 31 August 1994. He had helped persuade Northern Republicans that the democratic path was the only way to make political progress. For the worthwhile goal of peace, he was prepared to make the greatest personal and political sacrifices.

The greatest moment of achievement in the peace process was the historic meeting of John Hume, Gerry Adams and myself in

Government Buildings on 6 September, one week after the cease-fire. At the conclusion of the meeting, as we faced the world's press on the steps of Government Buildings, we issued the following statement:

> We are at the beginning of a new era in which we are all totally and absolutely committed to democratic and peaceful methods of resolving our political problems. We reiterate that our objective is an equitable and lasting agreement that can command the allegiance of all. We see the Forum as a major instrument in that process. We reiterate that we cannot resolve this problem without the participation and agreement of the Unionist people. We call on everyone to use all their influence to bring this agreement about.

A month later the Loyalist ceasefire was announced, and on 29 October 1994 I inaugurated the Forum for Peace and Reconciliation in Dublin Castle, attended by the SDLP, Sinn Fein and the Alliance Party.

John Hume is the most respected constitutional leader in Northern Ireland, both at home and abroad, because of his courage, common sense and moderation. He represents his people not only at Westminster but in the European Parliament at Strasbourg and in the United States of America. His native city of Derry is flourishing, largely thanks to his success in winning investment from America and Europe. He has always been strongly committed to the European ideal, and the role of regions like Northern Ireland in it. He has always urged participation in political dialogue, and the necessity of addressing all the relationships involved. The Downing Street Declaration is about settling relationships between the people of Ireland and seeking agreement among them. An agreed Ireland is the objective of negotiations that should follow the publication of the Framework Document, so that we can consolidate a just and lasting peace.

It was my privilege as Taoiseach to work closely with John Hume during the decisive phase that led to the breakthrough in the peace process. Without him, it would not have been possible. Only a willingness to take very great political risks, and to put one's leadership on the line in the supreme cause of peace, as well as an ability to hold one's nerve in adversity, were capable of

bringing about peace. John Hume will always be remembered
with gratitude by the Irish people for his courage, his vision and
his single-minded determination.

Introduction

The occasion was a star-studded dinner party on 14 August 1994 at Avondale, the late Charles Stewart Parnell's elegant country mansion, at Rathdrum, just south of Dublin. To keep alive the philosophy of Parnell – the formidable and popular leader who in Victorian times had sought to achieve constitutional goals by democratic means – a summer school had been established in the house. Although the meal had been arranged to bring together political leaders and commentators to discuss the challenges of Irish society, it was not their presence that was causing a tremendous buzz of excitement in the dining room but that of John Hume – the statesman who was on the brink of persuading the IRA to agree to a permanent ceasefire.

Opening the proceedings with a voice quivering with emotion, the United States Ambassador, Jean Kennedy Smith, paid a fulsome tribute to John Hume. 'I am privileged to be here for many reasons, but one stands out in particular. John Hume is a true constitutional statesman. He has that quality of leadership which has kept him true to his principles despite all the obstacles. Like Parnell he made his influence felt in Westminster and beyond to the European Parliament and the United States Congress. His pursuit of dialogue with Sinn Fein required remarkable courage, particularly in the face of widespread criticism.'

Shyly, Hume shuffled to his feet, acknowledged the applause, thanked President Kennedy's sister, then launched into a speech entitled 'Parnell's Legacy for Modern Ireland'. It was a rambling oration, but everyone was too mesmerized by the event to mind the style. There they were in the house of the greatest Irish politician of the last century; in the presence of the greatest Irish politician this century. Some wondered if John Hume had not already become the greatest Irish politician ever.

'Successful children', it is claimed, 'have many parents.' Several factors brought about the permanent ceasefire in Northern Ireland a fortnight after that meal. But, more than anyone, it was John Hume who had brought an end to the 25-year-long 'Troubles' in which 3,171 people had been killed and more than 30,000 injured. Crucially, his persuading the Secretary of State for Northern Ireland, Peter Brooke, to declare that Britain no longer had any selfish strategic interest in remaining in Ireland had deprived the IRA of its *raison d'être* for continuing the terror campaign. Subsequently his talks with Gerry Adams finally had the effect of bringing Sinn Fein and the IRA in out of the cold.

Unlike any other Northern Ireland politician during the Troubles, Hume possessed a post-Nationalist vision. He had advocated a new form of society, insisting that it was 'people who have rights, not territories'. His vision derived from his understanding of history. To him it seemed that victories in Ireland had never achieved durable solutions. The fundamental problem, as he saw it, was that there had never been a structured all-Ireland discussion and *agreement* on the future of the North. Having devised a political accommodation for the North within the larger context of Ireland and Britain, he advocated a range of innovative constitutional measures: the three-strand approach, cross-border bodies and an all-Ireland referendum. Such measures became integral parts of the 1995 Framework Documents.

A pacifist who had never been tainted by support for any form of violence, for nearly thirty years Hume had been a central figure in the province's political life. For much of that time he had been leader of the SDLP, a party which both trusted him implicitly as a person and respected his intellect. An attentive listener with a sharp analytical brain, he had the ability to dispel his colleagues' doubts with logical summaries which would leave them muttering: 'Now, why didn't I think of that?' Kevin McNamara, Labour's former Northern Ireland spokesman, claims Hume's real forte is as a lobbyist: 'He's a good committee man.' Never having possessed speech-making skills, Hume had instead concentrated on exerting his influence behind the scenes. For years he had used his uncanny political instinct to talent-spot persons whom he perceived as potentially useful for his purpose.

The key to Hume's success in politics has been that – in addition to being totally trusted within the SDLP – he has been consistent. Political acquaintances allege that effectively he has been making the same old speech for the past thirty years. SDLP members roll their eyes with disbelief and give a wry smile when they hear him deliver what has come to be dubbed 'the single transferable speech'. At BBC Foyle in Derry, Eamonn McCann – who has known him many years – mimicked it for me with a perfect John Hume accent: 'It is not territory which is divided, it is people who are divided; we are a divided people. Division can only be ended by agreement. Agreement threatens nobody. We must work towards agreement. My party is committed to agreement.'

That consistency has made Hume vulnerable to the accusation that he has basically been a rather dull one-issue politician. McCann observes:

> It's almost as if since the late 1960s John has been sailing through history in a sealed capsule and has suddenly emerged at the other end. On all the great political debates of the day about the collapse of Eastern Europe, the changing nature of social democracy in Europe and so forth, John has had nothing to say. Where would John stand, for example, on the question of the 'social context of the United States' at the moment, or the move away from bigger government in favour of *laissez-faire* states' rights? For a man who spends so much time in Washington – where he knows so many people and is closely associated with the Democratic Party and Ted Kennedy – it's remarkable that John has never said a word about this. I think that ideology passes him by. He's not a man of ideas. He's a man of moderate action with great political acumen, judgement and luck.

Those would be fair comments if Hume were in politics for the purposes of entertainment. It is largely because Hume did not allow himself to be distracted away from the task of securing a durable peace in Northern Ireland that peace has been achieved.

In contrast to Belfast-based politicians, who have tended to look to England and Scotland for inspiration, Hume, as a Derryman, has always taken a more global view. He has looked to Europe and America and has devoted much of his time to gaining and developing contacts there. In Europe, he put his fluency as a French-speaker and his position as an MEP to good use in garnering considerable economic development funds for the province. Meanwhile, in the United States he succeeded in making himself a trusted authority on Northern Ireland. It is because of the power that he has over the SDLP, his 'too-clever-by-half' intellect and the influence that he has in Dublin, Whitehall and the wider world that the gentle persuader is still mistrusted and feared by many Unionists.

A selfless devotion to public service is one reason why Hume travels incessantly, criss-crossing between Brussels, Strasbourg, Boston, Washington, Dublin and London. Another is that he is claustrophobic – so much so that in a car he never wears a seat-belt. His colleagues despair at his crazy nomadic life, but they say with a shrug of the shoulders: 'That's just John.'

Like many political leaders, Hume is a very private person. For understandable security reasons he has had his five children – Thérèse, Àine, Maureen, Aidan and John – educated abroad and has deliberately always kept them out of the limelight. His spouse, Pat (the 'wee wife', he calls her), is his diary secretary and his only really close confidante. Like the former Labour leader, Neil Kinnock, he has few genuinely trusted political friends. He is ill at ease with Unionists. But even close members of his family claim they do not really know him well. He relaxes best with the family of the diplomat Seán Donlan; Dublin film-maker, Noel Pearson; Oxford poet, Seamus Heaney; and Derry playwright, Brian Friel.

Of the Catholic Hume, one former minister told me: 'He's got a lovely sense of humour. He can be very, very funny. He tells the most amazingly funny stories when he's got a glass in his hand. When he's not going on about Irish politics, he's a delight to be with.'

My meeting with John Hume occurred while I was working on this book in Dublin in February 1995. I had been in Belfast and Derry earlier in the week, interviewing a broad range of his colleagues and acquaintances, when I received a call from his wife, Pat. John would be flying in from Brussels to attend the Peace Forum and could meet me beforehand. He arrived at the restaurant unshaven and looking travel-worn. A giant of a man, with his heavy ponderous step, dark crumpled suit and huge spectacles he resembled something between a penguin and an owl. Good-naturedly he apologized for being late. While we chatted and made our way to a table, heads swivelled around and a number of people could be seen mouthing the awestruck words: 'Look, that's John Hume.' Total strangers rushed up to shake his hand. 'All the best,' 'God bless you, sir,' they told him. Self-deprecatingly, Hume said: 'Ah, there's an awful lot of that.' Thirstily gulping down a large cup of black coffee, he began the interview by talking about his father. Speaking so quietly that I had to raise the sound level of the tape-recorder, he spoke of how his own political views had been formed by his non-sectarian Derry childhood. Within an hour, as McCann had predicted, he had effectively recited the single transferable speech.

It was understandable why Hume's long-standing acquaintances are rather baffled by him and regard him as an enigma. In several respects he is the custodian of his own legend. At the start of the interview he had told me that: 'Unfortunately, I've never kept any records, because I've never thought of myself as important.' Yet within weeks he had got his office to send me three envelopes bulging full of his speeches and writings. Those who have worked with him have admired his political instinct and talent for knowing where political power rested. What they have approved of less when there were gatherings was his tendency to alight on the most powerful and influential pace-setters and opinion-formers and opportunely cultivate them. Countless commentators have been disarmed by his apparently flexible language and have mistaken him for an honest broker instead of the Nationalist politician he really is.

Another round of coffee having arrived, the famous Hume sweet tooth began crunching on some sugary biscuits. The effect was remarkable. He instantly became relaxed and started enthusing about the political and economic links he had forged with the United States. Having hitherto regarded him as a modest and self-effacing character, I was surprised to hear him boast of all the honorary degrees he had been offered (a further four gongs since the ceasefire). I wondered, so what? Subsequently, his brother Patsy assured me that they caused delight because John regarded them as being 'another notch in Derry's bow'.

I better understood John's surprisingly self-righteous attitude from the next reply he gave. He maintained that the comparisons being made between peace in Northern Ireland and events in South Africa were irrelevant. He said: 'Who did I spend two hours with today in Brussels? The President of the Basque Congress. Coming in for talks with me. He's very interested in what I am doing.' Evidently he was proud that it was principally he who had resolved one of Europe's most intractable conflicts. Champions don't just play the game; they change it. The price of achieving that peace has been that his house has been fire-bombed, his cars destroyed and his family threatened. He wanted the world to know that he had been right to take the chances that he had to secure the ceasefire.

— 1 —

Citizen John

People look skywards when it rains in Derry and declare: 'It's an awful day, isn't it, you'd think John Hume would do something about it.' A Citizen Kane figure in his home town, Derry's favourite son commands such respect that many have come to believe he can achieve the near-impossible. The man in whom such remarkable faith is placed has risen from humble origins. John Hume's brother and sisters know surprising little of their family tree; however, they believe their ancestors may have come from the Strathclyde region of Scotland. Their grandfather was originally a Presbyterian who in the mid-nineteenth century had arrived in County Donegal in search of work as a stonemason. For a time he fished in Lough Swilly, but eventually he found permanent employment on the narrow-gauge Lough Swilly Railway. On marrying a Catholic girl he let his Protestantism lapse, but passed on to his successors the Scottish trait of purposefulness.

Born in 1890, Sam Hume was the youngest and reputedly the brightest in his family. At the age of ten he left school and Ireland and went to Glasgow to work as a riveter in the Greenock shipyards. In 1914 he joined the Royal Irish Rifles and served with them in France. When the war ended he joined up with the Irish Free State Army. The reasons for that surprising change of allegiance have never been explained. For most of the interwar years he was unemployed. Self-educated, he adored books and was exceptionally well read. His favourite hobby was conversation, and he would often be found on a street corner with other unemployed Derry men putting the world to rights. Yet although the conversation was certainly rich, their lives were being wasted.

Then a spell of work as a riveter repairing ships in a Derry yard provided him with the financial support he needed. Aged forty-six he married Annie Doherty, fourteen years his junior. Within a year – on 18 January 1937 – John Hume, their first child, was born in Sam's parents' home in a Derry slum: 20 Lower Nassau Street. In 1938 they moved to 10 Glenbrook Terrace, a small two-bedroomed house they rented from the Derry Corporation, in the Rosemount area on the edge of the city, less than half a mile north of the Bogside.

During the Second World War, Sam was at last given a job to do commensurate with his considerable intelligence. As a clerical officer at the Food Office (Derry branch of the Ministry of Food), he was put in charge of issuing ration books. Thus every ration book issued in Derry was marked with his distinctive copperplate handwriting. The war years provided him with a much-needed opportunity to boost his income, and it was then that Sam and Annie produced most of their children: Annie was born in 1938, and she was quickly followed by Harry, in 1939; Patsy and Sally in 1941; Agnes in 1942; and Jim in 1945. When hostilities ended, Sam hoped to continue his clerical duties at the Food Office; but, aged fifty-five – and a Catholic – he was unsuccessful. After this dismissal he would never work again.

Now permanently unemployed, Sam selflessly put his talent for book-keeping and letter-writing to good use by helping illiterate people prepare job applications and fill in official forms. Effectively he ran a personal advice centre for most of the town. In addition to that unpaid social work, he would also help local shopkeepers – be they Catholics or Protestants – with their book-keeping, usually for little reward. Seeing his father doing those public-spirited duties had a profound effect on young John, who later told me:

> My earliest memories of life were of my father writing letters
> for local people who had come to him for help. There was no
> age at which I was not aware of people's social and economic
> problems. In a sense that was natural to me.

Sam's politics were Labourite, decidedly non-sectarian and predominantly motivated by an impulse to help others. He was a man who practised Christianity in a very down-to-earth way. Patsy Hume maintains that in today's world Sam Hume would almost certainly have been a social worker.

Like her husband, Annie Hume was a kindly community-minded soul. If ever a neighbour was in trouble she would always be the first on the spot to voice her concern and offer a helping hand. She had never received a formal education, and the only thing she was able to write was her name. Even so, her eldest son claims she would utter the wisest sayings. 'John', she would tell him, 'always remember the bottle is half full, not half empty.' And, 'If you're reared in your bare feet, you'll never get pneumonia in the snow' – in other words it's what you get used to.[1]

One of the largest firms in Derry at that time was the Rosemount shirt factory. Annie was employed by them as an outworker. She would be at home all day with the family, then – having collected huge bundles of shirts from the factory – while all the family was in bed she would set to work as a patent-turner. Sitting up to the early hours of the morning she would earn a pitiful few shillings sewing collars and cuffs. Her hands became almost permanently covered in welts from using scissors. She would be paid for every twelve dozen shirts completed, which all had to pass an examiner's quality inspection. If the work was not up to standard they would be returned. Financial hardship was omnipresent in the Hume household. Each week the loan sharks' debt collectors would call at the door and Annie would find herself having to pay through the nose for their services.

John Hume entered Rosemount Primary School on 23 June 1941 at the age of four. In those days the practice was that pupils enrolled a short time before the summer holidays. In a sense that reflected the spirit of the times, since it gave new pupils a gentle introduction to the whole new world of school. He was met by the vice principal, Mary Ann Coyle – the school's only female teacher – who warmly welcomed him and helped divest him of his coat, which she hung on the rack outside her classroom at the end of the corridor. The popular Miss Coyle was a legend in her time and made an enormous contribution to the lives of so many in Derry who were fortunate enough to pass through her hands. In addition to being a very down-to-earth person, she taught with clarity and simplicity. Hume recalls that she made it her business to know just how intelligent her pupils were, also who they were, where they came from and who their parents were.[2] She recognized that in his early days at school a child could be influenced for ever in his attitude to education. Since education was the only way forward for the vast majority of children at Rosemount School there can be no underestimating the importance of her approach.

Miss Coyle taught John for his first three years at school and was consequently one of the major influences in shaping his attitudes to life and to the value of education. Even so, teaching conditions were primitive at Rosemount. The wood-panelled classrooms were sparsely furnished; there was no electricity, only gas – which was seldom used – and writing was still done on slates.

At school it was apparent that little John Hume was a quiet, mature, responsible and well-balanced lad who had natural powers of leadership. A rather serious and bookish child, he nevertheless mixed easily with his contemporaries and was a popular football captain. Like his friends he loved to read comics – *Beano*, *Dandy*, *Hotspur*, *Wizard*, *Rover* and *Adventure*. No one brought them all. They brought one and swopped it. Swopping was part of every-day life.

By now the war was in full progress. The threat of hostilities spreading to Ireland seemed very real and was greatly feared, especially after the Luftwaffe had bombed the Messines Park area of Derry in April 1941. Many children were evacuated to Donegal. But John, it seems, remained in Derry. At school he received lessons on safety and on the use of gas masks. When there were air-raid warnings he had the choice of going to shelters in Rose-mount Terrace, Lewis Street and at Brooke Park. It was hardly worth the journey as they were just small brick buildings with reinforced concrete roofs. Also to be endured was the daily issue of cod liver oil, provided in copious quantities by the Local Education Authority to improve child health.

Having had his first Holy Communion at the age of eight, John became an altar boy at the nearby St Eugene's Cathedral, a granite Perpendicular structure, with brass sidelights and impressive stained-glass windows. Here, most Sundays, he would serve Bishop Neil Farren. That year, too, he began an evening paper round to augment the family's meagre income. It brought in four shillings a week, but even the tips he earned he handed to his mother. Making deliveries in the streets of the Glen and Rose-mount districts of Derry enabled him to get to know many of the families there. The round also made him an avid reader of the *Derry Journal*. In those days children had no great awareness of the world beyond their own street or neighbourhood. Television did not exist and, indeed, like the vast majority of families in the Rosemount district, the Hume family did not even own a radio.

Sam Hume repeatedly emphasized the importance of education to his eldest son. Despite being handicapped by attending a school where the average size of class was between fifty and sixty pupils, the message evidently got home. The eleven-plus exam was the making of John Hume. Aged ten and a half, he sat it in 1947, the first year it was introduced in Northern Ireland, and he did sufficiently well to find himself in the top 25 per cent – high enough to be awarded a grammar school scholarship. Had he failed, or had he been born just a few weeks earlier, for the rest of his life he would almost certainly have been, like his father, unable to fulfil his intellectual potential. As it was, he became the only child in his family to pass the exam and receive a high level of education. The eleven-plus result was John's passport to St Columb's College, a Catholic middle-class establishment. Just outside the Derry city walls, it acted as something of a seminary, preparing its brightest pupils for the priesthood. The local authority paid John's tuition fees of seven pounds – a princely sum which Sam and Annie would never have been able to afford.

St Columb's was renowned for its stern discipline, but John rarely found himself in trouble. He was invariably top of his class, a position he maintained by diligently doing his homework late in the evenings on the wooden kitchen table when he had completed his paper round. Here the family worked together: John at his schoolbooks; Sam doing the voluntary clerical work; Annie earning a few shillings sewing shirt-collars. On the sports field John increased his reputation as an enthusiastic football player, and in the summertime played for the mainly Protestant Derry Cricket Club, applying his skill as a left-handed spin bowler. The experience of growing up in the Rosemount district and regularly mixing with Protestants moulded John's political outlook. He told me:

> When I was growing up I played every game. I played soccer, Gaelic football, I played cricket. In the cricket I obviously did a lot with the Protestants. At the end of the day anybody with any intelligence could see – and this has been my principal message throughout the twenty-five years that I have

been in politics – that it is the people of this island who are divided, not the territory. People can only be brought together by agreement and respect for diversity.

At that stage in his life he was more interested in religion than politics – an attitude that had been instilled in him by his father, who, John says, 'Was not involved in any way in politics. He regarded politics in Northern Ireland as too sectarian.' When aged only ten, John and his father had happened to find themselves caught up in a Nationalist meeting in a street. There were plenty of waving flags and speakers claiming Irish unity would be the solution to all their problems. Along with everybody else John was getting emotional. Suddenly his father, who was un-employed, put his hand on his shoulder and said: 'Don't get caught into that, son.' 'Why not, Da?' asked John. 'Because,' his father told him, 'you cannot eat a flag'. John learnt early to reject the idea that patriotism meant dying for Ireland, which was very closely allied to killing for Ireland.[3] Subsequently, John would often repeat that story to people he met. He told me: 'In those early days, politics was about flag-waving and my view was that politics was about more than that. But my basic attitude to the Irish unity approach was: "Well, how are you going to do it?" While you are waiting for it to happen – because you don't unite people in a week or a fortnight – politics should be about the everyday problems of the people: housing, jobs.'

John had the intellectual ability to climb out of the Bogside by opting for a career in law or teaching, but having grown up in a Catholic household he had a strong sense of spirituality and assumed his natural vocation was to become a priest. Indeed, at that time in Derry it was a tradition that the eldest son of a large family should go into the priesthood. When only seventeen he passed three GCE A-levels and then the Bishop's Examination. Having secured a university scholarship he prepared to cross the border to attend Maynooth College. As Maynooth was a recog-nized college of the National University of Ireland, John would be able to embark on a three-year undergraduate course in history with a view to doing a further four years of theological study.

The contrast between Derry and Maynooth could scarcely have been greater. Whereas the part of Derry from which Hume came from was oppressively crowded and working class, the college was something of a spacious country mansion. Even the trip there was an eye-opener on a world of wealth and privilege that John had never encountered. On the forty-minute bus ride from Dublin's O'Connell Street, Hume passed the Guinness Brewery and the grand houses at Phoenix Park and could see Trinity students sculling on the River Liffey.

Situated in the lush countryside some twenty miles west of Dublin, Maynooth was a small, attractive town, which had at its heart a bustling cattle market and a quaint assortment of nineteenth-century shops. The approach road to the college was a continuation of Maynooth's main street. Surrounded by rose gardens, playing fields and vistas where crows squawked in the treetops, the campus had a refreshingly healthy and purposeful atmosphere. Originally a manor house, the college had been extended by the architect Augustus Pugin, who had added an elegant granite quadrangle and a Gothic chapel.

For nearly two hundred years most of the priests serving the Irish Church had been students of Maynooth. Effectively, the college was one of Ireland's finest public schools. Of the hundred or so students in John's year, some sixty would eventually be ordained. Other contemporaries who dined with John in the lofty Pugin Hall eventually went on to become the best and brightest politicians and public servants of their generation. They included Michael O'Kennedy, who became Ireland's Foreign Minister, and Seán Donlan, who was to be Irish ambassador in Washington. Hume himself seemed destined for a high-flying career in the church. Although he was a working-class lad in an establishment traditionally peopled by the sons of affluent Catholic farmers and teachers, he fitted in well. He represented the college in a junior debating team and played football in the inter-class matches in the winter mud of High Field. Nevertheless, O'Kennedy indicates that something of a myth has developed about Hume's enthusiasm for sport: 'He was never a very active sportsman; he played a bit of soccer, but so did most the guys from Derry.'

The long days at Maynooth revolved around a strict regime of prayer and silent meditation, interspersed by lectures and dreary meal-breaks. The college's Russell Libary was home to one of the finest collections of manuscripts in Europe, but it provided little contact with the outside world. There was no television or even a regular supply of newspapers. Reputedly the only reliable source of information on current affairs was the Catholic periodical, the *Tablet*. However, the intellectually rigorous regime exemplified by that austerity was invariably tempered by a humane approach to life. Michael O'Kennedy recalls how the much-loved history tutor, Tomás Ó'Fiaich – who later became Cardinal Ó'Fiaich, Catholic Primate of Ireland – would come in, cadge a cigarette and talk to the students.

Like many other students, Hume was greatly stimulated by the intellectual climate at Maynooth. Ten years later he would confide to his business partner, Michael Canavan, that his experience in Maynooth had given him a tremendous grasp of philosophical reasoning, which taught him to reason on rational lines; it also had the effect of making him think for himself. Richard Burke, a European Commissioner for whom Hume worked as an assistant in the late 1970s, reckons it was Hume's decision to concentrate on studying humanities, rather than classics, that broadened his mind and improved the versatility of his thinking.

It was at Maynooth that Hume's aptitude for languages was extensively developed. He was the only student in his year studying French, so he was able to receive intensive tuition from the Alsace professor teaching the subject. Hume majored in French and history, taking logic and philosophy as subsidiary subjects. In exams at the end of his first year he came top in history. Ó'Fiaich reckoned Hume was the brightest student he had ever taught.

Within his first few terms at Maynooth Hume came to realize that a priestly life was unsuitable for him. That realization was partly brought on by a sense of obligation to provide his family with financial assistance. John never lost his sense of duty to them during the time he spent at Maynooth. Virtually every penny saved from the Bishop's Examination allowance and the Northern Ireland scholarship he was receiving was sent home. He also wondered if he was so committed to the church that he was willing to endure a lifetime of celibacy. Hume has always refused to discuss his reasons for deciding not to become a priest. When Sam knew what had been decided he took the surprising step of *encouraging* John to leave the seminary. John's sister, Sally, remembers Sam sagely telling his eldest son: 'It takes a big man to go into the priesthood, but a better one to admit he is not suitable.'

Illness marred his departure. Hospitalized with a stomach disorder, he was unable to sit his BA final examinations and therefore had to leave without a qualification. However, his time at Maynooth was far from wasted. It had given him an assured grasp of philosophical reasoning and taught him the skills of logical argument. Yoked to his growing interest in self-help was a formidable sense of self-belief.

— 2 —

Civil rights leader

Having left Maynooth as a 'spoiled priest', Hume was fortunate to find himself a temporary job teaching Irish history and French in the Christian Brothers' Technical School, Derry. When at last he did sit his BA finals he obtained an upper second class honours degree. Armed with that he straight away took up what could have been a permanent post at the newly opened St Colman's school in Strabane. For two years he taught youngsters who had flunked their eleven-plus. Because he was now again living in his parents' house in Glenbrook Terrace the job meant that every day he had to make the thirty-mile round trip to Strabane. Despite all the travelling, in the evenings he set about writing his National University of Ireland MA dissertation – supervised by post by Ó'Fiaich – on 'Social and Economic Aspects of the Growth of Derry, 1825–50'. The work was so authoritative that it was handed to writer Leon Uris to use as research data for the best-selling novel *Trinity* – which charts Ireland's history from the Famine to the Rising.

Leaving Maynooth had caused Hume to consider his future. He told me: 'When I came back I felt that I had a duty to give back to the people who weren't so lucky. My idea was that politics should be about self-help: we have heads and we have hands, and our heads and hands are as good as anybody else's. So let's stop complaining and use them.' The dissertation, and the unpaid community work with which he used to help his father, made him wonder if self-help schemes might be devised which could enable the peoples of the North of Ireland to improve their lot.

By this time, too, he had fallen in love with Patricia Hone, a blonde, level-headed Derry girl he had met at a dance. A bright lady with working-class roots, at the time she was studying in a

Belfast teacher-training college. Above all else Pat was attracted by John's sense of responsibility to his large family. After nine months of courtship they married in 1960. John was then twenty-three. Having started out together in the Waterside District of East Derry where Pat's parents lived, they moved to a bungalow in Beechwood Avenue on the edge of the Creggan district. Soon their five children began to arrive: Thérèse first, then Aine, Aidan, John and Maureen. Pat was more than just a wife; she became John Hume's closest political companion, and his political eyes and ears.

It has been assumed that the original idea for the Derry Credit Union came from Hume himself. In December 1984 he told the American journal *Commonweal*: 'The first self-help group that I started was inspired by my mother and her sisters. They had a system in Derry. I noticed that my mother was paying back so much a week, and if they put it all together every three weeks they would have a substantial amount of cash that they could be using for themselves. So I applied that principle to the community as a whole, and in 1960 we formed a credit department.' Then on 24 October 1993 he said in an interview with the *Sunday Business Post*: 'I got involved in the community, and one of the first things was founding the Credit Union movement when I was twenty-three. I got into that because of my family experience.'

In fact, according to the Derry Credit Union, the first Credit Union in Ireland was registered by Nora Herlihy in the South in 1958. Hearing of the scheme, Hume got together with a friend – Father Mulvey – and the innovative Bogsider Paddy Doherty and began to consider how it could be made to work in their town. Along with a local businessman, Michael Canavan, they recognized the need for a community banking system which would provide low-interest housing loans and encourage citizens to save. Having investigated the operation of such organizations in Germany and North America, in 1960, with a total capital of £7.50 (the sum of their joint savings), they gathered together seventy subscribers to establish the Derry Credit Union. From those humble beginnings, when Pat kept the new deposits in a till and John wrote out the receipts, the Derry Credit Union grew to an institution with 19,000 members in Derry, 425 branches throughout Ireland, and assets of billions of pounds. It could eventually claim to be the largest such cooperative in the world.

The Credit Union gave Hume his first brush with politics. The non-profitmaking organization catered primarily to the city's lowest paid, and by enabling such citizens to manage their financial affairs collectively, gave them self-confidence to tackle other problems together. It transformed the personal finances of thousands of people in Derry.[1] Although he received nothing but expenses for his efforts, when he was not teaching Hume was travelling far and wide throughout the province and Eire, speaking at meetings in praise of the virtues of the self-help organization. But it was always only Catholics who were interested. To the individually minded Protestants the Credit Union was a Catholic organization and therefore untrustworthy. They could not be persuaded to lend to it. For four years from 1964 Hume served as the all-Ireland president of Credit Union. Canavan recalls:

> John had strong connections with America because the Credit Union movement found the strongest expression in America and the Americans were very instrumental in helping the Credit Union in Ireland to become established. We knew American personnel. In fact John became world president of the Credit Union and he eventually went to America in that connection.
>
> Another one of the things that being in the Credit Union showed us was that Derry was very neglected in industrial development, particularly from government investment. So we decided to contact Irish-born directors of American, or English companies to see if we could interest them in coming to Northern Ireland. We were unsuccessful in that we could not get anybody to come.

Having obtained his Master's degree Hume returned to his alma mater, St Columb's, to teach French and History. But, realizing that his old school offered few prospects for the sort of promotion he needed to support a growing family, within a year he was itching to be on the move again. He applied for a job as Deputy Director of Education in the Londonderry Corporation Education Department. It was a bold, if a naïve move: traditionally the Unionist majority on the Education Committee meant there was no prospect of a Catholic obtaining a significant job with the local authority, as Sam Hume had found after the war. Even in the mid-1960s virtually nobody within the Guildhall was of Catholic origin. Of any job in any department of the Corporation – Health Authority, Road Authority, Electricity Authority, Parks, Libraries and Museums Authority – the most senior position then held by a Catholic was the School Meals Organizer. James Doherty recalls: 'John seemed to be easily the best qualified candidate and did an excellent interview, but even so the Education Committee voted against him.' Doherty and other Nationalist councillors turned the spurning of Hume into a *cause célèbre*, arguing that it was indicative of the institutionalized discrimination that the City Council was daily waging against Derry's Catholic majority.[2] The episode made Hume realize he could no longer hope that the local government system could be trusted to reform itself: to help bring about change he would have to get involved in politics. He later told me:

> We set up our own housing association. I was the first chairman of it. There was a local priest, Father Anthony Mulvey, who set it up and asked me to be the first chairman. In the first year we housed 100 families and the local council housed none. Then we set out to build seven hundred houses, but they wouldn't give us planning permission because it would upset the voting balance. The housing and living conditions of people at that time were awful. That's what led me into civil rights.

In 1963, hard on the heels of Viscount Brookeborough's replacement as Prime Minister of Northern Ireland by the Unionist Captain Terence O'Neill, a whole number of Westminster-funded development schemes began to be devised. To many in Derry the plans seemed to mean that rail and shipping services to Derry were being severed in favour of construction of a new town and motorways near Belfast. Of particular concern was the prospect of Derry being ignored as a site for Ulster's second university in preference for Coleraine – even though Derry was the province's second largest city. To many Catholics this seemed like a blatant attempt to bar Catholics from higher education. Even Derry Protestants were furious that the city was being sidelined. To harness the anger of both Protestant and Catholic communities Hume formed a 'University for Derry campaign' with himself as chairman. It had no real prospect of success, but for Hume it provided a rare opportunity to speak to a non-sectarian gathering.

A speech Hume made in a meeting held by the university campaign in the Derry Guildhall in early 1965 was the most electrifying he had yet delivered. Some say it effectively marked the beginning of his political career. He spoke of the need to unite the two communities for the good of the city in the longer term. Derry, he said, encompassed both traditions: the Protestant siege tradition and the native Irish tradition of St Columcille. To the Protestants it was the place where the battle had been fought; to the Catholics, the city where the battle was being fought.[3] This new approach to politics was perfectly in tune with the mood of the crowd and it won him a standing ovation. The speech established him as a leading public figure at the genesis of the Derry civil rights movement. In a speech at Queen's University, Belfast, he said that the Catholic community was witnessing the new plantation of Ulster.

Hume's skill for identifying and addressing the needs of working-class Catholics was demonstrated in an article he wrote for the *Irish Times* in May 1964. There he condemned the Nationalist Party for their ineffectual opposition in the Unionist-dominated Stormont and their failure to encourage the Catholic community to develop a sense of self-help. Such a dereliction of duty, he claimed, 'has led many Protestants to believe that the northern Catholic is politically irresponsible and therefore unfit to rule'.

Catholics of all shades of political thought are expected to band together under the unconstructive banner of Nationalism. This dangerous equation of Nationalism and Catholicism has amply contributed to the postponement of the emergence of normal politics in the area and has made the task of the Unionist ascendancy simpler. Disagreement with, or criticism of, the Nationalist approach inevitably brings down upon one's head a torrent of abuse. 'Castle Catholic', 'West Briton', are examples of the terms used.

A united Ireland, if it is to come, and if violence rightly is to be discounted, must come about by evolution, i.e. by the will of the Northern majority. It is clear that this is the only way in which a truly united Ireland, with the Northern Protestant integrated, can be achieved.

Those seminal thoughts were revolutionary. Practically for the first time ever a much-respected Catholic was calling for unity by *consent*. Hume was advocating a unity of *people* rather than of *territory*. It would take another thirty years for such views to become common currency.

Although friends of Hume at the time were urging him to go into politics, they have since come to realize that his not doing so enabled him to analyse the politics of Derry from a detached point of view. Canavan recalls:

> I remember very clearly, very early in 1963 and 1964, long before John went into politics, he wrote a series of articles at various times in which he made it clear that real unity in Ireland should embrace not just the land but the people and that the only unity worth working for was unity by consent. He underlined the principle of consent. He has never departed from that. He has always held that point of view. It's a remarkable and unshakable consistency.

The power of the Protestant ascendancy in the province was reinforced by electoral gerrymandering. The local government franchise in Northern Ireland included a property qualification and multiple votes for businessmen – limited companies were entitled to appoint up to one nominee for every £10 of the valuation of the premises, up to a maximum of six nominees.[4]

Catholic reluctance to practise birth control meant that the birth rate in Derry was one of the highest in western Europe. Despite the efforts of the Derry Credit Union, housing standards in the Catholic quarter of the city remained appalling. Often there were two or three families living in a single, two-up, two-down house: it was not unusual to find seventeen individuals living in one house with two bedrooms. Many of the houses were very old. Some Catholics had to live on the edge of the Bogside in complexes of houses which had been turned into flats with no proper sanitation or cooking facilities. Here there were instances of sixty or seventy people living in one building. The Creggan estate, which the government had had built in the 1950s, was overflowing. Since then insufficient public housing had been provided. Protestants on the city council, anxious to preserve their electoral majorities, ensured that no new Catholic residences were constructed outside of the Bogside. The problem was only slightly alleviated by the building of high-rise blocks of dreary council apartments, such as the Rossville flats in the overcrowded Bogside.

In response to the alleged discrimination in jobs and housing being practised by local government in rural Northern Ireland, a Dungannon doctor, Con McCluskey, and his wife began gathering evidence of such malpractice. In 1963 they effectively founded the civil rights movement in Northern Ireland by forming the Campaign for Social Justice. Their pamphleteering prompted Labour backbenchers at Westminster – who were already involved with the University for Derry Campaign – to form the Campaign for Democracy in Ulster. Willing at last to appear on a public platform in Britain, Hume readily accepted their invitation to speak to an audience of Londoners at Fulham Town Hall in July 1965. Meanwhile, the organizers of the Campaign for Social Justice had ventured into party politics by launching the National Political Front and then the National Democratic Party. The National Political Front aimed to displace the ineffectual Nationalist Party, which was perpetually shooting itself in the foot by demanding a united Ireland. When the 1965 general election for Stormont was fought, the NPF ought to have been the grouping to displace the Nationalist Party, but its challenge never materialized. The Nationalist Party emerged from the election with thirteen seats. Hume had been encouraged by Michael Canavan and other friends in the Credit Union to stand as an NPF candidate. But he was unwilling to commit himself to the NPF, which he believed to lack the wherewithall to overtake the Nationalist Party.

Employment as a teacher at St Columb's on the public-sector payroll would, he knew, be legally incompatible with being an elected representative. If he did get elected he would have to resign from the chalkface. It was therefore clearly prudent for him to find a means of supporting his family in the private sector. His self-help ethos made him something of a natural entrepreneur. Nevertheless, there were few who shared his vision; a scheme that he devised to bottle local spring-water was considered to be so daft it never got going. Ruefully he told me: 'I remember going around businessmen in Derry at the time saying I've got a great idea for an industry. They said: "What's that?" I said "Put water into bottles." They told me: "But there's enough water coming out of the taps." That was in the sixties. Look at the water industry now.' Having tried his hand at training for the priesthood and then teaching, in 1965, at the age of twenty-eight, Hume embarked on his third career: resigning from St Columb's, he became managing director of Atlantic Harvest Ltd. With Michael Canavan he had identified a market for processed fish from the River Foyle, one of the biggest salmon fisheries in western Europe. They discovered that the fish were caught, sent to Derry, then boxed and sent off to London, without being processed. If they could be processed in Derry, particularly as smoked salmon, this would give a good mark-up value with the prospect of an export business. Hume recalls: 'Michael Canavan says to me: "Well, if you can smoke a salmon I can set you up." So I gave up teaching and started the smoked salmon plant. It was all part of the philosophy of self-help from your own resources.' They established Atlantic Harvest in an old bakery in Corporation Street, near the old bridge. It was a modest operation, employing only five people, but it was highly effective. Fresh fish were brought from the local fishermen, then processed, filleted and smoked, and sold as an expensive delicacy. Canavan remembers that Hume was especially pleased that he was able to help the local economy: 'Although the numbers we employed were quite small – very small – the fact that we were buying fish from the fishermen meant that the benefits were spread across quite a large section of the community.'

Hume's energy and ability to deal with people – a skill which he had developed in the Credit Union – stood him in fine stead in the commercial world. He had a flair for trading. Claiming his produce was 'the best smoked salmon in Europe', he even managed to supply it to a group of supermarkets in London. Their big break came quite unexpectedly. Canavan told me:

By a strange chance the local MP at the time, Robin Chichester-Clark, had been at a dinner in Southampton. He was a Unionist MP for Westminster, but somebody had asked him about Irish smoked salmon and he knew that the Atlantic Harvest had been set up in Derry because he was the Derry representative. So he got in touch with us and told us that there was an opportunity. John went to Southampton to talk to the Cunard company who were running the cruises and got a contract for supplying smoked salmon to their ships.

The produce supplied by Hume to Cunard at this time could very well have been served at the tables of the wealthy by a steward who was later to become deputy leader of the Labour Party – John Prescott.

Atlantic Harvest became an early example of the benefits of a workable cross-border agreement between North and South. Through Atlantic Fisheries, Hume had first-hand dealings with the Foyle Fisheries Commission – a rare cross-border institution which had been established in 1952 to conserve and protect fish stocks. Sceptics might claim that while Hume was busying himself with the fishing industry an opportunity to influence political life in Northern Ireland peacefully was slipping away. In fact, Hume had already decided that he would eventually go into politics and had started Atlantic Harvest to help equip himself to make the transition. According to Canavan, it was fear of Sam's displeasure that was preventing John from stepping into politics: 'He was greatly influenced by his father. At that time politics was just two-dimensional – you were either a Unionist or an anti-Unionist and John's father would have been basically a Labour Party supporter. He said that "Waving the flag didn't put any food on the table" – that kind of thing. John therefore was reluctant to go down that road while his father was still alive.'

Nevertheless, although he was not actively involved in politics at that time, Hume's philosophy was taking shape. Some thirty years later in Dublin he explained to me:

> The creation of Northern Ireland was extremely undemocratic. People tend to forget that in 1912 the whole of Ireland was part of the United Kingdom. The UK Parliament voted for Home Rule for Ireland and the Unionists took up arms against it. As the leader of the Tories of the day Bonar Law went to Belfast and addressed a large Unionist gathering. His famous quote, which I have used a lot, is: 'There are things stronger than parliamentary majorities'. Then the sovereignty of the British Parliament was overthrown. Now if you look at the logic of Unionism, what is a real Unionist? Someone loyal to the Crown and Parliament? The fundamental basis of order in British society is the sovereignty of Parliament – and that was overthrown then. It resulted in the 1916 rising in the South, leading to partition and a line being

drawn on a map in a very careful way so that Northern Ireland was created where there was a two to one [Unionist] majority. Of course that meant they won. Then they wanted to make sure that they kept their majority. So they held all power in their own hands and discriminated. Sixty years of that led to the dreadful situation we had in the 1960s and 1970s and my own city was the worst example of that.

My fundamental approach to the problem was that there are two mind-sets, and those mind-sets exist in most areas where there is conflict in the world. There is the Unionist mind-set, which is in a sense the Afrikaner mind-set – the way to protect yourself is to hold all power in your own hands and leave everybody else out. That leads to widespread discrimination and in the end to conflict. My challenge to that mind-set is: 'Look, because of your geography and your numbers the problem cannot be solved without you, so come to the table and make an agreement that will protect your heritage forever.' Then there is the Nationalist mind-set, which is a territorial mind-set – 'This is our land, and you Unionists are a minority and you cannot stop us uniting.' My challenge to that mind-set throughout the twenty-five years has been that it's people who have rights, not territory. When people are divided they can only be brought together by agreement.

Soon after the Northern Ireland state was created Derry had, for electoral purposes, been effectively divided in two. The bulk of the urban population, crowded into the Catholic ghetto on the west side of Derry, were held to be in the Foyle constituency, while the City constituency had its boundaries extended eight miles east into the countryside of County Derry to create a Protestant majority. A revision of the local government electoral system in 1966 provided for twenty-four elected representatives in Derry from three sectors – Waterside Ward, North Ward and South Ward (which included the Bogside). By that division, the 20,102 anti-Unionist voters of Derry that year returned eight representatives to the City Council, and the 10,274 Unionist voters returned sixteen representatives.

In the face of continued discrimination against Catholics by local government, protest groups were mushrooming. The most prominent was the Northern Ireland Civil Rights Association (NICRA), founded in February 1967 with five declared objectives:

> to define the basic rights of all citizens;
> to protect the rights of the individual;
> to highlight all possible abuses of power;
> to demand guarantees for freedom of speech, assembly and associations;
> to inform the public of their lawful rights.

Other groups were coming under the control of Republican left-wingers. Such organizations gradually became a magnet for disaffected students who were inspired by the activities of student demonstrators in Germany and France. Hume steered well clear of them. Rising to prominence as an agitator was Eamonn McCann, a young tub-thumping left-winger who had been associated with the Irish Workers Group and frequently clashed with Hume in the Columcille Debating Society. He and a group of fellow-travellers had taken over control of the Derry branch of the Northern Ireland Labour Party, then formed the militant Derry Housing Action Committee, which throughout 1968 had used intimidation tactics to disrupt Corporation meetings at the Guildhall. The culmination of that agitation was intended to be a march on Saturday, 5 October through the city walls to the centre of Derry. Hearing that the Protestant Apprentice Boys were threatening to demonstrate simultaneously, the Minister of Home Affairs, William Craig, announced a ban on all marches in Derry – a step which had the fatal effect of gaining wider Nationalist support for the march.

On the appointed day several hundred demonstrators – many of them ordinary young working people – gathered near the Waterside Railway Station by the river in east Derry. As they made their way along the narrow Duke Street heading towards the Craigavon Bridge, they were halted by a cordon of uniformed police, who, muttering 'Fenian bastards', took two steps forward and struck down the leaders with batons. One of the most memorable pictures ever screened of the Troubles was of a Catholic businessman raising his arms, pleading with the constables 'in God's name', only to be brutally clouted in the stomach. Also among the injured was the MP for West Belfast, Gerry Fitt, who had brought three Labour MPs over from the UK to witness the demonstration. The marchers paused for speeches but were then attacked by baton-charging officers of the RUC. As the crowd dispersed on to the Craigavon Bridge the police attacked Saturday afternoon shoppers. Hume had been on the march, but had not been one of its leaders. When the police attacked he had been fortunate to discover an escape route down some steps. To many Nationalists it seemed as though the protestors had been deliberately set upon by the RUC in a Protestant area. That night fighting broke out at the Diamond in the centre of the walled city and attempts were made to erect barricades in the Bogside.

The prospect of further demonstrations being organized brought forward a wider – and more moderate – circle of civil rights volunteers who wanted to be involved with planning the protests. Outnumbering McCann's militants, they effectively took control of the protest group and, at Michael Canavan's insistence, renamed it the Derry Citizens' Action Committee. Canavan became its secretary; James Doherty, its treasurer; and Hume, its vice-chairman. Hume reckoned that if an efficient stewarding system could be devised the Citizens' Action Committee might become the nucleus of an effective protest movement in the style of that led by the recently assassinated Martin Luther King. McCann contemptuously denounced the newcomers as middle-class and middle-of-the-road. With the new management in control, on 19 October the Committee organized a mass sit-down in the city centre. Mercifully the 5,000-strong peaceful demonstration passed off without incident. By then the malcontents' demands had crystallized. Along with their call for 'one man, one vote', they insisted on the disbandment of the Protestant Ulster Special Constabulary (the B Specials); a repeal of the Special Powers Act; an end to discrimination in housing and jobs; and a universal franchise in the local elections.[5]

A more challenging confrontation was planned for 16 November, when the steps of the 5 October march were to be retraced. Hume's hope that such public demonstrations might stimulate a mass movement for reform received a boost just before the event when the Protestant Bishop of Derry, Charles Tyndall, offered to open the ancient city's St Columb's Cathedral for an ecumenical vigil. For a while it seemed there might be grounds for optimism. On 16 November, effective stewarding allowed the 17,000 marchers to avoid confrontation with the police. The stewards themselves halted the march at the police barriers in Carlisle Square; the crowd then made their way individually through the city gates and reconvened in the Diamond.

Within a week Stormont's resistance to calls for civil rights had crumbled. Captain Terence O'Neill unveiled a five-point programme of reforms which in essence acceded to the campaigners' demands. An ombudsman was to be appointed; the company vote in by-elections was to be abolished; the Special Powers Act was to be repealed. Most significantly, the Derry Corporation was to be replaced by a development commission. Hume joined in the celebrations, but he knew as he did so that pressure was growing for a Protestant backlash.

Spearheading that Protestant agitation was a minister in the Free Presbyterian church, the Reverend Ian Paisley, who perceived the gains made by the civil rights protestors to be a threat to Protestant hegemony. Counter-demonstrations were organized. To no practical purpose the militant People's Democracy sought a showdown with the Paisleyites, and to that end organized a march from Belfast to Derry. On 4 January 1969, as the 800 or so marchers reached Burntollet Bridge, on the outskirts of Derry, Loyalist extremists struck, hurling stones and other missiles down on the young Catholics.

I was told by Eamonn McCann:

About six miles out on the road to Belfast, local people organized by Major Ronald Bunting – who at the time was Ian Paisley's second in command, so to speak – attacked the march. There certainly was a very large contingent of RUC people that they had travelling in Land Rovers and wearing riot gear. What was significant about what happened was that as soon as the march was attacked, they simply took off and left the march at the mercy of the attackers. A number of them joined in the attack before scarpering off. It was the behaviour of the RUC rather than the attack on the march that was significant. It was the fact the RUC did this which caused such bitterness in Derry and catapulted even moderate Nationalists into refusing to accept the legitimacy of the RUC as a police force.

Film of the police during the ambush established in the minds of many Catholics – especially in the South – that the RUC were not impartial, but were on the side of the Unionists. The Burntollet incident was the first full-scale direct clash between Catholic and Protestant citizens. That weekend the Bogsiders vented their anger by rioting against the RUC. Barricades were erected on the main roads to the Bogside; although within a week Hume had arranged for them to be dismantled, already he could only watch as the violence spread. An NICRA march which he attended on 11 January in Newry degenerated into a riot.

At the age of seventy-seven, suffering from liver failure, Sam had died on 24 June 1967. Out of respect to his father, and in accordance with his mother's wish that he devote his spare-time energies to the Credit Union, John continued to decline invitations to enter politics. Then in 1968 he decided that the time had come to challenge the Neanderthal Nationalists head-on. Having resolved to put himself forward as an Independent candidate at the next Stormont general election, he turned down invitations to stand in Westminster by-elections for Armagh and then Mid-Ulster. When only just turned thirty-two, he stood as an Independent for the Foyle constituency, in the February 1969 Stormont election. He later said to me: 'When I fought my first election, my election manifesto spoke of the need to take housing out of the hands of local politicians who were abusing it for discriminatory purposes. They needed to set up a centralized housing authority. I also asked for a mandate to found a social democratic party.' That grouping, he had written, should be 'a non-sectarian political movement based on social democratic principles with open membership'.

At the count in Coleraine County Hall it was evident that Hume and his young turks were changing the old order in Nationalist politics. Paddy Gormley, a long-serving Nationalist MP, was ousted by an Independent candidate – Hume's colleague on the Citizens' Action Committee, Ivan Cooper. It was ironic that Cooper – who was a lapsed Unionist – should have defeated Gormley, who only three years earlier had been urging the Nationalist Party to base itself on social democratic principles.[6] The results that election night were not so much proof of the breakdown of sectarianism as evidence that many in the Catholic community had come to recognize that a new course of political action was required.

As bundles of ballot papers were amassed on the counting tables it became clear that Hume was set to win a historic victory. His main opponent, Eddie McAteer, the Nationalist Party leader who had represented Mid-Derry and Foyle for twenty-two years, was devastated as the comfortable 3,454 majority he had won in 1965 evaporated to be replaced by a commanding 3,653 majority for Hume – an unexpectedly large margin. Hume had also decisively outpaced the other challenger, Eammon McCann, who polled a mere 1,993 votes. The disconsolate McCann stood staring at the meagre pile of ballot papers stacked on his table. McCann's supporters – many of whom were not eligible to vote – were deeply resentful that Hume had used the civil rights movement to springboard himself into Stormont over the head of their hero. Some of McCann's supporters angrily predicted there would be a sellout of the civil rights cause when Hume got to Stormont. Keen to refute that allegation, in his victory statement Hume vigorously pledged that the fight for civil rights would go on by democratic means. The day after he was elected he resigned from Atlantic Harvest and prepared to take his seat at Stormont.

— 3 —
Stormont

Electoral success was a pyrrhic victory for John Hume. The price of putting his head above the parapet rapidly proved to be sickeningly high. Even during the election campaign every window in his Atlantic Harvest factory had been shattered. Offensive hate-mail was soon dropping through his letter box – as much from Nationalists as from Unionists. Often it was obscene; sometimes it was more sinister, advising him and his family to get out of town. He feared more for his wife Pat and the children than he did for himself, but he was still resolved to adhere to his ideals. He told his friends: 'I would be cheating myself and my family if for safety's sake I forsook them. How could I face my children if I abandoned my convictions?'[1]

Fortunately for him, Pat was willing to throw herself heart and soul into the role of an MP's wife. It was in 1968, when the civil rights campaign really got going and her fourth child (John) had just been born, that she first considered giving up teaching. The four months' maternity leave she received placated her, but later, when Hume was elected to Stormont, she did give in her notice, and became his unpaid secretary, organizing his schedule and typing his letters. Within three months, however, she found she missed teaching too much. Repeatedly pressed to return as a part-timer and knowing there was a serious shortage of teachers in Derry, she felt unable to refuse. It meant on weekdays she still had to leave home after breakfast and return at four with lessons to prepare. While she was out at work a neighbour would be employed to guard the Humes' bungalow home in Beechwood Avenue.

The demands of schoolteaching and mothering did not prevent Pat from being quietly concerned about John's safety. Outwardly it showed only in the many cigarettes she used to smoke. She would go to bed around midnight and read a book till John returned. The nocturnal Hume would often be out till all hours, talking to journalists or spreading the gospel of peace in the Bogside. Even so, Pat never knew if he might be attacked by one of the many sick characters who used to threaten him on the telephone. She could never sleep until she knew he was safely home.[2]

Meanwhile, in those early months of 1969, Hume had taken his seat at Stormont. In his maiden speech on 5 March he called for action to tackle the basic problems which had prevented the emergence of a just society in the North of Ireland.

> We have had sentiment for quite a long time and no action. It was the vast amount of sentiment and the lack of action that created, or was partially responsible for the creation of, the impatience that has led to the activities of the last four months.

Predictably, the main subject of the speech was public housing. Calling for the scrapping of the practice of allocating rented accommodation according to religious denomination, Hume suggested the creation of a central housing authority.

> The only final way to remove injustice in housing is to take all housing problems completely out of the hands of local government and put them into the hands of a central housing authority working through local committees with tenant representation. This would not only remove it from the political arena and prevent people and homes from becoming political tools but would also ensure professional attention at every level of housing problems.

Although, of course, he had served no political apprenticeship by being elected to the Derry Council, at Stormont he certainly soon showed that he knew how to make an impact. A month after his election, with other opposition MPs he attempted to prevent the Unionists from bulldozing through the Public Order Bill. When they tried to silence him by closing the debate in which he was speaking, he took the astonishing step of organizing a sit-in protest. For that disruption – during which he sang 'We shall overcome' – he was suspended from Stormont for a week.

Before the Stormont elections, Hume had hoped that O'Neill's five-point plan of concessions would enable the Civil Rights Association to change tack to heal the wounds caused by the campaigns. But that optimism was soon dashed. The promised voting reforms and housing concessions brought no tangible benefit to the youths of the Bogside, many of whom were unemployed. Hume's fear was that hooligans would jeopardize the future of the newly won liberalism, which needed to be carefully conserved.

On Saturday 19 April the Civil Rights Association prepared to march from Burntollet to Derry to maintain the momentum for reform. Threatened with attacks from a Protestant mob they cancelled the demonstration, but CRA supporters waiting for them in the centre of Derry were not informed of this decision. In Guildhall Square they were attacked with truncheons by RUC officers, who, while chasing them to the Bogside, broke down the front door of an elderly Catholic man, Samuel Devenney, and caused him to have a heart attack. Hume was arrested but released without charge during the night.

Believing that the RUC were planning to invade the Bogside, the next day Hume organized an evacuation of the most vulnerable ghetto-dwellers to the Creggan estate, where the women and children were given shelter. He telephoned Robert Porter, the Minister of Home Affairs in Belfast, and warned him that the menfolk of the Bogside were planning to return in two hours and that if the police had not been removed by then he 'could not be responsible for the consequences'. There followed ninety minutes of tension before – with half an hour to the deadline – the police were instructed to withdraw from the Bogside to a point within the city walls. But a thousand-strong mob of Bogsiders, furious at having to leave their boarded and shuttered houses, marched towards the walled city.[3] At Butcher's Gate, where the demonstrators were scowling virtually eyeball-to-eyeball with the RUC, Hume scrambled on to a traffic bollard between the warring parties and dissuaded his followers from taking violent action. It was a momentous speech in which he persuaded them to disperse and trust him to obtain justice on their behalf.

Hume's reputation as a voice of moderation was subsequently bolstered in September by the publication of Lord Cameron's report into the disturbances in late 1968 and early 1969. Hume was the one politicians strongly praised by the Commission. The situation in Derry after the demonstration on 5 October 1968 had, the report claimed, been stabilized mainly by his activities; and his success in persuading the Bogside crowd not to riot against the police at Butcher's Gate on 20 April had been 'an astonishing achievement'. The Derry Citizens' Action Committee, of which he was chairman, had acted with moderation and restraint throughout, the report said, adding: 'For this, much – if not most – of the credit must go to Mr John Hume who from the beginning has taken the lead and shown himself both responsible and capable.' The report brought him to the attention of national newspapers in the UK. The *Daily Telegraph* diary prophetically noted: 'If the splintered opposition at Stormont came together in a formal alliance Mr Hume could well emerge as the leader.'[4]

Unfortunately, Hume's influence did not spread as far as Belfast. On the day of the Butcher's Gate incident the province's capital experienced the worse violence since the civil rights troubles began. Petrol bombs set alight nine post offices and a bus station, while explosives planted by Loyalists damaged a pipeline from Belfast's Silent Valley reservoir.

As spring turned to summer, Hume feared that the traditional Orange parades on 12 July and 12 August might provoke serious rioting. The 'Glorious Twelfth of July' Orange marches celebrating the Battle of the Boyne were larger than ever before, with more Union Jacks and more feeling than ever that year. They prompted disturbances in Derry and nearby Dungiven, but passed off reasonably quietly. On 12 August some 30,000 Orangemen were expected to march in celebration of the relief of Derry in 1689. In the past Catholic spectators had jeered amicably as the Loyalists, with their fife and drum bands, marched past. But in 1969 the event was likely to be a powder keg.[5]

Hume's attempts to get the parades called off were hampered by accusations of hypocrisy in the stance he was now adopting on public marches. Had he not only a few months previously been insisting that the NICRA had the right to demonstrate peacefully? Campaigning to get the parade banned, he contacted the Taoiseach, Jack Lynch, who was concerned, but insufficiently alarmed to take action. Before travelling to Whitehall to lobby the Home Office, Hume was out on the streets trying to soothe angry teenagers who had threatened to throw stones: 'Boys, what has violence ever achieved?' They told him: 'We would never have had the Republic without it.' In London, the Home Secretary, Jim Callaghan, was unable to see him so he met Callaghan's deputy, Lord Stonham. Claiming that the Ulster government had effectively lost control of the situation in the province and that responsibility now fell on the Home Office, Hume urged the minister to ensure the march was banned. He invited Stonham, or Callaghan, to visit Derry to assess the situation for themselves. Later he met Labour MPs and prompted more than a hundred of them to table a Commons motion calling for the 'immediate presence' of Home Office observers in Northern Ireland and the withdrawal of the B Specials from Derry.

Back in Derry, Hume's influence had waned. A new group, the Derry Citizens' Defence Association, had been formed to organize defences against Protestant mobs which – it was feared – might try to invade the Bogside in the wake of the police incursions. Just as Hume had dreaded, the 12 August parade was regarded by many Catholics as being highly intimidatory. Hume, Cooper and McAteer endeavoured to keep the warring tribes apart but were swept aside as the Protestant gangs entered the Bogside. Having been continuously pelted with stones and petrol bombs for nearly two days, the police eventually retaliated by firing CS gas. One such round hit Hume full in the chest as he tried to calm tempers around Rosemount police station. Almost simultaneously sectarian violence was breaking out in Belfast. What came to be known as 'the Troubles' had begun.

The civil disorder was already having wider implications. In response to concerns that it could spread south of the border, Jack Lynch went on television in Dublin and declared: 'The Irish Government can no longer stand by and see innocent people injured.' As a practical measure he announced that the Irish army would be establishing field hospitals in Donegal – just over the border from Derry – in order to treat Bogsiders who had been injured in the disturbances. Although the gesture was a comfort to the Derry Catholics, in Belfast it fed the paranoia of working-class Unionists. Unable to comprehend that the disturbances had been a response to persecution, they became convinced that there was a hidden Republican agenda which was causing the Catholics to rebel. Enraged by the broadcast, in Belfast a Protestant mob crossed from the Shankhill to the Falls Road and burnt down an entire row of houses.

In Derry the Bogsiders were terrified that the B Specials were going to invade the ghetto accompanied by a Protestant mob. With the province lurching towards civil war the Stormont government had no option left other than to ask Whitehall for troops to be deployed in Derry and Belfast. The Home Secretary, James Callaghan, assented to the demand with what was to become a historic understatement: 'It will be easy to send troops to Ulster, but a totally different thing to withdraw them later.' Fewer than 1.5 million people lived in Northern Ireland, but for the next twenty-five years the province would be a significant factor in the British political scene.

The troops of the Prince of Wales's regiment who were first deployed on the streets of Derry on 14 August 1969 were greeted with cheers and cups of tea from the Bogsiders, who – for the moment – regarded them as an impartial peacekeeping force. Had it not been for the misery of the past few days, the situation on the streets of Derry would have seemed like a clip from the Ealing comedy *Passport to Pimlico*.

Of that time, Canavan recalls:

When the British troops arrived in Derry, Paddy Doherty and myself, as leaders of the Derry Citizens' Defence Association, went down to the police headquarters at Victoria Barracks and asked to see the person in charge. A senior RUC official came out, we introduced ourselves and said that we wanted to talk to Colonel Todd [the officer commanding the troops in Derry]. Colonel Todd told us that his purpose in Derry was to restore order and to administer justice impartially after that. So we said that we thought we could do that ourselves because we were members of the Defence Association and we could use their authority, provided the police and the B Specials were kept out of contact with the Bogside and only the army was on the perimeter. Colonel Todd agreed to that, so we went ahead. With the people accepting that was the best way forward, the Defence Association went ahead and ran Free Derry – which was an area of about 880 acres and 25,000 souls.

Relations with the army were businesslike and often good-humoured, although there was little apparent progress made on the Bogsiders' demands for the disbandment of the B Specials, the disarming of the police, the abolition of Stormont and the repeal of the Special Powers Act.

In late August, Hume successfully persuaded the Home Secretary to make a visit to Derry while on a fact-finding trip to Ulster. Having briefed him the evening before in Belfast, he greeted Callaghan at the entrance to the Bogside, then escorted him through the crowds to the centre of the ghetto. When they paused at Grandma Diver's house for a cup of tea, Hume told Callaghan what the crowd wanted to hear. The Home Secretary then went upstairs and from a first-floor window made a moving speech in which he admitted inequalities had been perpetrated in the past and promised justice in the future. Callaghan's courageous, albeit appallingly belated, visit to the province's trouble spots was a great success – largely because of his insistence on seeing everything and meeting everybody from the Roman Catholic archbishop to the Reverend Ian Paisley.[6]

Already a tradition was beginning to be established of British ministers being persuaded to articulate John Hume's ideas. The nine-point 'Downing Street Declaration' which Harold Wilson issued on 19 August after he had shown it to the Northern Ireland Prime Minister, Major Chichester-Clark in London, pointed to the need to stand down and disarm the B Specials, called for an impartial investigation of the police system and asserted the right of all citizens in Ulster to the same freedom from discrimination enjoyed by all other citizens of the United Kingdom. Subsequently, on 10 October the inquiry into the RUC by Lord Hunt recommended the disbandment of the loathed B Specials and the creation of a new volunteer force (which eventually became the Ulster Defence Regiment) under regular army control. While those reforms were taking effect, the restrictions around Free Derry melted away and the RUC again patrolled the streets of the Bogside. It was agreed that the barricades should be removed and replaced with lines painted across the roads.

Convinced that the Nationalist sectarian philosophy was outdated, Hume believed the time was approaching when it might be possible to found a new party based on social democratic principles. What Northern Ireland needed, he thought, was a normal left/right political structure, rather than the existing religious one. During 1969–70 he articulated those views in a column he regularly wrote for the *Sunday Press*. In the autumn of 1969 he reportedly declared in a interview with the Hamburg newspaper *Die Welt*: 'The programme of the Labour Party is ideologically too Socialist, even today. I should like to found a party which is politically more in the centre, representing moderate Socialism and completely open as to religion.' Like a young musician divulging the name of the band he would like to form, he even went so far as to announce that he would like it to be known as the Social Democratic Party of Ulster. Unfortunately, he had not yet discussed such a grouping with opposition MPs and so subsequently claimed he must have been misunderstood by the German reporter.

Hume recognized that, if they were to mount an effective challenge to the thirty-nine Unionist MPs at Stormont, the thirteen other MPs needed at least to give themselves the semblance of a businesslike opposition group. Accordingly he persuaded most of them each to shadow a minister. Paddy Devlin recalled to me: 'Every time we prepared to ask questions at Question Time, we would sort them out beforehand. We beat the Unionists easily because they were quite slow on their feet and we were politically well-read. They imagined that in Question Time if they were asked a question and it was a one-question answer that would be the end of it. But we had cottoned on to the way that the political system worked in Westminster. Instead of hitting them with one question we would follow it through with a lot of questions. They were knocked off their feet and they didn't know which way to turn. They didn't know how to cope with the supplementaries. So that encouraged us to become even more organized.' Hume began to attempt to create a political party by persuading the opposition MPs to meet informally at weekends in Bunbeg on the west coast of Donegal. The civil rights MPs – John Hume, Paddy O'Hanlon and Ivan Cooper – formed a political nucleus to which the ex-Nationalist Austin Currie and eventually Paddy Devlin gravitated. When Senator Paddy Wilson and then the Northern Ireland's only Catholic MP at Westminster, Gerry Fitt (the Republican Labour leader), agreed to come on board it was evident there was a sufficient area of common ground on which to establish a new party.

Having agreed a manifesto, the Social Democratic and Labour Party was launched in Belfast on 21 August 1970 with Gerry Fitt as its leader and John Hume as its deputy leader. At the press conference Hume declared that the party would be left-of-centre, and its aims would include equal pay for equal work; civil rights for all citizens; encouragement for cooperatives; and introduction of proportional representation. Most controversially, the SDLP saw its primary goal as the eventual reunification of Ireland. The party was convinced that Ireland could not be reunited by violence: the people of the North would have to give their consent to any unity with the South.

They declared: 'The SDLP's aim is to promote cooperation, friendship and understanding between North and South with a view to the eventual re-unification of Ireland through the consent of the majority of the people in the North and South.'

The formation of the SDLP was a death knell to the old Nationalist Party, the NDP, which disbanded in October 1970. But it also had the effect of uniting the existing opposition at Stormont and thereby caused a hardening of the religious divide there. Hume's response to the rising tide of violence in the spring of 1970 was to issue a statement reaffirming his belief that the central problem in Northern Ireland then was what it had always been: a deep barrier between the people built on prejudice, distrust and intolerance. 'Surely now is the time for all of us, irrespective of our political views, to stand against a threat which could destroy the whole community and in which the only right left to us will be the right to bury our dead. The choice facing us is clear – reconciliation or destruction.' In a Stormont debate in May he had no compunction about denouncing the firebrand MP for Bannside, the Reverend Ian Paisley, for seeking government approval to turn four B Special drill halls over to the Ulster Special Constabulary Old Comrades' Association. Fearing that the B Specials would revert to the old-style Ulster Volunteer Force, he insisted that drill halls were meant for drilling, not to keep 'government storm-troopers in action should they be needed'. Paisley, he claimed, was dictatorial.

The Unionists, however, had good cause to be wary of Hume. By October he was openly advocating a united Ireland. Speaking opposite the leader of the Ulster Unionists, Brian Faulkner, in a Cambridge Union Society debate on the motion 'This house would unite Ireland', he made a strong plea for unification, insisting it was the only way of achieving permanent stability and peace.

> Northern Ireland was created by drawing a line on a map in such a way as to ensure a permanent sectarian majority for one section of the community in the north-east of Ireland. Northern Ireland must be ended. Unification would be in Britain's interest as well. The real challenge of unity is not only for the Catholics. To the northern Protestants we are saying join in partnership to end all this and create a new vision.[7]

To Hume it seemed that the SDLP was the only institution which could bring about reform in Stormont. Endeavouring to ensure it an effective voice there, he began to call for elections to the Assembly to be by proportional representation; he further called for elections to the executive to be by the same method. To neutralize sectarianism there should be a bold system of power-sharing; but he had doubts as to whether that could be achieved under the premiership of Brian Faulkner, who was sworn in as Northern Ireland's Prime Minister in March 1971. Indeed, it seemed likely that under Faulkner there would be a swing to the right in Ulster. In June, speaking to an SDLP meeting in Derry, he urged the British government to admit that the 1920 Act and the system of government created by it at Stormont had been an abysmal failure:

> We are asked to believe that the present Unionist government at Stormont will solve our problems – a government which is led by one of the chief architects of Northern Ireland's sick society and only eighteen months ago one of the staunchest defenders of the injustice-ridden Unionist system. How can people be expected to believe that the man and the party that caused our problems are the man and the party to solve them.

Within a month the hope he entertained that Stormont might be able to curb the army's excesses had vanished. In Derry that July the army shot dead two youngsters they believed to be carrying arms – although none were ever found. Along with other

SDLP MPs, Hume demanded that an inquiry be held. But it soon became clear that Stormont would be unable to deliver even that. Stormont's weakness and partisanship were confirmed in the following weeks when the army raided scores of houses in Derry and Belfast and rounded up hundreds of Nationalist agitators, many of whom had never been associated with terrorist activity. The immediate effect of interning those persons under the Special Powers Act was to prompt many young working-class Catholics in Belfast and Derry to apply to join the IRA. It further caused numerous Catholics who had hitherto merely believed that Stormont should be boycotted to believe that it should be brought down.

This anger found expression in the formation in early August of the Assembly of the Northern Irish People. Having already – in conjunction with the NICRA and SDLP – incited council tenants to embark on a rent strike, it now demanded that Westminster dissolve the Stormont government. Hume was unanimously elected its President when it convened in the hastily converted ballroom of an ancient castle in Dungiven for its first meeting. The Assembly, which included representatives of all the opposition parties who were boycotting Stormont, was composed of more than fifty MPs, senators and councillors. In his opening speech to the breakaway 'parliament', Hume ironically quoted from the words of the Unionist Lord Carson, who in 1912 had mobilized citizens to oppose Home Rule for the whole of Ireland's thirty-two counties: 'We don't recognize the authority of the Stormont government, and we don't care tuppence whether this is treason or not.'

The protests against internment and torture had their lighter moments. In October, Hume, together with Paddy O'Hanlon and Austin Currie, impulsively took a plane from Belfast to London to carry out a 48-hour hunger strike outside 10 Downing Street. Hume forgot to change his shirt and they had almost no sleeping gear. Worse still, they had forgotten to weigh themselves beforehand. The burly O'Hanlon and 14½-stone Hume quipped: 'It's a great way to get thin.' But for the eleven-stone Austin Currie the protest was an ordeal. 'I'm afeared we're going to lose him, y'know,' Hume said with mock concern. 'He's going to disappear altogether.' To the amazement of the trio, the policeman standing guard outside Number 10 was consistently agreeable and good-humoured, joking with them. It made a change from being called 'Fenian bastards' by the RUC.[8]

The brushes with authority became more robust on 18 August, when Hume and Ivan Cooper attempted to prevent the army from moving into the barricaded Creggan estate. The day began inauspiciously when a gunman was shot dead as 1,500 soldiers made a dawn raid on the Bogside and Creggan districts to remove the twenty-three barricades which had stood there for nearly two years. In Lone Moor Road, not far from Hume's West End Park house, some 300 Catholics had gathered to prevent the army's incursion. Fearful that a riot might ensue, Hume organized a sit-down and singing protest. While the crowd sang 'We shall not be moved' he approached the officer commanding the company of Marines – among whose number was the future Liberal Democrat leader, Paddy Ashdown – and made a bargain. They agreed that if the green berets withdrew from the sight of the crowd he would make sure the protestors dispersed peacefully within thirty minutes. He explained that deal to the crowd, who gave it their full approval. While army headquarters were being informed of the decision the Marines retreated. Minutes later, when a second company of troops came into view, the protestors reckoned they had been tricked. Hume strolled over to the Artillery major commanding them and told him of the agreement he had made with the other military commander, suggesting similarly that if he moved his own troops back he could make sure the crowd dispersed within thirty minutes. The major put Hume's request to his commanding officer, but when his brigade commander checked Hume's story about the arrangement with the Marines no confirmation was available. On hearing that fresh instructions had been issued to clear the road the crowd became emotional. Hume told Major Gahan: 'If you drive your vehicles along this road you will have to drive over my dead body.' He then walked to the middle of the road and sat down in front of an armoured car.

When Hume had been joined by the rest of the crowd, the Artillery major warned the protestors by loudhailer to disperse. Rubber bullets were then fired and a water cannon was aimed at the crowd. Rising to his feet, Hume was knocked down by a powerful jet of purple dye. On impeding a snatch squad's arrest of Hugh Logue – a civil rights leader who had allegedly been throwing stones at the troops – Hume and Ivan Cooper were hauled out of the crowd and arrested. After an hour during which they stood dripping wet they were bundled into an RUC van and driven to a barracks where, with Michael Canavan, they were charged under section 31 of the Special Powers Act for failing to comply with an order to disperse given by Her Majesty's Forces. A special criminal court duly found them guilty and fined them each £20.

A friend of Hume's, Charles Hill – a young lawyer sympathetic to the civil rights movement – advised John that the case was worth contesting on a number of grounds. Hill prepared an appeal based on the fact that under the 1920 Government of Ireland Act the Northern Ireland parliament did not have power to legislate in respect of the army.

> The point that I drew John Hume's attention to I had used a similar argument in a court case previously. However, as I had won that on other technicalities the court did not decide the matter. Therefore I told John that in my view, the proper way to do the case was to appeal to the High Court on the basis of the untested point. I thought it would be an extremely interesting constitutional case, and so it proved to be. It's probably the most important case in the history of Northern Ireland, and it meant that the legislation carrying the powers of the Northern Ireland parliament needed to be changed.

Determined to challenge the army's authority under the Special Powers Act, Hume took the case to the Court of Appeal and got the convictions quashed: the court ruled that the army had no authority under the Special Powers Act to order the dispersal of an assembly that might lead to a breach of the peace.[9] It had been a bold move and it had paid off. Particularly impressed were a group of some fourteen Labour MPs at Westminster who took a close interest in Northern Ireland. The swiftness of the government's response made parliamentary history and illustrated to them what a real upset Hume had caused. One of their number, Kevin McNamara, claimed:

> Hume's case had shown the actions of the British army were illegal. Therefore they had to make it legal. They did it by

a one-clause Act in longhand. It's a most unusual thing to happen. Suddenly out of the blue appeared this Bill, written in longhand. The government's business for the day was completely changed. The Bill to legalize the army's actions was a manuscript Bill and it went through both Houses in one day. Not many people can achieve that.

For practically the first time in living memory it was necessary to rush a retrospective law through the House of Commons overnight. The case had shown there could be no managing of the security position when there were two parliaments with control over two security forces. Hill maintains that Hume's decision to take the case to court had the eventual consequence of bringing down Stormont and introducing direct rule.

The drive to remove the barricades on 18 August had been part of a crackdown by the security forces, whose most drastic step had been to commence the policy of internment. Hume condemned the measure as a knee-jerk blunder by Stormont which would only have the calamitous effect of provoking many young Catholics into siding with the Nationalist gunmen. Soon thirty prominent Catholics had resigned from public life in Derry in protest against internment. There being nothing he could do at Stormont to prevent the defections, Hume journeyed to the prison ship *Maidstone* in Belfast harbour, where several of his constituents were being held. He was refused permission to go on board, but a special caravan was brought alongside so that he could talk with them. Having spoken to them, he complained to the authorities that they were suffering from severe overcrowding and lack of exercise. In January 1972 he attended a demonstration on the shores of Lough Foyle at Magilligan, where the army had established a huge internment camp. With the demonstration threatening to degenerate into a battle between troops and protestors, television cameras recorded footage of Hume arguing the right for the march to take place there.

The presence of the British army on the streets of Derry had become an irritant for the mild-mannered John Hume. In November he was detained by troops who were clearing an obstruction in Lone Moor Road. After he had refused to be searched, two soldiers were detailed to stand in front of him with maxi shields to protect him from youths who were throwing stones at the troops. When the commanding officer eventually arrived, a brief conversation ensued and Hume continued his journey to a shop, muttering: 'It has reached a ridiculous stage when a person cannot leave his home and go sixty yards to buy cigarettes without being searched by soldiers.'

As 1971 drew to a close Hume remained determined that the SDLP should continue its refusal to sit in the Stormont parliament or help the Home Secretary, now Reginald Maudling, prepare reform plans. In a lengthy article for the *Irish Times* he asserted that despite the hopes of the constitutionalists in the early 1920s, when the Government of Ireland Act was enacted: 'There does not yet appear to be a full realization at Westminster that the first step towards a real solution is the acceptance of the failure of the system and of the need to abolish it.'[10] The British army, he argued, was now defending Unionist power and privilege by means of searches and internment:

> There can be no solution through a continuation of such policy. It will only harden Catholic opinion even further to a point where the emotional fellow-feeling of Southern Irishmen will spill over into their total involvement as well.
>
> British policy in Ireland is dictated, as it has been since 1912, by the threat of the right-wing Unionists. There can be no real solution till the British government faces up squarely to this threat. The remarkable thing is that every possible way has been tried to bring Northern Ireland into the twentieth century except this, for when the power of the threat is broken, the solution to the Irish question will be remarkably easy.
>
> To do so does not require military action but political action. The action that is necessary is the abolition of the system of government to which the threat gave birth.

It would be several years before he would encounter a British government which had the courage to withstand the power of the Unionists.

In every sense of the phrase, Hume had established himself as a professional politician. Despite the momentous and brutal events that were occurring in the province at that time, Hume somehow possessed sufficient inner calm to plan ahead strategically. In

February 1971 he published an article in the current affairs journal *Fortnight* setting out his vision of how, and indeed why, a united Ireland might come about as a consequence of developments that were taking place in Europe.

> It was probably inevitable after the bitterness of the happenings at the beginning of the century that the attitudes to the border on both sides should largely be an emotional reaction, rather than a reasoned position. The result has been that to many Irish unity has come to mean the conquest of one state by the other rather than a partnership of both where both traditions combine in agreement to create a new society in Ireland, a pluralist society where all traditions are cherished and flourish equally.
>
> It must be quite astonishing and puzzling to outsiders to note that while countries like France and Germany, who only twenty-five years ago were engaged in mutual carnage, are today building bonds of friendship, in Ireland there is little or no sign of the communities coming together. It seems somewhat contradictory that each part of Ireland seems willing to participate separately in the planned integration of Europe, but not in the planned integration of this little island.

— 4 —
Labours of Sisyphus

Sensing that an illegal Civil Rights Association parade in Derry on Sunday, 30 January 1972 would end in violence, Hume and many SDLP supporters had deliberately stayed away. When the crowd reached Free Derry Corner soldiers of the Parachute Regiment opened up with rifles. To Father Denis Bradley, a Bogside priest who was standing by, it seemed like a massacre. He saw nobody shooting at the troops. One paratrooper beside him fired at least eight shots at people fleeing. He grabbed him and shouted: 'For God's sake, stop!', but the squaddie shrugged him off. The priest administered the last rites to about four people.

Hearing the shots in his home in West End Park, Hume hurried to the scene. By the time he got there thirteen men and youths were lying dead in the streets. At the nearby Altnagelvin hospital, where the bodies and the seventeen injured were taken, he found himself running back and forth telling people that their relatives were dead. One of those killed was his next-door neighbour. Overwhelmed with grief and anger, Hume denounced the atrocity as 'another Sharpeville'. In a press interview he was reported to have exclaimed: 'It's a united Ireland or nothing!' These words became notorious and have been used against him ever since. Later, when I asked him what he meant by it, he categorically denied he had ever uttered them.

> I never said that. The one quote that has always been used against me is the one I never made. You've got to realize the absolute mood at the time. Can you imagine the anger in those streets? And I'm their only representative. I had to channel that anger to make sure that there was no more violence. I was interviewed about 'Bloody Sunday'.

Remember there was still a Northern Ireland government and they were using the British troops. The question that the interviewer asked me was: 'What's the reaction to people in the Bogside to what has happened?' I gave my reaction, and one of the points I made was that we've lost all confidence in any Stormont government. I think – this is my memory – the interviewer said: 'You mean it's a united Ireland or nothing.' And I said: 'That might be the mood.' But the way they reported it then was: 'Hume says: It's a united Ireland or nothing.'

Hume claims that day was probably the worst of his life. The anger in Derry was very deep and he was worried it would spill over. On the Free Derry Corner killing ground that afternoon, soldiers were bombarded with acid bombs, bottles, bricks, nail bombs and at least one canister of CS gas as they fought to control the angry mobs. Already troops were duelling with snipers firing from rubble around the Rossville flats. When they had fired rubber bullets to disperse a crowd and got through they found two men shot dead on a rubble heap. Two and a half years earlier, the army had been deployed on the streets in Northern Ireland to defend the Catholic minority. Now they were shooting them.

The massacre firmly established Hume's house as a bridgehead for any visiting politician or journalist seeking a calm and reputable viewpoint on the Bogside. The day after the funerals of the Bloody Sunday victims his home was a feeding station of hot stew on a cold day for many. The place was filled with politicians – Gerry Fitt, Garret FitzGerald, Charles Haughey, Brian Lenihan, to name but a few. As the local elected representative, Hume attended the wakes of all the victims.

Learning that Whitehall's response to 'Bloody Sunday' was to appoint the Lord Chief Justice, Lord Widgery, to carry out an inquiry into the shootings, Hume promptly condemned the inquiry for seeking only to examine the area in the Bogside and Creggan districts of Derry in which the disturbances took place. Expressing his mistrust of the British system of justice, he called for an international commission to be established. The Widgery inquiry, he claimed, was an absolute insult to the people: 'Because of its terms of reference it excludes any investigation into whether or not the shooting was the result of a military plan or government policy. All the senior people involved in the affair will be excluded from the scope of the investigation, and so will get off scot free.' He was thus not surprised when the inquiry eventually reported that it was the march organizers and not the paratroopers who were at fault.

Convinced more than ever that Stormont needed to be brought down, on the Sunday following the shootings Hume and the five other SDLP MPs attended a civil rights march in Newry, County Down. The event was illegal, and for their attendance they and twenty other participants – including the MP Bernadette Devlin – were summoned to appear at the magistrates' court in Newry. If convicted, they might be liable to a six-month prison sentence. A problem for the RUC was that Hume lived in a part of Derry where the police had dared not go alone for several months. A Derry police sergeant telephoned him to ask if he would go to the city centre to collect his summons, but Hume refused. In desperation to serve the order, the RUC used Saracen armoured cars to deliver it to his house.

Meanwhile, in Whitehall and Belfast there had been a tremendous amount of political activity going on in the attempt to save Stormont. When the SDLP commenced its boycott of the Northern Ireland parliament, its members were approached by a senior Conservative who conveyed an offer of secret talks at Downing Street. The SDLP were sounded out and asked if they would look favourably on the idea of a community-type government at Stormont which would have a Deputy Prime Minister drawn from the opposition side and some Cabinet posts for opposition members. They rejected the proposals, stating that the first step in any real solution was the abolition of Stormont.[1]

For a while it seemed as though the SDLP was gaining ground. On 24 March 1972 the Heath government took the first step towards suspending Stormont for a year by persuading Brian Faulkner to resign as Ulster's Prime Minister. The dissolution of the Stormont Assembly effectively meant that the parliament building was shut down. The prospect of direct rule from London loomed nearer when the Northern Ireland Office was created, with the new Cabinet post that came with it going to William Whitelaw. Accompanied as it was by the promise of a phasing out of internment – although no date for the ending of it was given – this move should have given some of the Republican paramilitaries a sense that they should now work for peace and give the new deal a chance.

In early March 1972 the Leader of the Opposition, Harold Wilson, received a message through an intermediary (Dr John O'Connell, a member of the Dáil) indicating that some of the leading 'friends' of the IRA were anxious to discuss the problems of the North. Accompanied by the shadow spokesman on Northern Ireland, Merlyn Rees, in a mansion on the edge of Dublin's Phoenix Park on 13 March he secretly met a delegation consisting of David O'Connell, Joe Cahill and John Kelly. Talking with them until nearly 1.30 a.m., Wilson became impressed by their intellect but appalled by their lack of negotiating skills. A meeting of minds was clearly impossible. They were worlds apart; their respective key words had quite different meanings. 'Violence' to Labour was what 'peace' was to the IRA. The IRA leaders wanted an amnesty for political prisoners; Wilson told them that if 'political prisoners' meant those who committed murder he would not accept it, nor would any British government.

Having heard Wilson stress that constitutional talks could only take place between 'elected' representatives, David O'Connell insisted that they must be between the British government and 'our friends'. Wilson asked if the IRA would trust anyone to speak for them in any talks that were held, given that constitutional talks could only be between elected representatives: 'What would your friends feel about my friends in the SDLP?' Claiming that the SDLP had completely lost touch with the IRA, Joe Cahill reacted sharply and abruptly: 'Our friends hold very strong views. No one substituted for them in the fighting and they do not want a substitute in the talking.' The discussions got nowhere; but Labour had usefully managed to break the taboo on contacts with the IRA, and thus held the door ajar for future talks.[2]

Already that year the IRA had attempted to commence some dialogue with the British government, clumsily making their demands known via another go-between, the Stormont MP Tom Caldwell. Responding to grass-roots Catholic pressure, that summer they organized a press conference to announce an offer of a temporary ceasefire. On the British side, a hunger strike in the Crumlin Road prison by IRA inmates who were demanding political status was also forcing Whitehall towards the negotiating table.

Trusted for his integrity by both the Northern Ireland Office and the IRA high command, Hume was the natural choice for the role of intermediary. He soon found himself commuting between Whitelaw and the IRA's leading negotiators Seán MacStiofáin and Dáithí Ó'Conaill. Having had discussions with the terrorists in Free Derry, he passed on to London the IRA's conditions for talks. There was scant prospect of the Whitehall side agreeing to name a date for eventual British withdrawal from the province, although they were willing to accede to the demand for political status. The IRA were particularly keen to secure the release from Long Kesh of Gerry Adams.

Before his detention Adams had notionally only been a barman in the Duke of York pub in the centre of Belfast. According to the security forces, Adams had joined the IRA in the mid-1960s. In the early 1970s he was the commandant of the 2nd (Ballymurphy) Battalion of the Belfast Brigade and later the Brigade's commanding officer. The British authorities, however, have never been able to provide evidence of Adams ever having been an IRA volunteer, and he himself has always denied ever being a member.[3] Whatever his history, in 1972 he was considered by the Republicans to be an effective negotiator. Whitelaw having authorized his release, on 26 June the IRA was sufficiently influenced by Hume's powers of persuasion and agreed to commence a ceasefire.

Ten days into the cessation of hostilities the IRA were rewarded by a meeting with Whitelaw. On 7 July, six of them – including Martin McGuinness, the commander of their Derry brigade – were covertly flown by the RAF to London for secret talks with Whitelaw in Paul Channon's Chelsea house on the banks of the Thames. But the meeting lasted for less than an hour. The IRA team demanded that the British leave the province within two years and wanted a decision on that from the Cabinet's next meeting. Clearly there was no real prospect of reaching a lasting agreement: Britain would not agree to withdraw its troops on or before January 1975, nor would the IRA abandon their demand for a repeal of the Special Powers Act. The fragile ceasefire was shaken when several Catholic families were prevented by rioters from occupying houses allocated to them on a Belfast estate, and the army arrested some IRA activists who were at the scene.

The IRA Army Council were on the verge of cancelling the ceasefire, when they heard that Harold Wilson – who had been encouraged by reports he had heard of the Whitelaw talks – wanted to meet them again, this time at his home in Great Missenden in Buckinghamshire. Three IRA members, including Joe Cahill, flew in a chartered plane to a nearby private airfield on 18 July. The meeting was barren from the start. Such was the Provisionals' political naïvety that they had only made the journey because they believed Wilson was empowered to negotiate on behalf of the British government. They could not distinguish between British politicians, regarding them largely as interchangeable members of the same conspiracy. On 21 July the IRA ended the ceasefire with spectacular savagery. That 'Bloody Friday' they detonated twenty-six bombs in Belfast, killing eleven people and injuring 130.

Whitelaw now pushed ahead with an attempt to find a new political solution. But because the British government continued to refuse to specify when internment would finally be phased out, the SDLP – along with other opposition groups in Ulster – refused invitations to attend an all-party seminar Whitelaw was planning to convene in Darlington. Hume spelt out their misgivings in a Dublin newspaper article in which he argued that if the possibility of a condominium or a Council of Ireland was to be discussed, then Dublin should be represented. As there was to be no representation from the Republic, the conference was guaranteed not to produce a lasting solution. He claimed: 'It is the intention to parade the disagreements, so as to justify an imposed solution.' The 1920 settlement had been imposed; a settlement in 1972 had to be arrived at by involving all parties, North and South, through discussions based on genuine grievances. Even the timing of the Whitelaw conference, he alleged, had more to do with the Conservative Party conference than ought to be the case.[4]

In a last-ditch attempt to persuade the SDLP to participate, Heath invited John Hume, Gerry Fitt, Ivan Cooper and Austin Currie to talks at Chequers. When they met, Heath was intransigent, brushing aside their complaints that the remaining internees were being kept as 'hostages' against the behaviour of the IRA. When tea was wheeled in Paddy Devlin asked the Prime Minister: 'Could you pass me one of those muffins?' – grumpily adding: 'It looks as if that's all we're going to get from you today.'

In the absence of the SDLP making its views known at Darlington, Hume made several key public speeches in which he reiterated his argument that a settlement could be durable only if it had majority acceptance throughout Ireland. That recommendation formed the centrepiece of a policy paper, *Towards a New Ireland*, which the SDLP published to further its call for a system of proportional representation. Although the Chequers talks had seemed unproductive, Whitelaw had been sufficiently impressed by Hume's reasoning to include the SDLP's views on consultation with the South in a Green Paper, *The Future of Northern Ireland*, which he published in October to outline proposals for a settlement. When a White Paper on the Whitelaw plan was eventually produced, it promised – as the SDLP had requested – that the future elections to the Assembly would be by means of a system of proportional representation.

The result of the June 1973 elections to the Assembly, which Whitelaw had just enlarged, was good news for the SDLP. While the two centre parties – the Northern Ireland Labour Party and the non-sectarian Alliance Party – had performed disastrously, Fitt's group captured an impressive record 22 per cent of the vote and secured nineteen seats in the 78-member Assembly. Unquestionably the SDLP now represented the majority of the Catholic electorate. In complete contrast to the old Stormont, not one of the Unionist parties would be able to hold an overall majority in the Assembly. But when the Ulster people voted that March in a border referendum similar to that which had been put to the people of Gibraltar, they expressed their preference on sectarian lines, with nearly 99 per cent expressing a wish to retain the traditional tie with Britain. The result had been distorted by the SDLP's call to its supporters to boycott the referendum; nevertheless it indicates that there was still only minority support for the type of Nationalism advocated by the SDLP.

The White Paper and the SDLP's showing in the Assembly elections meant that when the power-sharing Executive was eventually named in November, the SDLP for the first time had a stake in the government of the province. Hume was appointed Minister of Commerce, and Gerry Fitt became Deputy Chief Executive. Austin Currie received the Local Government, Housing and Planning portfolio; Paddy Devlin got Health and Social Services; Ivan Cooper, Community Relations; and Eddie McGrady, Executive Planning and Coordination. Even Oliver Napier, a Catholic member of the Alliance Party, was given a portfolio. However, determined to express their opposition to the notion of Catholics in government by bringing down the power-sharing experiment, William Craig and Ian Paisley formed a Loyalist coalition.

Although Hume recognized the need for conciliation with the Protestants, he was in no mood to let the militant views of Craig and Paisley pass without censure. During an Assembly debate in November he eloquently attacked Craig, the Vanguard Party leader, for allegedly doing much to bring about a wave of anti-Catholic sectarian assassinations in the province.

In a bid to save the Assembly, in December 1973 Whitelaw's newly appointed successor, Francis Pym, convened a conference at Sunningdale, the Civil Service's staff college in the Berkshire countryside. The SDLP approached the conference with the intention of getting all-Ireland institutions established which would ultimately lead to a united Ireland. In contrast to the Unionists, the SDLP had prepared their case well in advance. Their planner, Paddy Devlin, told me: 'We always prepared beforehand. Any time we had a delegation or had to write a letter we discussed every aspect of it in advance. We would always bring in people who had specialized knowledge, whatever the subject. I was the planner for all that, Hume was the talker.'

The actual negotiation took place in the conference room in Northcote House, a fine manor house at the centre of the complex. The conference quickly broke into five sub-committees to discuss the main topics: finance of the Executive, the Council of Ireland, the status of Northern Ireland; law enforcement; and policing. Soon it became apparent that the proceedings were becoming ensnared by discussions in Hume's and Paddy O'Hanlon's Council of Ireland committee. As a consequence the conference would be unable to complete its deliberations in the allotted two days.

The Unionists insisted that the only circumstance in which they could accept the need for a Council of Ireland would be if there was a formal declaration by Dublin recognizing Northern Ireland's constitutional status. Hume was the *de facto* leader of the SDLP delegation – despite Gerry Fitt's presence – and it was he who spearheaded attempts to resolve the deadlock. He was in his element, flitting between sub-committees, wheeling and dealing with Ted Heath and Garret FitzGerald in smoky rooms until the early hours.

In the final communiqué, which was signed on the fourth day

in the main hall at Sunningdale College, no mention was made of the issue of law and order, on which no agreement had been reached. This was largely Hume's fault. He had been insistent that the power-sharing government should have control over the security forces, whereas Heath was implacably opposed to any devolution of authority on security.

Nevertheless, at the conference there was a widespread recognition of the need to suppress terrorism. It was agreed that to facilitate cooperation between the North and the South an all-Ireland Council of Ministers should be established. The assumption was that eventually it would exercise executive functions.

On Friday night Ted Heath threw a lavish seven-course dinner party for the delegates in Downing Street. The SDLP delegation were in a boisterous mood – they seemed to be on the verge of achieving much of what they had been campaigning for over the years. It appeared that the deal reached would ensure they had a sustained run in office and thereby enabled them to transform the nature of northern politics for ever. On the return coach journey to Sunningdale they sang Irish songs at the tops of their voices.

For the first time European Community influence was featuring in the Northern Ireland equation. All participants at the conference had been aware that a working model for a Council of Ministers already existed in the EEC. Nevertheless, that 'Irish dimension' was to prove to be fatal: it failed to appease extremist Nationalists, and enraged many Unionists. Mistrust was unwittingly added to in an hour-long BBC interview with Hugh Logue in which hope was expressed that the Council of Ireland could eventually lead to political understanding between North and South. Hume subsequently claimed that the news bulletin summary of the views expressed was a distortion, but the damage had been done.

Such misunderstandings were hardly surprising. In recent months Hume had been under immense personal strain. He had suffered from exhaustion during discussions at Stormont prior to the Sunningdale conference, and had had to be admitted to Derry's Altnagelvin Hospital with blood poisoning of the wrist. It should have been treated some time earlier but because of pressure of work he had hitherto avoided going to hospital. The ailment was not serious and after a few days of treatment he was discharged.

Financial worries were also pressing down on him. He had been involved in a motor accident in which he drove his car across approaching traffic in Derry and collided with a motorcycle, knocking over the rider and causing him leg injuries. Subsequently, in 1973, the Ulster High Court ruled that he should pay the accident victim damages of £12,500 – in those days a considerable sum of money.

Most worrying of all was that in January of that year his ten-year-old daughter Aine had nearly been kidnapped. A girl closely resembling Aine had been bundled into a car as she left St Anne's primary school in the Rosemount area of Derry and driven into the country. The child heard her abductors talking about her classmate Aine and assumed they had planned to abduct Hume's daughter. After she had been released on a deserted road between the River Foyle and the border, Derry police interviewed Hume and Aine.

Hume's own life was sometimes in danger. Twelve months later he was attending a meeting in a private room in the Dunowen Hotel, Dungannon, with Gerry Fitt, Seamus Mallon, Paddy Devlin and Austin Currie. Suddenly a gang of masked men armed with pistols walked in the hotel's front door, planted a 20 lb device in the foyer and fled. The SDLP members realized what was going on after hearing a lot of shouting. Without hesitation they all fled the premises. As they were evacuating, Mallon realized a jacket containing some important papers had been left inside. He ran back and collected the coat just five minutes before the bomb exploded, causing extensive damage to the building.

When the power-sharing Executive finally took office in January 1974, Hume immersed himself in his duties as Commerce Minister. In this first – and only – government post he carried out his duties with energy. The Commerce portfolio was ideal for him as it enabled him to start to implement his theory that economic development, if administered fairly, could bring the Catholic and Protestant communities together. Moreover, he hoped that Unionist reservations about the South might be lessened if economically tangible improvements could be made on an all-Ireland basis. In search of overseas investors he frequently travelled to America and Europe, opening a promotional office in Brussels.[5]

However, the Executive had found itself in trouble as soon as it had taken office. Many Unionists had become alarmed that the proposed Council of Ministers might become a slippery slope towards a united Ireland. The Ulster Unionist Council having rejected the Sunningdale agreement, the Unionists split into two groups: the Faulknerite Ulster Unionist Party and the Paisleyite United Ulster Unionist Coalition – which had been formed specifically to fight the Sunningdale agreement. In the February 1974 British general election the UUUC swept the board, winning all eleven Unionist seats. The best the SDLP could do was retain Gerry Fitt's seat in West Belfast. On 14 May, immediately the power-sharing Executive had won an Assembly vote on the Sunningdale agreement, with UUUC backing an Ulster Workers' Council was formed to organize a general strike with the intention of bringing down the Catholic-influenced Executive.[6]

Operating from William Craig's Vanguard Party Headquarters, the UWC coordinated a barricade-building programme and a series of walkouts to bring everyday life in the province to a halt. Mass absenteeism and threats of arson attacks meant that shops and factories closed down and the public transport system virtually came to a standstill. Even cross-channel ferries to Stranraer could not sail. Soon, nearly half of Ulster's workforce of around half a million people were refusing to report to work. Milk was ruined, cattle starved and schoolchildren missed exams. Most serious of all was the drastic cut in the level of electricity supplied by the power stations. With the electricity supply dwindling all the time, on 19 May Labour's new Northern Ireland Secretary, Merlyn Rees, declared a state of emergency.

As Commerce Minister, Hume was responsible for seeing that vital supplies of oil reached the province's petrol stations. He devised a plan to restore some movement to Ulster's paralysed industries; but there was little that he could do without the support of the armed services. Frustrated, he vented his anger on the British government, accusing them of being too timid to break the strike and demanding that they deploy troops to restore essential services. On Sunday 26 May, when the strike was nearing its climax, the six SDLP ministers gathered for an all-day meeting at a secret venue in Belfast. The outcome was an ultimatum to the government, drafted by Hume: send troops in to break the strike or they would resign. Hume reckoned that if it was not accepted his own position would become intolerable.

The reality was that the army was in no position to operate and maintain the power stations. Already all 800 members of the Electrical Power Engineers' Association had voted to walk out if they attempted to do so. On the morning of 27 May, Merlyn

Rees made ready to declare his acceptance of the plan Hume had drafted to get the petrol pumps flowing again. No sooner had he done so than the UWC announced an identical plan for negating the initiative. Clearly the mole who had been supplying the UWC with a stream of valuable information during the strike was a well-placed official in the Northern Ireland Office. At 11 a.m. the UWC announced the general strike had become total.

On Tuesday morning the road to Stormont was jammed with tractors driven by farmers demonstrating in support of the strike. The Executive met at 11 a.m. for ninety minutes and decided by majority vote that negotiations with the UWC must commence. Hume, Fitt and Currie abstained. Faulkner then met Rees, who told him that the British government would not negotiate when it was cornered. That lunchtime Rees announced that Faulkner had resigned along with the Unionist members of the Assembly. The Assembly ended its last session that afternoon with an SDLP spokesperson claiming: 'Power sharing has worked and the idea of power sharing has worked.' When the MPs who had refused to resign were paid off, Rees assumed responsibility for the preservation of law and order in the province. Effectively, direct rule had returned.[7] The 'spirit of 1912' had been triumphant. There was now an identifiable limit on the power of the British government: in future the only constitutional changes it would be able to introduce in the province were those with which the organized Protestant population were prepared to agree.

Like many Nationalists, Hume remains convinced that the strike could have been defeated. He told me:

> I've no doubt at all that had the British government at the time stood firm against the Loyalist Workers Strike the Sunningdale agreement would have stood firm and we would be in a much better situation today. When the strike started they had very little support because most people went out to work. One thing that gave it strength was that in the power stations they were switching off the power. Had the government of the day – the Secretary of State – taken very firm action it wouldn't have lasted two days. There were people trying to go to work in Belfast and they were being stopped by barricades.

The strike had shown the SDLP the extent of Unionist opposition to their ambitions. During the course of the walkout they had gone as far as to risk the integrity of their party by agreeing to abandon their cherished ideal of a powerful Council of Ireland, and to accept instead a temporary Council of Ministers without any real power. Even so, during the strike they had committed the tactical blunder of spending too much time in Dublin. Talks that Paddy Devlin and Ivan Cooper had had there with the Foreign Minister, Garret FitzGerald, much to Rees's annoyance, made them seem subversive and further alienated the many Loyalists who reckoned power-sharing was a conspiracy.

Hume had for several years been refusing invitations to stand for a seat at Westminster, but, prompted by the collapse of power-sharing and his growing recognition of the need to influence British ministers, in September 1974 he finally decided to put himself forward. Selected as the SDLP candidate for the Derry constituency which the UUUC had won in February with a majority of 9,390, he knew he would have a tough fight on his hands. He was not surprised in the general election that autumn when the result was virtually unchanged. The SDLP again came second, with Hume a virtually hopeless 9,020 votes short of toppling the UUUC candidate William Ross. Elsewhere in the province there had been few upsets – except in South Down, where the ex-Tory Enoch Powell was elected as a Unionist.

Chastened, but still convinced of the need for some form of representative government in Northern Ireland, Merlyn Rees set about devising a successor to the power-sharing Executive. In June, Hume formed part of an SDLP delegation that travelled to 10 Downing Street to impress upon Harold Wilson the need for the new set of proposals to have an 'Irish dimension'. Hume seemed to have forgotten that it was the Council of Ireland – on which he had foolishly been so insistent at Sunningdale – that had been the principal cause of the Unionists' hostility to the power-sharing Executive. Hume told the Prime Minister: 'If there is to be a real solution it must involve concern for both sections of the community and concern for North and South.' When a month later the Rees plan was published in the White Paper *The Northern Ireland Constitution*, Hume was annoyed to find that his views had largely been ignored. The centrepiece of Rees's attempts to create a government run by both communities was to be a

78-member 'Constitutional Convention'. The proposals added to the growing sense of unease and disillusion with the Labour government felt by many Catholics. To Hume, the Convention was merely the old Assembly renamed. In the first major speech by a prominent constitutional Nationalist figure on the White Paper he savagely attacked Labour, declaring at an SDLP meeting in Derry that the proposed convention would be 'used by the Loyalist coalition simply to restore its lost ascendancy under the propaganda mantle of a democratic majority'.

A continuing source of friction between the SDLP and the British government was the practice of internment without trial, now well into its third year. In November 1974 Hume made a speech in Derry in which he appealed to Labour's Tribune group to arrange a visit to the Long Kesh prison camp to see conditions for themselves. Bitterly disappointed that the Wilson administration had not ended internment, he declared:

> The issue has exposed the double standards in the British Labour Party and makes one seriously question their so-called Socialist conscience. On the one hand we have the left wing of the Labour Party publicly agonizing over the Simonstown naval base in South Africa. We have even had Cabinet Ministers breaking the principle of collective responsibility on the same issue to let the world know that their socialist hearts are in the right place.

He argued that it was dishonest to say that internment was needed because of violence in Ulster. The facts showed that internment increased rather than decreased violence and merely acted as a recruiting agent for terrorism.[8]

> In the past few years, we have had howls of rage from some people over the internment of a single British journalist in Rhodesia, backed by a massive publicity campaign in Britain itself, and we have had unrelenting opposition to the Greek colonels for imprisoning people without trial.
>
> On the other hand, here in Northern Ireland, within the UK, under their own government, we have an internment situation unparalleled in Europe and an internment centre that makes Colditz look like a holiday camp, and there is not

a cheep from one of them. Yet this is an issue which has put the present British government in the dock before the European Court of Human Rights at Strasbourg. The last people who were there were the Greek colonels.

The White Paper's failure to fill the political vacuum that had developed since the Loyalist workers' strike caused the gulf between the SDLP and the RUC to widen. In an infamous local television interview Hume alleged that many of the province's policemen were 'scoundrels'. The remark was furiously seized upon by Unionists and cited as evidence of the SDLP's unfitness for government. It drove Captain Austin Ardill of the Ulster Unionist Party to remark: 'The SDLP's latest attack is yet another example, if such were needed after their years of anti-authority and riotous posturing, of how utterly impossible it will ever be for this belligerent minority to be willingly accepted by the law-abiding majority to participate in the government of this province.' Harry West, Faulkner's successor as Unionist Party leader, added to that, saying: 'We ask all law-abiding citizens in Northern Ireland to appreciate our stand against sharing power with those such as John Hume or even entering into negotiations with them. How can we negotiate with those who were instrumental in destroying the security in the province and are still adamant on undermining the security forces?'

The political vacuum also caused strains to develop within the SDLP about what the party's attitude to the RUC should be. The official SDLP policy was still to withhold support from the overwhelmingly Protestant RUC until there was a form of government acceptable to both communities in Ulster. Hitherto rank-and-file members had supported the leadership line, but at the annual conference in Belfast in January 1975 the official policy was rejected by sixty-two votes to fifty-three. The vote was interpreted as a victory for SDLP moderates who wanted to reform (rather than disband) the RUC. Among the principal speakers against the party executive was Sean Hollywood, who had been defeated in South Down by Enoch Powell in the general election. He claimed that the party's attitude was defensive and stagnant and said the SDLP should be meeting the Police Federation as well as the police authority. Nevertheless, Hume dictatorially insisted that as only 115 of the 450 delegates had been present the vote did not represent party thinking and there would be no major revision of policy.

The SDLP have persistently been criticized for only cooperating with the RUC on a day-to-day basis, and refusing to have strategic planning discussions with them. I asked Hume if that policy might have been unwise. He replied:

Well, I think that first of all, the basis of order in any society is agreement on how you govern. When that is absent you are always going to have instability and the police are going to be seen as being on one side or the other – which is what happens in Northern Ireland. Our view throughout was that it is not a policing problem, it was a political problem. Until such time as the political problem was resolved, our position throughout was that we fully and unequivocally supported the police in upholding the rule of law. Our only qualification was that they should do so impartially.

Could he not, I asked him, have assisted the police by encouraging Catholics to join the RUC?

No, because it is pointless suggesting things that people won't do. Policing is a *symptom* of the overall political situation. The basis of order is agreement. We have to find that *first* and then from that will emerge the institutions that are appropriate to govern the North.

For Hume, life in the fast lane continued to be personally hazardous. In September 1975, the car in which he was being driven by Donegalman Eamonn Gallagher – an official at the Irish Department of Foreign Affairs – collided with another vehicle on the main Dublin–Derry road near Castleblayney. As usual, the claustrophobic Hume was not wearing a seat-belt. Fortunately his injuries were only bruises and slight shock; even so, he had to be whisked to St Vincent's Hospital in Dublin, where he was kept under observation for a couple of days.

Virtually nowhere was safe for him. A year earlier he had been waiting in the lounge at Belfast airport for a flight to London to meet Rees when two men grabbed him by the arm, saying they wanted to take him away for questioning. Fearing Hume was about to be abducted, Paddy Devlin, who was seated close by, shouted out to a couple of RUC security personnel that the men should be stopped and questioned. The RUC constables sprinted after them and apprehended them at a door. Currie claimed he had seen the men who approached Hume carrying Ulster Volunteer Force badges, but the constables were satisfied that they were no would-be kidnappers, but plain-clothes soldiers on escort duty, and let them go.

With no prospect of Rees's package including a provision for an intergovernmental Council of Ireland, the Convention had few attractions for the SDLP. Still angry that the British government had made so little effort to counter the Loyalist workers' strike, in their manifesto for the October 1974 general election they called for Britain to declare its intention to withdraw from Northern Ireland. But out of office the SDLP had little influence. Thus when in January 1975 the Provisional IRA arranged a short ceasefire they did so without using Hume or any other SDLP member as an intermediary. Instead they again contacted Harold Wilson's office via Dr John O'Connell. The power-broker that time had improbably been a Protestant clergyman, the Reverend William Arlow. A truce was declared, but it was never accepted by the South Armagh brigade of the IRA, who within three weeks launched a series of attacks. Their killing of four soldiers in a bomb explosion near Forkhill, Co. Armagh, effectively ended the ceasefire.

In the run-up to the October 1974 general election Brian Faulkner's Unionist Party of Northern Ireland attempted to distance itself from the Sunningdale agreement by issuing a document declaring that they rejected the Council of Ireland concept. But they now had to pay the price for Faulkner's participation with the SDLP in the five-month power-sharing agreement. In the general election, although William Craig's Vanguard Unionist Party secured only 2 per cent of the poll other Unionists were swinging further to the Right. Ian Paisley's Democratic Unionist Party (DUP) went from strength to strength. The UUUC took 57 per cent, and the marginality of the Alliance Party was reinforced with 5.1 per cent; the Northern Ireland Labour Party (NILP) took only 1.6 per cent. In the May 1975 elections for the Constitutional Convention the UUUC took 58.4 per cent of the vote and forty-seven seats, thus gaining a substantial majority that enabled them to dominate the Convention. The DUP took twelve of those seats and the Official Unionists nineteen. The SDLP inauspiciously lost two seats in the strong Republican areas of South Derry and South Armagh, but still ended the day with a creditable seventeen seats – enough to maintain its status as the chief opposition party.

The Convention had been established with the aim of bridging all divisions and pursuing conciliation. But with the Unionists having refused to allow SDLP members to have seats on its executive, in November 1975 the Convention was suspended. In an attempt to find a compromise arrangement, interparty talks were held under the Convention's independent chairman, Sir Robert Lowry. William Craig appealed to other Loyalists to support a proposal for a referendum on an emergency coalition government consisting of the SDLP and the Unionists. For so much as proposing voluntary cooperation with the SDLP, Craig was expelled from the UUUC.

The Convention resumed meeting in February 1976, but no common ground could be found between the parties. All the while it was under threat. Hume accused the Provisional IRA of using anti-internment demonstrations to engage in violence and place the Convention under the same pressure as that which had led to the downfall of the power-sharing Executive the previous year. Despite warning of the dangers of increased violence and of greater unemployment and economic problems, Craig stood little chance of winning enough support for his proposal. In a Stormont debate on 3 March 1976 he made an eleventh-hour appeal to the Unionists, denouncing Ian Paisley and his group for not trying to make the Convention work: 'We are placing people's lives in danger on an ever-increasing scale. Nobody wanted the Convention to fail more than the IRA'.[9] Hume said that he wished more members of the Unionist Coalition had shown the moral courage to stand up against Paisley's demagoguery. His attack on Paisley was filled with venom. At one stage Hume took members back to the days of 1969 when the Trouble began. Pointing his finger at 'that man', he recalled that Paisley had once said: 'I would rather trust the Devil himself than the RUC.' Across the chamber he shouted of Paisley: 'He is the best friend the IRA ever had because he feeds them with his extremism and in return they feed his extremism as well.' Paisley did not retort, but his wife Eileen – also a Convention member – shouted back at Hume at one point: 'You are a twister, a political Jesuit twister.'

Two days later, on 5 March, the Convention was finally dissolved and direct rule from London continued unchecked. Dishearteningly, Ulster was no nearer to peace than it had been in August 1969. Nevertheless since the Troubles had begun Hume had accomplished much. Not least of his achievements had been to develop the SDLP from a civil rights group into Ulster's principal opposition party. His career had come to be a mirror image of Paisley's. In contrast to Paisley, who was a destroyer – wrecking the power-sharing Executive and then the Constitutional Convention – Hume was a builder, who had attempted to create an all-party consensus. Now that his career as a politician at Stormont was effectively at an end, he would have to try to secure a lasting peace in Northern Ireland by seeking assistance overseas.

Martini politician

When the Constitutional Convention ended in 1976, Hume, along with other leading SDLP figures, found himself in the wilderness. Nevertheless, their drive for public duty remained undiminished. Hume told me: 'If we all just disappeared all you would have had was violence versus violence. So, in order to keep politics alive, we in the SDLP called ourselves constituency representatives. Those who had been elected stayed on as constituency representatives – but with no income.' Unemployed, and with five children to raise, for most of that year the family was dependent upon Pat's meagre income as a teacher. John Bradley, who is now the headmaster of Hume's old primary school, told me:

> The Hume finances went through a very bad phase after the closing down of the Northern Ireland Assembly. John was out of work entirely and during that period Pat went back to work – she was a qualified teacher – she taught for a number of years in St Anne's School in Upper Nassau Street, Rosemount. The school was a primary school so Pat taught everything to her form – Primary 6 year.

Salvation for Hume came from the other side of the Atlantic in the form of an invitation to lecture at Harvard. Eagerly accepting the poorly paid temporary associate fellowship, for two months in late 1976 he taught conflict studies to university students at the Centre for International Affairs in Boston. While he was there he lived in Dunster House, which for a time was also the hall of residence of Al Gore, who later became a Senator and then Vice-President.

Hume had begun to forge links with the United States in 1969 when he crossed the Atlantic to put right the false impression of Nationalism that Bernadette Devlin had been presenting. When visiting, in March 1972, as a Stormont MP, he had tried to counter what he regarded as the British 'propaganda machine' and endeavoured to make Ulster a presidential issue. He told me:

> I always regarded the American dimension as being very important for a number of reasons. One, because of the size of the Irish community. They always had a romantic notion of Ireland and a very simplistic one: 'Get the British out and the problem will be solved'. There's a lot of support for that. So it was essential that I spent a lot of time going to America to oppose violence and to seek economic assistance.

When he was Minister of Commerce the United States was his first destination when he went on an overseas industrial promotion tour to try to stimulate confidence in Ulster's future. In April 1974, in meetings with business leaders in New York, Detroit, Boston, Pittsburgh and Milwaukee, he appealed to Irish Americans to use their influence to encourage more American investment in the province.[1] In Washington he told a meeting of congressional leaders that more needed to be done to ensure that the thousands of donated dollars that were pouring into the Irish Republic and Northern Ireland did not support the purchase of guns and explosives: 'I would ask some of my fellow countrymen in this land to consider, when they subscribe to IRA funds, whether they would themselves fire a gun or throw a bomb – for that is what their dollar will do.'

In the United States the Ancient Order of Hibernians, a formerly responsible organization which had grown into a virtual IRA support group, reportedly sent the Provisionals $1 million in 1972. A former chairman of the Order claimed that Hume had personally been given $150,000; Hume strenuously denied the allegation, claiming that a donation of $100,000 had indeed been made, but to a welfare charity of which he was chairman. The Northern Ireland Resurgence Trust – founded by the Heinz foods supremo, Dr Tony O'Reilly – assisted self-help groups in promoting jobs and industrial and housing projects in needy areas in Northern Ireland. Its annual report was freely available to verify Hume's defence.

By far the most significant step came with the ties Hume managed to secure with the Kennedy clan. Having come to regard Ulster as Britain's Vietnam, almost since the outset of the Troubles, Senator Edward Kennedy and the Speaker of the House, 'Tip' O'Neill, had naïvely been calling for the withdrawal of British troops from the province. In 1969 Kennedy had sent a telegraph to the Northern Ireland civil rights chairman: 'Today the Irish struggle again, but not alone. Your cause is a just cause. The reforms you seek are basic to all democracies worthy of the name. My hopes and prayers go with you.' As a Catholic who talked the politics of non-violence, Hume was someone to whom Kennedy could relate.[2] The two men first met in November 1972 when Kennedy was visiting Germany as a member of the US delegation to the North Atlantic Parliamentary Assembly. Having received an invitation by phone from the Senator, Hume overcame his dislike of flying, borrowed the air fare from the Credit Union and flew to Boston. In deference to Kennedy's wish to avoid the press, the meeting took place at a secret dinner party in the home of a witty old friend of Hume's since Maynooth college days, Seán Ronan, now the Irish Ambassador in Bonn. The Hume and Donlan families had become great friends and regularly went on holiday together.

Hume and Kennedy instantly established a rapport. According to Michael Hand: 'They were both convivial and enjoyed sharing a drink or two. Hume used to like partying. Harmless fun. Hume used to be the life and soul of a party – singing and telling stories. Kennedy was attracted to that sort of thing. They got to know each other well.'

By 1975 Hume was working closely with Kennedy to persuade Irish Americans and the American government to press Britain for an initiative on Northern Ireland. Realizing that Hume was a force for good, and thus needed to be nurtured, Kennedy had played a part in getting him the lectureship at Harvard. While he was in the States the Kennedy clan treated him almost like one of the family, and their endorsement helped cement his ties with other senior American Democrats. Hume got paid relatively little while he was at Harvard, but that did not stop him spending much of his time attending meetings and seminars paralleling the work of the Irish Embassy, which was trying to convert Irish American decision-makers in Boston and Washington to the Dublin view.

Sam and Annie Hume, John's parents,
in the yard of their Derry home

Hume gained his BA in French and History after
leaving Maynooth. He was subsequently awarded
an MA at the National University of Ireland

St Patrick's College, Maynooth, where John Hume studied
for almost three years to be a priest

John and Pat, Derry, 1960

A rare moment of relaxation; Hume with four of his five children: (*left to right*) Thérèse, Aidan, Aine and John (*Belfast Telegraph*)

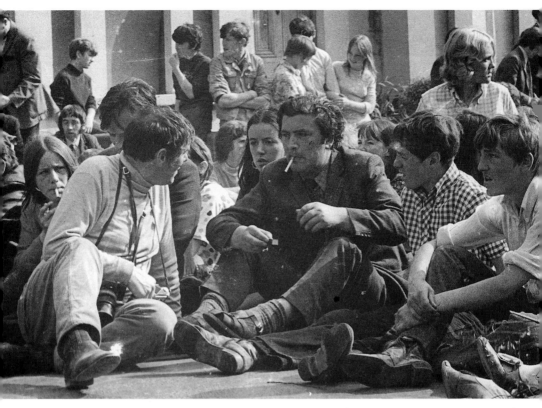

The start of a peaceful protest at Laburnum Terrace, Derry, August 1971.
Hume leads the singing of 'We Shall Not Be Moved' (*Willie Carson*)

Later that day Hume was covered in purple dye by the army and arrested
on Westland Street with fellow MP Ivan Cooper (*Willie Carson*)

Price of principle. Hume inspects an SDLP office wrecked in an arson attack. During the Troubles his cars and house in Derry were also firebombed (*Belfast Telegraph*)

He was especially keen to further the efforts of the Taoiseach, Liam Cosgrave, to cut off financial support to the IRA. His efforts had their reward when in New York on St Patrick's Day in March 1977 – at his suggestion – Edward Kennedy, Tip O'Neill, Hugh Carey and Daniel Moynihan made a combined appeal to Irish Americans to refuse to support organizations which indulged in violence in Northern Ireland.

Of those barnstorming years, Hume said:

I built very strong friendships with Ted Kennedy, Senator Daniel Moynihan, Tip O'Neill and Governor Carey. They became known as the 'Four Horsemen of the Apocalypse'. They kept in regular contact with me and took advice from me on the Irish scene. That led to the foundation of the Friends of Ireland congress as well, whose first chairman was Tom Foley, who later became Speaker. When Tip was Speaker he came over and visited me on the streets of Derry as well. He and I became very close friends. About six months before he died he wrote of his five heroes in the world. I was one of the five. Jimmy Carter was one. Tip was a great friend. The 'Four Horsemen' idea led to the tradition of issuing statements every St Patrick's Day. They always consulted me as to what should be in the statements. The first one was Jimmy Carter's in 1977 calling on the two governments to work together.

The 1977 'Four Horsemen' statement gained sufficient credibility in Washington to enable Hume to progress to influencing the policy of President Jimmy Carter. With Hume advising on tactics, the White House prepared a speech which Carter delivered on 30 August stressing the need for the 'Irish dimension' in seeking to solve the problems of Northern Ireland. Significantly, the President hinted that if a political settlement could be reached, US government funds might be made available for economic development in the province. When interviewed in Derry about the declaration, Hume characteristically did not take any credit for it himself. He enthusiastically claimed that because of the offer, politicians should redouble their efforts to find an agreement:

It underlines the encouraging and valuable good will for all
the people of Northern Ireland in the United States. Coming
as it does in a month when unemployment figures have
reached their highest point since 1938, it shows the people
what the real prize of agreement can be – a prize that could
help us eradicate once and for all our serious economic and
social ills.

Anxious to demonstrate what the benefits of partnership could
be, Hume urged the Northern Ireland Secretary, Roy Mason, to
sponsor the sending of a joint Unionist and Nationalist trade mission to America to promote industrial investment. The Official
Unionists' vice-president, the Reverend Martin Smyth, welcomed
the idea and said they 'would be happy to see a joint delegation
going to the United States'. But to IRA supporters in America,
even the prospect of Ulster attracting investment before a unified
Ireland had been achieved was anathema. In April 1978 Leaders
of the Ancient Order of Hibernians wrote threatening letters to
executives of major US corporations saying they should be wary
of investing in Northern Ireland because most of the new jobs
would go to Protestants. Ominously, the letters said they should
be concerned about the possible safety of their plant and their
executive personnel in Northern Ireland, and warned of the
dangers of being singled out by paramilitary groups. Hume was
furious that the campaign might sabotage the effort he had been
making for years in America to counteract Provisional IRA propaganda and to seek investment to provide jobs.[3] He claimed:

It is imperative that these misguided people are made aware
of the facts. We had to persuade some Irish Americans in the
past that their money was not going to spill, but save, blood
in the North. Now we must convince some AOH members
that if they in any way prevent new jobs from coming here
they will be prolonging the agony.

That year Seán Donlan became Irish Ambassador in Washington. Having encouraged the development of the non-violent
interest group Friends of Ireland, with Hume's assistance he was
influential in getting the 'Four Horsemen' to stiffen their
St Patrick's Day message in 1979 with a plea for the British

government to give some consideration to the question of allowing the island of Ireland to be divided into a confederation.[4] In January 1979 Hume made a nationwide speaking tour of the United States, urging audiences to recognize that violence was not a cause but an effect of the Troubles in Northern Ireland. By then he had become a regular visitor to the United States, and would usually travel there once or twice a year. Already he had established the tradition of getting prominent peace-loving Irish Americans to make reformist speeches on St Patrick's Day. In support of that he made it his custom to visit the United States for a week or so each March.

The eventual effect of Hume's efforts to persuade Irish Americans to take a more responsible attitude towards the problems of the North was that Nationalists in Ireland gradually came to focus their attention on seeking to achieve their ambitions by purely political, rather than partially terrorist, means. For his efforts, in 1979 Hume was feted at an Ireland Fund dinner in the Madison Hotel – one of Washington's finest. A hush fell over the crowded room when Senator Edward Kennedy got to his feet at the rostrum to pay tribute to his old friend, declaring: 'He has made a significant difference in the moderating of the extreme elements in the US. In this way he has been a great service to all the people here and in the North. John Hume is one of the finest and most creative political leaders of our generation, a man of extraordinary courage, wisdom and understanding.' The audience greeted those words with loud and prolonged applause. Throughout the speech Hume had sat motionless, his eyes slightly downcast. The applause he responded to with a shy smile and a wave.

Already Hume had begun to wonder if a solution to Ireland's partition problem might be found within a European context. His opportunity to discover the means in Brussels and Strasbourg by which that might be done occurred in June 1977 when he was appointed political assistant to Richard Burke, Ireland's Commissioner with responsibility for Consumer Affairs.

For Hume, the job was a godsend. In addition to providing him with some financial security, it enabled him to mix with a galaxy of European political talent. According to Burke, he had good working relations with the *chef de cabinet* and other cabinet members. They were a closely knit team and Hume fitted in well. Also part of that entourage was a distinguished RTE television journalist, and an Irish civil servant, Michael Lillis, who would later go on to play a leading role in the establishment of the Anglo-Irish Agreement. Hume told me: 'Dick Burke offered me a part-time job as his special adviser in the European Commission. That of course was very valuable to me, in addition to helping me in a difficult financial time. I built a lot of major contacts in Europe and I got to know the European scene inside out. That's been valuable to me ever since.' Again, when the chips were down it was from abroad, not from Britain or the Ulster Unionists, that rescue came – an experience which understandably strained Hume's loyalties further. From *Who's Who* it would seem that after the Constitutional Convention collapsed in 1976 further financial salvation for the Humes came from abroad in the form of a year-long job acquired for John Hume via Dick Spring – a prominent Irish Labour party politician, later to be Irish Foreign Minister – as a research fellow in European Studies at Trinity College, Dublin. However, Trinity College has no record of his ever having worked there.

As Burke's assistant, Hume continued to live in Derry but regularly travelled to Brussels and other European capitals. Burke was the Commissioner with special responsibility for setting up relations with the European Parliament prior to its first direct election. Hume used to go with him to Strasbourg on each occasion and would act as a lieutenant. Doing so enabled him to see the operation of the parliament at close quarters. He was commissioned by Burke to assess the attitudes of European Union member governments to consumer issues; strengthen links with the European Parliament; and prepare the ground for a high-level EC conference to examine the implications for consumers of recent changes in the economic climate. Hume's appointment had a clear political significance as it effectively gave the Common Market and its institutions their first direct link with the Catholic community in Northern Ireland since the UK joined the European Community. It certainly had a profound effect on Hume's political thinking. He told me that it reinforced in his mind the perception that in the history of the world, Europe was the best example of conflict resolution.

When you think back fifty years, thirty-five million people died right across the continent. Who could have forecast that?

And that was not the first time. Who could have forecast then that there would be a united Europe? Now the Germans are still Germans and French are still French. How did they do it? By recognizing that difference is not a threat. Recognizing that difference is natural. There are not two human beings in the entire human race who are the same. These are some of my favourite repeating phrases: 'It's an accident of birth what you are born and where you are born and whether that accident is race, creed or nationality, it should never be a source of hatred or conflict. The answer to difference is to respect difference.' What they did in Europe was to build institutions which respected their differences – the Council of Ministers, the Commission – but allowed them to work their common ground together. Economics. They built with their sweat and not their blood, and by doing that began the healing process. Now that's precisely what I want to do in the North. Create institutions that allow people to work their common ground together.

The province had found itself with no direct political representation at the EC level since the Ulster Unionist MEP, Rafton Pounder, lost his seat in the European Parliament after the February 1974 general elections. A Conservative group subsequently offered to give up one of their allotted Strasbourg seats to an MP from the Ulster Unionist coalition but the offer was not accepted.[5]

When in May 1979 Hume's next opportunity – albeit another hopeless one – to stand for Westminster in a general election arose, he did not put himself forward. Instead he concentrated his energies on getting elected to the European Parliament in the June 1979 European elections. The British government had become as anxious as the Irish government to see his political career survive. Cynics wondered if the third European parliamentary seat the British government created for Northern Ireland had been made specially for him. Promising in his election manifesto to get special regional aid for the province, he won convincingly, fighting to gain a share of the province's European contingent of three MEPs with the Unionists Ian Paisley and John Taylor. When counting under the proportional representation system was completed, Harry West – the leader of the Official Unionist party – was eliminated and the party's second-choice candidate, John Taylor, had to struggle to fill the third available seat. The DUP leader Ian Paisley, campaigning as the man who would protect Ulster against the Catholics of the Common Market, topped the poll with 170,686 votes. Nevertheless, as the SDLP candidate, Hume was comfortably elected on the third count.

Immediately he resigned from Burke's staff. Without that job he probably might still have been unemployed. In that position and with no experience gained of Europe he would have lacked credibility as a candidate. Fortunately he had fallen on his feet. A decade later he would publicly acknowledge his debt of gratitude to Burke, saying: 'I owe my success to that down there man who gave me that job in Brussels.'

Europe had become a significant element in John Hume's political life. From now on, as an MEP he would spend some 100 days a year on the continent. In Derry he was able to expand the level of service he gave to his constituents. An office was established at 24 Strand Road, where his wife Pat and his faithful chief of staff, Denis Haughey, could assist him with constituency business. On being elected, Hume joined the bureau of the European Socialist Group, and put himself forward to serve on the ACP–EEC joint committee which dealt with economic aid to the third world. In his maiden speech he expressed the hope that the European Parliament would take a close interest in the underlying causes of the Troubles in Northern Ireland.

> It seems to me not very logical to think that one can discuss the purely security aspects of a problem without also discussing the political situation which has given rise to those security aspects. I therefore look forward to their joining with me, not just in discussing some aspects of this problem, but in bringing on to the floor of this House a full-scale discussion of a problem that has poisoned relations between two of our Member States at least for the past decade and, as we all know, for many years before that, because it seems to me quite illogical that we in this House should pass comment on what is happening in other parts of the world far outside this Community and refuse to face and discuss a serious political problem within our own boundaries. I must say it is foolish to assume that you can solve problems like this by security measures alone. There is a deep political

problem there that has to be faced up to and has to be resolved, and I would welcome a full-scale discussion of it in this House at a future date.

The main focus of his attention was the European Parliament's Committee on Regional Policy and Planning, of which he became a member. His fluency in French and the experience he had gained of Brussels bureaucracy while Richard Burke's adviser proved to be invaluable in the manoeuvres he needed to engage in to win EC grants. As a consequence of his lobbying a substantial portion of the £25 million needed to build a new bridge across the Foyle came from Brussels, as did cash to develop both Derry's harbour and its airport. In the past there had been official approaches from Northern Ireland for the setting-up of a Commission Office in Belfast, along the lines of the EU offices in Cardiff and Edinburgh, but without result. Hume lent his weight to the campaign to get one established.[6] Although in Ulster Ian Paisley and John Hume were great rivals, in Europe Hume was able to establish a working relationship with the mercurial churchman. With John Taylor, however, a *modus operandi* could never be found.

By 1979 Hume had established himself as a tough and experienced campaigner who had a far wider international reputation and much closer ties with influential politicians in Brussels and America than even the ministers at the Northern Ireland Office.

Humespeak

Although he was now spending much of his time abroad, in September 1976 John Hume took an active role in talks in which the SDLP aimed to find areas of common ground with the Official Unionists. With Paddy Devlin he proposed that the functions of the Secretary of State for Northern Ireland should be discontinued and his powers transferred to a resident in Northern Ireland, to be called the Lord President, who would oversee a Cabinet representing all parties in the province. That Cabinet would control policing and other powers by agreement with Whitehall. The SDLP contingent also suggested that the North and the South should negotiate directly on matters of common concern, and that any government institution in the North should aim to have the full support of people in both North and South.[1]

The Reverend Martin Smyth and the Unionist negotiator, Captain Austin Ardill, had agreed with most of the SDLP's proposals for denuding the Secretary of State of his powers. However, the talks suddenly broke down on the question of power-sharing, with the Unionists accusing the SDLP of refusing to give up the idea of that sacred goal. As had so often been the case, the Official Unionists gave into pressure from hardliners within the UUUC coalition to end the talks. The DUP and other elements within the United Ulster Unionist movement had been violently opposed to the talks and feared a sell-out. Hume reacted vigorously by making the content of the talks public.

Despite the province's war-weariness, such was the lack of genuine common ground in politics that even the popul-arist Peace People movement eventually disintegrated. It had originally been sparked off by an accident in August 1976 in Belfast's staunchly Republican Andersonstown district, in which three children died when hit by an IRA gunman's car. Outraged by the senseless killing, the children's aunt, Mairead Corrigan, and Betty Williams, who had witnessed the accident, formed the Women's Peace Movement. Paddy Devlin dismissed it as a nine days' wonder, but Hume was not so sure. Eventually calling themselves the 'Peace People', the movement organized marches in Dublin and Belfast and throughout the province. In Derry, Protestant and Catholic women together marched over the Craigavon Bridge. Furious that the Peace People were sapping their already wilting support, the Provisionals transformed the statement on the movement's signs as 'Seven Years is Enough' into 'Seven Hundred Years is Enough'.

For their efforts Corrigan and Williams were awarded the 1976 Nobel Peace Prize. They went on long foreign tours and accepted degrees, to advertise their cause as being 'a non-violent movement towards a just society'. Despite their efforts – which included the founding of a Peace Assembly – personal differences were eventually to cause the Movement's demise. Meanwhile, in Ulster the killings continued.

In August 1977, news that the level of unemployment in the province had reached its highest point since 1938 increased the SDLP's sense of frustration. At Westminster they reckoned the British government was entering into 'shameful pacts' with Unionist MPs. Disgruntled that their prospects of returning to any form of power-sharing were the poorest they had been since the dissolution of the Constitutional Convention, the SDLP leaders refused invitations to attend official receptions which had been organized for the Queen's Silver Jubilee visit.

The years of opposition were increasingly straining party unity. The divisions were highlighted in September, when Paddy Devlin, one of the party's founder members, split with his old comrades, alleging that the SDLP had reverted to sterile Nationalism. To Hume's anguish, another high-ranking rebel was the SDLP's chief whip, Austin Currie, who in the May 1979 general election stood as an Independent in the Fermanagh and South Tyrone constituency, and in doing so lost the seat to an Independent Republican.

For years, on the advice of successive British ministers, Gerry Fitt and others in the SDLP leadership had been holding back from declaring that the unity of Ireland was the party's ultimate aim. However, in 1977, while Hume was away in America, SDLP extremists had been making a flurry of 'green' statements calling for an immediate declaration from Britain that it intended to withdraw from Northern Ireland. Quarrels were breaking out more frequently than ever between urban members such as Gerry Fitt and the county Nationalists.

Judging that a shift towards Nationalism would best hold the party together, for the SDLP's annual conference in November Hume produced a distinctly 'green' document – *Facing Reality*. Laying renewed stress on the Irish dimension, it called on the British government to declare a long-term aim for Northern Ireland and to enter talks with Dublin and local politicians about fresh initiatives. Adopted by the conference, *Facing Reality* called for cross-border economic cooperation on a scale unheard of since the Sunningdale agreement.[2] The majority of the SDLP rank and file favoured committing the party to an aim of a federal island, but Hume's document proved to be sufficiently hard-line to keep even the most extremist of them at bay. Nevertheless, he did not relax. Seeking to gain wider support for the party's new radicalism, following an SDLP meeting in Dungannon he went on Irish radio to declare it was high time that the Taoiseach, Jack Lynch, and other Fianna Fáil politicians made known exactly what they meant by Irish unity.

Adding to the SDLP's sense of frustration was the stance the Opposition leader, Margaret Thatcher, was taking on Ireland. Accompanied by Airey Neave, the shadow spokesman on Ulster, she visited the province in June 1978 and made a strongly pro-Unionist speech, describing power-sharing as 'not a phrase I have heard used by either side at Westminster'. To the dismay of the SDLP she ruled out the prospect of a power-sharing local assembly on which they had pinned so much hope. Hume bitterly attacked her proposal to restore an upper tier of local government and rejected her invitation to the SDLP to participate on such committees, claiming that she ignored the fact that the abuse of local government powers was the original cause of the unrest.

Official Unionists were disappointed that Mrs Thatcher made it clear that if the Conservatives were elected at the next general election they would not rush into restoring self-government to the province on the scale they would like.[3] Even so, Hume claimed her visit would serve only to increase the difficulties the govern-

ment was having in getting the Unionists to start talks on a political solution. He described her speech as irresponsible and accused
her of coming to Northern Ireland with the sole intention of brib-
ing the Ulster Unionists in order to secure power herself. 'This
is a blatant attempt to play the Orange card yet again. Anybody
who has serious views about resolving the crisis here must look
at all sections of opinion. Mrs Thatcher made no attempt to see
any parties other than the Unionists.'

Soon after the Conservatives had come to power in the 1979
general election it became apparent to numerous SDLP members
that fears that the Thatcher administration would impose a settlement on Ulster were unjustified. However, when the new Secretary of State for Northern Ireland, Humphrey Atkins, began
planning an all-party conference as a first step towards finding a
solution to the political deadlock in the province, further strain
was put on the unity of the SDLP. Whereas Gerry Fitt favoured
a step-by-step approach which would endeavour to get all the
parties concerned to agree on a new Northern Ireland government
and then deal with the question of the relationship with the South,
the SDLP membership unanimously wanted discussion of the
'Irish dimension' to be the minimal requirement for the SDLP's
participation in such talks.

In his working document and in the news conference to launch
it, Atkins made Fitt's job impossible by categorically stating that
Irish unity was not to be discussed. It had been decided to exclude
the unity issue from the conference agenda largely because it was
that which had helped to bring down the power-sharing Executive
of 1974. Predictably, the SDLP executive voted against attending
the talks. Bitterly disappointed that he had been unable to deliver
to Atkins the promise of SDLP attendance at the talks, on 22
November Fitt called a press conference at Westminster and
announced his decision to resign as SDLP leader. He complained
that the party had been taken over by the Provisionals.

As Fitt's deputy, John Hume automatically became acting
leader. In many respects, that was what he had been since the
SDLP was formed. In 1969 the new party needed a figurehead:
as a force in the civil rights movement, Hume had been by far
the most capable person to lead the party, but Fitt, as the only
founder member who was a Westminster MP, was reckoned to
be more likely to supply the fledgling group with the kudos it

needed to be taken seriously as a political party. Now it was Hume who was the party's star attraction. In June he had become the SDLP's first MEP, winning a huge majority in the European elections. Furthermore, the other leading lights of the party were in no fit state to prevent support for Hume gathering pace like an avalanche. Austin Currie had wrecked his own chances by standing as an Independent in the general election; Frank Feely, the Newry representative of the SDLP, was relatively inexperienced; and Seamus Mallon, who had been elected to the Assembly in 1973 and had become the chairman of the constituency representatives, was currently recovering from a bout of ill-health. Thus it was no surprise when, a week later on Wednesday, 28 November, at the hastily convened meeting of constituency representatives, Hume was unanimously elected leader. Seamus Mallon, the Armagh schoolteacher, became his deputy. They disagreed on the speed with which Britain should withdraw and the type of Irish state there should be, but despite that were able to work together.

The 43-year-old Hume had become the undisputed political head of Northern Ireland's constitutional Nationalists, but there was scarce time for him to celebrate his victory. An immediate task for him was to keep even the prospect of talks alive. Influenced by Enoch Powell, Jim Molyneaux's Official Unionists had made it plain they would not take part in Atkins's proposed conference. Only Oliver Napier's non-sectarian Alliance Party and Ian Paisley's DUP were left as willing participants, but without the Official Unionists – who were numerically the largest party in the province – the conference would be a meaningless exercise.[4] Having convened a weekend meeting of SDLP executive and constituency representative colleagues, Hume had talks at Stormont Castle with Humphrey Atkins to try to break the deadlock. Already he doubted that the government was really serious about its objectives and wondered whether the conference was merely intended to silence American critics of its inactivity. When he met Atkins his suspicions were confirmed. It was apparent that no serious thought had gone into the initiative; certainly there had not been the widespread talks with party leaders that Atkins had been claiming. The constitutional conference that Lord Carrington had just convened at Lancaster House to solve the apparently intractable problem of Zimbabwe's independence was proving to be a considerable triumph. But in sad contrast, the prospects of the Ulster talks being a success were virtually nil.

Privately, however, the party leaders were in a mood for compromise and were anxious to find a form of words to get the conference moving. After further discussions at Stormont with Atkins, Hume eventually agreed a formula which he hoped would enable progress to be made. He accepted that the conference should not be seen as an end in itself but rather as a means of identifying methods by which Westminster might hand over responsibility for certain powers to locally elected representatives. Private assurances were given that the SDLP would be free to put papers containing its own proposals to the conference, and that such offerings would be discussed. Wisely, Hume was careful to carry his party with him, and convened a meeting of the SDLP executive to get the concessions approved. This breakthrough had been possible because the DUP had adopted a rather more conciliatory stance as a result of its wish to help the new Tory government in its search for a political solution. A further and particularly significant factor in this shift had been Hume's personal links with Ian Paisley.[5] The two men were now the undisputed giants of contemporary Ulster politics. Each had won an overwhelming victory in the June parliamentary elections. In Brussels and Strasbourg, and when they inevitably met at airports and on trains, their contacts were cordial. I was told by the *Belfast Telegraph* journalist Barry White, who knows both politicians well, that relations between them are quite ambivalent. Nevertheless, they have learnt to respect each other's political abilities and have come to maintain a reasonable working relationship.

Eventually, on 7 January the constitutional conference began with eighteen representatives – six from each of the three parties – seated around a table at the Stormont parliament building. At Atkins's suggestion it had been agreed that there should be 'parallel talks': the first conference would deal with areas where agreement was possible, such as the form of voting for any new assembly; the second would discuss various subject matters in detail. Knowing that Paisley was attending only to 'ensure that there was no conspiracy to break the union', Hume was not surprised when the Reverend furiously withdrew the DUP from the entire proceedings. Technically the constitutional conference was merely adjourned, but effectively it was dead. From the outset Hume had been highly pessimistic about the prospects of the talks reaching any form of agreement; nevertheless he had hoped it might be the start of a continuing process.

More than ever Hume was convinced that the British government had to be persuaded to abandon the constitutional guarantee it had effectively given to Ulster's Unionist majority in 1949. In 'Unity Should Be UK Policy', a carefully thought-out article he wrote for the *Guardian* of 18 February 1980, he claimed that as long as Britain continued with its present policy there would be absolutely no incentive for the Unionist political leadership to talk to anyone. 'We are not asking that Great Britain pull out and leave us to it, but that she should join the ranks of those who would persuade the Unionists that their future lies in a stable and firm political association with the rest of Ireland, and that she should use all her power and influence in that persuasion.'

Some attitudes in Dublin were changing, as was noted by the influential Conservative backbencher Michael Mates. He told me:

The turning-point was the murder of Mountbatten on 27 August 1979. That brought home to the Irish the fact that the IRA were as much an enemy of their state as of ours. Then Jack Lynch came over here and had to make an act of public apology for what had happened in his country. He came over for Mountbatten's state funeral. That was one of the turning points because when he went back from here he started giving completely different sets of orders particularly to the Garda who became much more cooperative. He caused there to be a reassessment of the IRA threat, as it affected the Republic. That changed a lot of things.

It was Charles Haughey, who had replaced Jack Lynch as Taoiseach in December 1979, whom Mrs Thatcher met at the Anglo-Irish summit on 21 May 1980 to discuss the question of Irish reunification. Hume was heartened to recognize elements of the cherished 'Irish dimension' in the Green Paper which the British government published in July; but within an hour of seeing that discussion paper Paisley and Molyneaux predictably rejected the power-sharing executive idea which Whitehall had proposed as a means of restoring democratic government to the province. Hume conveyed his party's mood of despair at an afternoon meeting with Atkins at Stormont. There he again insisted that a route beyond the impasse could be found only by removing the constitutional guarantee on Ulster's place within the United Kingdom. It was a point which Haughey had also been making.

Meanwhile, a crisis was looming in Ulster regarding demands for convicted terrorists to be granted political status. Since 1972, when Whitelaw had agreed to allow such inmates 'special category' status, the British government had steadily been phasing out their privileges and introducing a policy of criminalization. In the Maze Prison – the former Long Kesh camp – inmates had been treated like prisoners of war and had been allowed their own organization and discipline.[6] Their refusal to wear prison uniforms led to the 'blanket' protest; then the prisoners' refusal to leave their cells for fear of being attacked by the warders when using the bathrooms eventually developed into the 'dirty protest'. Since the warders refused to clean out certain cells in the H-blocks with prisoners present, the cells soon became virtual open sewers. The worldwide adverse publicity for the British government that the 'dirty protest' attracted in 1979 encouraged IRA prisoners to escalate their squalid martyrdom into a hunger strike.

The hunger strike began in late October 1980 when one INLA and six IRA prisoners began refusing food. Hume feared that the protest would cause an escalation of sectarian tension and confrontation on a scale not seen for years. He also saw his chance to win some kudos for the SDLP by attempting to mediate to bring the strike to a close. The two crucial points of the prison regime on which he recognized the British government needed to concede were the right to wear civilian clothes and the right to free association. He reinforced those demands by quoting a European Court of Human Rights ruling that: 'Governments, as the custodial authority, are required to safeguard the health and well-being of all prisoners whether protestors or not.' Meeting in Newcastle, Co. Down, the annual conference of the SDLP overwhelmingly supported an emergency motion deploring the 'ineptitude' of the government's handling of the affair and called on the authorities to permit the prisoners to wear their own clothing.

During talks in London with Atkins in December, Hume urged the Secretary of State to look at humanitarian reform with a view to defusing the situation. Subsequently he issued a statement appealing to those on hunger strike to call off their protest. At

Hume's suggestion a representative of the Northern Ireland Office travelled to the Maze and presented a proposal document to the prisoners. By offering a compromise on prison clothing, the initiative was sufficient to bring about a halt to the hunger strike at Christmas. But when – contrary to Sinn Fein's advice – Bobby Sands, the IRA prisoners' commanding officer in the Maze, decided the clothing issue was an all-or-nothing matter, preparations were made for the next hunger strike.

In the months that followed Sands' commencement of a hunger strike in March 1981, there were scores of demonstrations by H-block supporters. Throughout the province there was a huge upsurge of civil disturbances in which thousands of petrol, acid and blast bombs were thrown. Some of the worst rioting was in Derry, where during one week there was disorder every day. Attempting to establish a 'Free Derry' no-go area reminiscent of the early 1970s, youths in the Bogside built road blocks around the ghetto with paving stones and barbed wire. One of the oldest-established shops in the area, which had served the ordinary people of the city for generations, was burned out. For the people who lived in the riot areas, many of them elderly, it was a nightmare existence. Just a few hundred yards from Hume's house on the Bogside two youths were killed in an accident involving an army Land Rover. With tension in the district as high as he had seen it for many years, Hume claimed the army was extremely irresponsible for recklessly firing off plastic bullets. But he also condemned 'those who bring young people on to the streets to riot at the present time and in the present atmosphere.'

The SDLP's credibility as a conciliatory Nationalist grouping had been severely eroded by the additional tide of Republican extremism that had flowed from the Maze hunger strike crisis. As many young Catholics had rapidly come to regard support for the National H-Blocks Committee as an article of faith, the SDLP found itself greatly compromised when Frank Maguire, the Nationalist MP for Fermanagh South, suddenly died and the now emaciated Sands put himself forward as an Anti-H-Block candidate in the ensuing parliamentary by-election. At the last minute, in response to death threats from the Provisionals, Maguire's brother decided not to contest the election as an Independent. Unfortunately, the SDLP's Austin Currie heard news of that decision fractionally too late to submit his own nomination papers.

In the absence of the SDLP fielding a candidate to split the Nationalist vote, on 9 April Sands – with Sinn Fein campaigning on his behalf – was elected with a majority of 1,446 to serve as a Westminster MP.

That summer another hunger striker, Kieran Doherty, was elected to the Dáil. When, following Bobby Sands' death, an election was called in Fermanagh South in August 1981 the SDLP again failed to field a candidate. This time, however, on Hume's instructions, it deliberately abstained. The result was a win for the Sinn Fein candidate, Sands' former election agent Owen Carron. Albeit only for tactical reasons, the Republicans were increasingly turning to democratic institutions to gain propaganda for themselves.

One of the many who criticized Hume for avoiding a confrontation with Sinn Fein was the eminent Irish socialist Dr Noel Browne, who claimed: 'In betraying representative democracy in favour of the men of violence, Hume has become one of them.' In the polarized atmosphere of Ulster at that time, by taking too moderate a line Hume had put the SDLP in mortal danger of being squeezed out by pressure from both sides. The pro-Sinn Fein weekly *Republican News* falsely alleged that Hume was secretly in favour of internment, and had instructed members of his party to distance themselves from the H-block campaign; on the other side were the Official Unionists, who in August launched an attack on the SDLP, claiming it was no longer regarded in either Northern Ireland or the Irish Republic as a moderate Catholic party. In an attempt to discredit the SDLP's reputation it produced what it called the 'Hume File' – a collection of newspaper cuttings about recent political decisions by the SDLP. Even the former party leader, Gerry Fitt, had turned on his old comrades by becoming an Independent Socialist MP and thereby leaving the SDLP without any formal representation at Westminster.

All the while Hume had been searching for wider answers to Ulster's problems. Convinced that the search for peace in Northern Ireland was intimately linked with the winning of better living and working conditions, in June 1981 he persuaded the European Parliament in Strasbourg to accept unanimously a report calling for a detailed study to be conducted by the Commission into the province's economy. Compiled by the Committee on Regional Policy and Planning, the study found that so far Britain's membership of the European Community had made no significant impact on the economic circumstances of Northern Ireland; but, to Hume's satisfaction, it recommended broad social measures to offset the dismal jobs and industry situation.[7] Hume also continued to use his position as an MEP to curb some of the excesses of the conflict. In May 1982 a motion he tabled calling for the use of anti-riot plastic bullets to be banned was overwhelmingly approved by the European Parliament. A few months later he persuaded the European Community to ask its Political Affairs Committee to investigate the political situation in the province. To ensure that the committee, chaired by the Danish Liberal Nils Haagerup, carried out its brief he persuaded the Socialist group in the European Parliament to establish a working party on Northern Ireland to monitor it.

Partly as a consequence of the pressure that Hume's influential friends in Washington had been putting on the British government, since her meeting with Charles Haughey in May 1990 Mrs Thatcher had increasingly felt the need to have more dialogue with the government in Dublin. That December the two premiers met and decided to establish a practice of holding twice-yearly summits. Hume had lost a powerful friend when Haughey was swept from office in June 1981 by a Fine Gael–Labour coalition led by Dr Garret FitzGerald; nevertheless at the second summit in November 1981 Thatcher and FitzGerald agreed to form an Anglo-Irish Intergovernmental Council. To supplement that, the new Secretary of State, Jim Prior, convened a Northern Ireland economic conference. Predictably, the Official Unionists and Democratic Unionists refused to attend – in Ian Paisley's case, because he believed the meeting could facilitate the creation of a parliamentary tier to the Anglo-Irish Council.[8] To Hume's disappointment, Dublin's support for Argentina during the Falklands War temporarily put a freeze on any genuine wish Mrs Thatcher might have felt to develop the Council further. Nevertheless the first step had been taken.

Although he was enthusiastic about the Intergovernmental Council, Hume was convinced that the British government's latest devolution plans stood no chance of furthering political progress in the province. A White Paper was published in April 1982, outlining the structure of the new Stormont Assembly in which six committees would be formed, in proportion to party strengths, to scrutinize government policy and to draft legislation. Also envisaged was a second stage where legislative power could be transferred to the Assembly. However, that would require the agreement of 70 per cent of Assembly members – a degree of consensus that was unlikely ever to be achieved. Hume dismissed the Prior initiative as ill-thought-out, and the body proposed as 'an unworkable and powerless assembly with powerless committees'. The Assembly would leave the SDLP with even less influence over the conduct of the province's affairs than its predecessor had wielded in the Sunningdale period. For weeks Hume and much of the SDLP considered boycotting the Assembly elections which Prior was preparing to hold in October. Finally, after a seven-hour-long closed meeting in August, at Hume's direction the constituency representatives decided by twenty-five votes to fifteen to contest the election, but to take no part in the Assembly unless there were radical changes to the government's plans. Basically, the SDLP's plan was to seek a mandate from its supporters to hold itself ready but aloof until there was an institution of which it could approve.

Hume's argument for involvement in the election had been that to remain a political force the SDLP needed to fight elections and provide some sort of leadership.[9] Realistically, he feared that if the SDLP did not make a significant showing it would be at risk of being usurped as the democratically elected voice of Ulster's Catholics by Sinn Fein. On the hustings he sought to distance his party from Provisional Sinn Fein, saying: 'The people have for the first time the opportunity of stating very clearly where they stand on the issue of violence and non-violence. We have had a campaign of violence for the past twelve years by the Provisionals. They are clearly seeking a mandate to justify that in retrospect and to justify its continuation.' Hurling a huge amount of effort into the election, Sinn Fein spent £27,000 on its Assembly campaign, compared to Hume's mere £1,390. Their reward for that effort was 64,000 votes – 10 per cent of the total number cast – an impressive achievement compared to the Alliance's 59,000 and ten seats, and the SDLP's 119,000 and fourteen seats. Like the SDLP, Sinn Fein had no intention of taking its place in the 78-member Assembly, yet by winning five seats and getting its leading members – Danny Morrison, Martin McGuinness and vice-president Gerry Adams – elected it had gained valuable democratic legitimacy. Its successful challenge for the Nationalist vote brought despondency to the SDLP, several of whose senior figures began to wonder if the party should radically rethink its future. Clearly there was going to have to be a fundamental battle within Ulster's Nationalist community on the question of how Irish unity could be achieved.

Hume's scepticism about the Assembly, and about the willingness of its Loyalist members to share real power, was soon proved justified when Official Unionist members insisted that John Cushnahan, a leading member of the non-sectarian Alliance Party, would be 'unacceptable' as chairman of the education committee because he was a Catholic. Incidents such as that were sufficient evidence for Hume to denounce the Assembly at the SDLP's annual conference in January 1983 as a 'meaningless charade'. The party unaminously backed his call to take no part in the Assembly. Hume was now surer than ever that Irish unity should be the central plank of the SDLP's policy commitments.

When launching the SDLP's Assembly election manifesto on 1 October 1982, Hume announced a plan to create a 'Council for a New Ireland' in conjunction with the Republic's Dáil. Effectively he was re-proposing the idea which he had originally mooted in the 1970s. Such a conclave – made up of members of the Dáil and those elected to the Assembly – would, he envisaged, have the task of examining the obstacles to the creation of a 'New Ireland' and producing 'an agreed blueprint' so that a debate on real alternatives could begin within the Anglo-Irish framework.[10] The proposed body would challenge the assumption that underlay all British policy: namely, that any settlement of the Irish question in an all-Ireland framework threatened the basic interests of the Protestants. In conversation with me he explained at length the origins and significance of that initiative.

> I wrote an article for *Foreign Affairs* in 1979. The key thing there was that it was the first time that anybody had suggested this new strategy. Up until then all the internal attempts had failed. This was a new strategy, which I called 'The Irish Question, the British Problem'. In other words, this isn't just an Irish problem; this is a British–Irish problem. What we need to do is get *both* governments working together rather than have the megaphone diplomacy across

the Irish Sea. This was the first time that this argument started. That was our strategy throughout the eighties.

In addition to that, another of our arguments was that what was called Nationalist Ireland had to rethink its attitudes about the simplistic romantic Nationalism. For that reason, in the 1982 election to the Northern Ireland Assembly we made clear that we wouldn't be taking our seats because there was no internal solution. We used it to get a mandate to call for the setting up of a Council for a New Ireland that would re-examine Nationalists' attitudes and their relationship with the Unionist people.

About the time of our manifesto for the 1982 Assembly election I wrote an article in the *Irish News* about it. Then after the election we came to Dublin and argued with the parties here and eventually the government here agreed to set up the Forum for a New Ireland – as they called it; we called it the Council for a New Ireland. The whole purpose of that was to re-examine Nationalist attitudes. If you look at it – the Forum report – the most important part is the section which deals with principles and realities. Some of the parties in the South insisted that there had to be solutions at the end of the day. So they advocated a united Ireland, a federal Ireland. But our view was that in order to engage the Unionists in dialogue it would be better to stick to the principles and the realities, to see if we could get the Unionists to agree to those, and then – having agreed to the structure – give expression to them. That was our strategy. The parties in the South were still Nationalistic in the old sense. However, it was a valuable exercise. Because it led directly to the Anglo-Irish Agreement.

In media interviews he set about cajoling Garret FitzGerald and Charles Haughey to support the Council for a New Ireland. On Channel Four's *Meet the Press* programme he repeated his now familiar visionary line of argument: 'I do not see a solution in a victory for anybody over anybody else. I see a solution in an agreement which respects all the different traditions in Ireland. The Unionists' interests must lie in coming to terms with the rest of the people in Ireland rather than waiting to be conquered by numbers.' Broadening the scope of his argument, he claimed that it was in the South's financial interests to bring the Troubles to a peaceful conclusion: 'I believe the evidence is already there in the cost to the South's economy of providing border security and in the crime rate growing in the cities of the South because so much police work has to be devoted to the border.'

Hume hoped that by opening up the whole debate on the Irish question the Council would make an impact not only on Irish opinion but also on British and international thinking. In search of allies, he wisely invited to the SDLP's twelfth annual conference in Belfast the Irish Labour minister Ruari Quinn, a close associate of the Deputy Prime Minister Dick Spring. Quinn read a message to the conference saying that Spring supported the proposed Council without reservation. The position was reinforced by the SDLP's chairman, Sean Farren, who claimed it was time Britain stopped tinkering around with half-hearted measures: 'As in the Falklands crisis, failure to take courageous political action in Northern Ireland while there is still time is only storing up much greater problems for the future – problems which will inevitably prove tragically costly in terms of life, property and community relations.' He insisted that only when a new Anglo-Irish frame-work was created could progress be made: 'We believe that within such a framework, a completely new and dynamic partnership will develop to unite the suffering people of Northern Ireland and to give them the confidence to cooperate fully in facing their great common social and economic problems.'

Subsequent to a trip Hume made to Dublin for talks with Fitz-Gerald, Spring and Haughey, in March 1983 the Irish government announced that it would be backing the creation of his Council for a New Ireland, and providing facilities at Dublin Castle for it to have its first meeting in May. This decision was provoked by Mrs Thatcher's angry reaction to the European Parliament's decision to proceed with its investigation into Northern Ireland's political and economic problems. For the foreseeable future she had evidently closed her mind to any non-British discussion of Northern Ireland's problems. When the Council met to draw up plans for reunification, Hume hailed his brainchild as the most significant initiative in Ireland since 1920. It intended to sit for much of the summer with the hope of producing a report at the end of the year which would show that Unionists could be accommodated within a new Ireland and that a way could be opened to changing the relationships within the island of Ireland and between Britain and Ireland.[11] Although Sinn Fein was not invited, and the Workers' Party, Alliance Party and the Northern Unionists refused to take part, the delegations meeting at Dublin Castle represented four out of five voters in the island of Ireland. Paisley predictably dismissed the idea as merely 'an international conspiracy against the Ulster people'. Contrary to appearances, there were real differences of emphasis between the Irish parties as to what the Council should achieve. FitzGerald hoped it would produce models for the future, while the Opposition leader Charles Haughey saw it as the first step in a process leading to round table negotiations and Britain's eventual withdrawal from the North. For too many years the Republic's political parties had merely talked about a united Ireland; now they were going to have to look carefully at what the consequences of that unity might be.

FitzGerald and Haughey considered that a principal function of the Council for a New Ireland would be to boost the flagging fortunes of the SDLP. As they saw it, the British government's failure to be more sensitive to the SDLP's problems had been directly responsible for the building up of popular support for the Sinn Fein at the expense of moderate Nationalist politicians. They feared that Prior did not regard the SDLP – as they did – as the last political bulwark against the IRA. It seemed to be vital to show that Hume was making progress so that the SDLP would retain political support. Already weak and demoralized, the party would be further endangered in the forthcoming British general election unless something could be done to restore its credibility with the Catholic community in the North.[12]

Hume was no less concerned. Determined to tackle Sinn Fein head-on, in an aggressive speech at the SDLP's annual conference he launched an eloquent attack on the Provisionals' strategy of pursuing votes in tandem with the campaign of violence.

From this moment onwards, let the stark choice be clear. A vote for these people – and let their own words say it – is a vote for 'unambivalent' support for the armed struggle.

Translated into the reality of the streets, that is a vote for killing industrialists and destroying investment in a community starved of work, a vote for killing working men

and women in the Protestant community who have donned
uniforms and see themselves as the defenders of the Protestant tradition and way of life in this island.

It is a vote for the murder of public figures as they leave
their places of worship, and a vote which encourages young
people to use the Armalite rifle and to spend the best years
of their life in prison. We want to hear no more lies about
two wrongs making a right, no more use of one atrocity to
justify another.

The general election was to be fought on new constituency
boundaries which gave the province seventeen seats instead of its
previous twelve. Sinn Fein's strategy was now to replace the SDLP
as the main voice of the Catholic population. Having secured
64,000 votes in the Assembly elections, they aimed to get
100,000 in the general election – enough, they hoped, to win three
seats. Gerry Adams was likely to capture Gerry Fitt's old West
Belfast seat, and Sinn Fein also had a chance of winning Mid-
Ulster, as well as Fermanagh and South Tyrone.

Despite a shortage of funds, the SDLP took on their opponents
with a zeal which had not been apparent in the Assembly elections.
Hume's deputy Seamus Mallon, who was standing in Newry and
Armagh, appealed to Northern Ireland voters to rescue the name
of Republicanism from those who had disgraced it: 'The Owen
Carrons of this world, who have threatened to destabilize the
Republic of Ireland, have hijacked the aim of Irish unity which is
deeply held by the vast majority of people on this island.' Sinn
Fein, meanwhile, was conducting a vigorous registration drive to
mobilize the Nationalist electorate – traditionally renowned for
abstaining. Having been condemned by the SDLP for taking a
'brutal and thuggish' approach to politics, they responded by
accusing Hume's party of being tired, discredited part-timers. By
continuing with their terrorist actions during the election campaign, the IRA foolishly deprived Sinn Fein of potential support.
In one horrific incident they shot a woman while she was trying
to protect her husband – an English soldier holidaying in Derry –
from gunmen. The killing brought forth the wrath of the Catholic
establishment. Even Derry's Bishop Edward Daly appealed to
voters not to support Sinn Fein at the election. In West Belfast,
SDLP candidates pointed to an IRA bomb outside a police station

– which injured fifteen people and caused some £1 million worth of damage – as evidence of the Provisionals' intentions. The outrage reinforced Hume's campaign theme that the stark choice for Catholic voters was between building with the SDLP and destroying with Sinn Fein.

SDLP premises were themselves targets for attack. The party's advice centre in the Falls Road had its windows broken and an attempt was made to force the door. In Derry, SDLP workers were subjected to harassment and the party's posters were removed from many areas of the city. In an attempt to disrupt the SDLP's campaign there, one Saturday morning a lighted object was thrown through a window of the SDLP office: the building was severely damaged by the resulting fire and 3,000 of Hume's own leaflets and posters were destroyed. The Provisional IRA were suspected of having made the attack. Canvassing in the Creggan estate the next day, Hume brushed it off, claiming it would not affect his campaign: 'Something like this will make our workers more determined.'[13] He was no stranger to intimidation and bomb attacks; the previous August his Victorian terraced house overlooking the Bogside had been attacked by youths who threw petrol bombs and stones.

His resilience was rewarded in the election result: he won the newly formed Foyle constituency with 46 per cent of the vote and an impressive 8,148 majority. Sinn Fein's Martin McGuinness could only manage third place. Elsewhere in the province the results were disappointing for the SDLP, which had polled 17.9 per cent, not far above Sinn Fein's 13.4 per cent: the gap between the rival Nationalist parties had shrunk from 8.7 per cent in October 1982 to 4.5 per cent. Gerry Adams had replaced Gerry Fitt as MP for West Belfast and the night ended with Hume as his party's only MP. The SDLP had fallen far short of their seemingly realistic ambition to win four seats. Of his own achievement Hume jubilantly declared: 'For the first time in three hundred years a Catholic is representing the city of Derry at Westminster.'

Squaring the circle

Some mornings, commuters might see Hume reading a newspaper and eating breakfast in a café next door to the Falkland Islands office in London. Although when in the company of other Irish MPs he would invariably be in a jolly mood, he hated being in London. He did not enjoy Westminster, and spent as little time there as possible, confining himself to matters which affected Northern Ireland. On 13 July, speaking in a Commons debate on capital punishment he argued against the reintroduction of the death penalty, claiming that the 'instability of the present time would be nothing to the reaction if the death penalty were reintroduced. If you want the IRA to win, hang them.' Influentially, his contribution helped harden the vote against the reintroduction of hanging.

Hitherto, a few government officials and ministers apart, few people in Britain knew anything about Hume. The image most politically aware Britons had of him dated back to the early months of the Troubles, when the burly Irishman with dark wavy hair had been seen on television news bulletins appealing for crowds of civil rights demonstrators to behave calmly. Nor did he seek personal fame now; but, as an original thinker and a dynamo of energy, he could not but help make an impact at Westminster. He was soon attempting to have a bust erected in honour of his hero, the influential parliamentarian Charles Stewart Parnell, who had asserted that Irishmen could never achieve unity until they had conciliated the Irish Protestants. Hume was amazed to find that no memorial existed to him. The Speaker told him that no taxpayers' money was available, so Hume persuaded a group of Irish businessmen in London to pay for the bronze and commissioned the Breton sculptor Yann Goulet to create it. The room that Parnell had used had come to be occupied by Annie's Bar, the one watering hole where politicians and lobby correspondents were allowed to mingle, but Hume did not consider that place to be an appropriate location for the bust.[1] Eight years later, with the assistance of the veteran Labour MP Eric Heffer, he got it sited in the Westminster corridor where the old Irish Parliamentary Party used to meet.

On 28 June 1983, as the member for Foyle, Hume rose nervously in the House of Commons to make his maiden speech, declaring: 'It is a commentary on the politics of the north of Ireland that never before has someone with either my religious or my political persuasion stood in the House to represent the city of Derry.' He went on to set out his stall, claiming that Foyle had the highest rate of unemployment of any British constituency, with 38 per cent in Strabane and 28 per cent in Derry. If the government, he said, were to take the economic crisis in the north of Ireland seriously and make a sensible and determined attack on the problems of youth employment, they would also be making a determined attack on the problems of extremism.

> There is no greater example of the reasons for extremism in Derry than that we now have a generation of young people who were only four years old in 1969 and 1970 and have grown up in a society in which they have always seen security forces and violence on the streets, in which they have been continually searched simply because they are young people, and in which – when they reach the age of eighteen – they have no hope of any employment because they happen to have come of age during the deepest economic crisis for a long time. Therefore, there are resentments, and there are sadistic people who play upon these resentments, point to a British soldier and say: 'Get rid of him and all your problems will be solved.'

With some bitterness he claimed that most MPs were relatively unconcerned about what happened in Northern Ireland. Certainly they did not consider the province to be 'as British as Finchley' – as Mrs Thatcher had incorrectly been reported to have once described it.

I should like Hon. Members to take any part of the United
Kingdom over the past decade and to imagine the following
things happening. Imagine 2,000 people maimed and injured,
and £430 million spent on compensation for bomb damage;
two new prisons built and a third under construction; the rule
of law drastically distorted, with the introduction of imprison-
ment without trial; senior politicians and policemen murdered
and innocent civilians murdered by the security forces and by
paramilitary forces. Imagine a shoot-to-kill policy for people
suspected of crime being introduced from time to time instead
of their being arrested. Imagine jury courts being disbanded,
plastic bullets used on the streets and innocent children killed.
Imagine paramilitary organizations engaging in violence and
the type of interrogation methods that led to the British
government being found guilty in the European Court of
Human Rights being introduced. Imagine hunger strikers
dying in prison in Yorkshire and a representative of the paramilitary being elected to this House to represent Yorkshire.

If those things had happened on what is commonly called
the mainland, can anyone tell me that those events would
not have been the major issue in the general election campaign? Can anyone persuade me that any speech made since
that election would not have referred to that issue? However,
the only Hon. Members who have referred to it were leaders
of two parties in Northern Ireland. Nevertheless, we are told
that we are as British as Finchley.

In fact, he claimed, Britain had psychologically withdrawn from
Northern Ireland: 'Britain and Northern Ireland would be
healthier places if that psychological reality were translated into
political reality.' He argued that MPs who represented the Loyalist
tradition had a lot more thinking to do:

Their consistent stance on Northern Ireland has been to protect the integrity of the tradition in an island in which they
form a minority. I have no quarrel with that objective. Any
country is richer for diversity. I quarrel with the methods of
protecting the integrity. Put crudely, that method dictates,
'We must hold power in our hands.' That is precisely what
has been said. It is a violent attitude. It is an attitude which

demands the exclusive exercise of power. The leaders of that tradition have consistently maintained that view, but it invites violence. It is not possible permanently to exclude an entire section of the population from any say in the decision-making process.

The Republican tradition, he told the House, had also taken a rather simplistic approach.

Its argument had often been presented in emotional and romantic terms. Its simplistic definition of Irishness was extremely sectional. It was based substantially on two power-ful strands of the Irish tradition – the Gaelic and Catholic – to the exclusion of the Protestants. That narrow definition made the Protestant tradition feel excluded from that notion of Irishness. In its more extreme form, it was thought right not only to die, but to kill, for that version of Ireland.

The solution he advocated involved denying the Unionists their historic right of veto; being inspired by the European Com-munity's (albeit belated) role in reconciling postwar Europe; and the building of structures which enabled different traditions to live in peace, harmony and unity in a new relationship with Britain. He told the House that central to all of that should be the creation of an all-Ireland Assembly.

Hume's prime concern in the summer of 1983 was to ensure that the Council made progress. Almost immediately it had run into difficulties on the question of economic integration. Eco-nomic reports clearly showed that the South lacked the where-withal to aid the recovery of the six war-torn counties. To concentrate thinking on the vexed question of constitutional change, Hume personally drafted a seminal memorandum, entitled 'The Fundamental Problems', in which he asked why constitutional Nationalists had been unable to persuade Britain to reassess its position on Ireland. He suggested that while British neglect and lack of interest had been significant, the historical reality was that the main problems had been posed by the Loyalists in Northern Ireland. Urging the Forum's members to take into account the Unionists' ethos and misgivings, he floated the idea that the Catholic church's influence in government affairs should be scaled down. When the memorandum was leaked, the latter proposal angered a number of SDLP members, and right-wing Catholic groups. Even more infuriated, when they saw the entire text, were the Unionists – particularly by the section which recommended that the Council consider three different constitutional models: joint sovereignty, a federal system and a unitary state. Thereafter, at Hume's suggestion, the circulation of all working documents was tightly controlled by a steering committee and the Chairman of the Council, Dr Colm O'hEocha.[2] In public Hume continued to preach his creed that victory for either side was no solution to the Irish problem: the result had to be by accommodation and agreement.

With unemployment in Ulster at 21 per cent and still rising, Hume knew he must continue to turn to the wider world for help in attempting to solve the province's problems. In September 1983 he tore himself away from the Dublin Council to go on a nine-day promotional tour in the United States and Canada. Organized by the Northern Ireland Industrial Development Board (IDB), the trip by academics, bankers and trade unionists was a major component in an advertising campaign to sell the economic potential of Ulster to North America. Accompanying Hume on this mission was his political rival, Ian Paisley. Hume did not object to Paisley's presence; indeed, he was glad of the opportunity to underline to American businessmen that divisions in the Ulster community did not extend to economic matters.

The prospect of having to fight Sinn Fein in the June 1984 European elections filled the SDLP with fear that a further erosion of its support could have catastrophic consequences for its credibility. The campaign was expected to be a fight for the hearts and minds of the Catholic community. Speaking at the SDLP's annual conference in Belfast that January, Hume rallied his troops, reminding them they were the only people in the province who were standing up against a tide of nihilism. He claimed:

Sinn Fein insults people by assuming that they would not see the irreconcilable contradiction between the bomb and the ballot paper. Sinn Fein policy is the policy foreseen by George Orwell, the policy that the bigger and more blatant the lie, the more people you are likely to fool. Every one of us sees the unravelling of the structure of civilization going on in our own local community. The most basic roots that hold people together in civilization are being hacked away by the violence of the Provos and the lies of Sinn Fein.

Noting that the economy was in tatters and society in a state of almost terminal disintegration, he told the SDLP they must offer leadership during those dark days in Northern Ireland.[3]

> People know the IRA have bombed thousands of jobs out of existence and have kept thousands of other jobs out of Northern Ireland by murdering industrialists and they are not impressed by Sinn Fein's exploitation of the IRA's dole queues.
> The individual and communal memories of young people recall only the Troubles, only violence, tension and hatred. The economic situation offers them little hope. It interacts powerfully with the political scene. Thus many of the young – the hope and anchor of the future – have become the easy prey of the cult of the Armalite.

In April 1984 the battle began inauspiciously for the SDLP when Hume's election headquarters in Derry was destroyed by fire only two days after opening. Nevertheless, the party was assisted in its campaign by the refusal of Neil Kinnock's Labour party to establish its own party organization in Ulster. Kevin McNamara, a leading advocate of Irish reunification, had successfully persuaded Labour to give every encouragement to Hume's party. Relying on his own superb record as an MEP, in contrast to all other candidates Hume based his campaign squarely on Europe. When the votes had been counted he was delighted to find his strategy rewarded by his getting 60,000 more votes than Sinn Fein's Danny Morrison. The SDLP had captured 22.1 per cent of the poll, compared to Sinn Fein's mere 13.3 per cent. Effectively the SDLP's standing had increased by 4 per cent since the general election. The gain had been made in part as a consequence of many Catholics deserting the Alliance Party to help defeat Sinn Fein. Delighted with the result, which he interpreted as an emphatic victory for non-violence, Hume claimed: 'There is no doubt that the Sinn Fein momentum has been halted. I think the increasing contradictions between the Armalite and the ballot box will continue to weaken them.'

Hume again outpolled the Official Unionists' John Taylor to take the second of Ulster's three European parliamentary seats, an achievement which further heartened the SDLP. A matter of some concern, however, was the performance of the Democratic Unionists' Ian Paisley, who had topped the poll with a massive 34.3 per cent and reversed the DUP's recent decline at the expense of the Official Unionists.

The SDLP continued to be at loggerheads with the British government on the question of what it regarded as the security forces' bias against Nationalists. In the Commons, Hume reprimanded Mrs Thatcher for making a Christmas visit to a barracks where eight members of the Ulster Defence Regiment had just been charged with the sectarian murder of Catholics. Partly because of fear of being identified too closely in the Nationalist community with the government's security policies, in January 1984 a meeting of the SDLP's constituency representatives decided not to allow the party to accept an invitation to meet the RUC Chief Constable, Sir John Hermon, for talks on security strategy. Knowing that since a massacre in a Darkley church the Official Unionists had been boycotting the Assembly as a protest against government security policies, Hume agreed with the representatives and dismissed the invitation as a cynical 'cover for impartiality'.

In June he warned of a crisis of confidence over the perceived partiality of the judiciary and the security forces. A political row had been caused when Lord Justice Gibson, the senior Lord Justice of Appeal in the province, had acquitted three policemen of the murders of three unarmed IRA men who had burst through a police roadblock. Gibson had further infuriated Nationalists on both sides of the border by declaring that the case should never have been brought to trial. Describing the Judge's remarks as 'deplorable', Hume issued a statement:

> There is a general belief that members of the security forces are above the law and beyond its reach. That view is corroborated by the near 100 per cent acquittal rate in charges brought against members of the security forces. This acquittal rate contrasts oddly with the overall acquittal rate of between 12 and 15 per cent in cases involving civilians accused.[4]

At a similar trial involving an RUC officer on a murder charge, Mr Justice MacDermott had acquitted the accused and complimented his marksmanship. Hume alleged that there appeared to be a policy of reserving trials involving members of the security forces for certain judges. No Catholic judge had presided over such a trial in recent years. Garret FitzGerald echoed those concerns, claiming that the police in Northern Ireland had lost the confidence of most Catholics because of recent security operations. In Strasbourg, Hume continued with his efforts to curb what he considered the excesses of the security forces by voting – as he had done in 1982 – for an emergency motion which called on Britain to stop using plastic bullets in Northern Ireland. Rather melodramatically, he claimed: 'If governments ever reduce themselves in their methods to the level of terrorist organizations, they are promoting terrorism itself on a very wide scale.'

After twenty-eight private sessions, thirteen public sessions and fifty-six meetings of the steering group, the Council report was finally published in Dublin on 2 May 1984. Hume called it 'an extraordinary day in the history of our island'. Exploring the possibilities for a future Ireland, it noted that the problem being dealt with was a divided island with a divided society. The recommended solutions were, just as Hume had originally suggested, a federal/confederal state, a system of joint authority or a unitary state. The last of the three was the option favoured by Charles Haughey and the 'greenish' fraction. In Washington, FitzGerald had outlined the Council's conclusions to a joint session of Congress, and was subsequently rewarded with the news that the US Senate and House had voted unanimously to back the report.

But in Northern Ireland there was little appetite for change: the Official Unionists and the Alliance Party published pamphlets explaining why the Council's report should be rejected. Even so, they were careful not to compound the problems of the SDLP needlessly, still fearing that the party might be replaced by Sinn Fein as the majority voice of constitutional Nationalism.[5] Ian Paisley's DUP had no such qualms about rejection of the report outright, thereby both increasing Nationalist hostility towards Unionism and helping Paisley to increase his majority in the European elections.

Privately, Mrs Thatcher took the Official Unionist line on changes to the constitutional status quo, but nevertheless in July allowed Parliament to debate both the Forum report and the Official Unionists' document *The Way Forward*. In the debate, Hume spoke of the need for a fundamental rethinking of attitudes by the Unionists – particularly in terms of their differing opinions of others with differing loyalties. Merely holding up their hands in horror at the prospect of change, he warned, was bound to lead to further violence. Her resolve hardened by the bombing of the Grand Hotel in Brighton, Mrs Thatcher made her views on the report known to Garret FitzGerald at an angry meeting at Chequers in November 1984. At a press conference afterwards she curtly declared: 'A unified Ireland was one solution that is out. A second solution was confederation of two states. That is out. A third solution was joint authority. That is out. That is a derogation from sovereignty.'

Those offensive 'Out, out, out' remarks appalled Hume, and also made him realize how little Thatcher understood Ireland or the Irish people. Struggling to stifle his fury, he issued a lengthy and considered statement in which he accused the Prime Minister of 'paralysing progress' and deliberately trying to cut the ground from under the feet of the political parties which had drawn up the Council report.

> The intransigence and extremism of Margaret Thatcher has fuelled the anger and bitterness upon which violence in Ireland feeds. There is now no credible political force on the Unionist side in Northern Ireland which will accept anything short of majority rule, or which will agree to any form of political recognition of the Irish identity of the minority.
>
> We may yet be driven to the conclusion that no serious business can be done with this particular British government. The Nationalist minority in the North has outgrown the Northern state. The British government may still prevail over us, but they should bear this in mind: You do not have our consent. You have never had our consent. All your military might cannot force our consent.

Dr Cahal Daly, Bishop of Down and Connor, echoed those views, warning that the alienation of the Catholic community was leading to anger and despair.[6] He claimed that the situation in Northern

Ireland was deteriorating dangerously and that the summit had been a 'humiliating setback for Nationalism'.

The rejection of the Forum proposals faced Hume with a serious tactical problem. Having hurried with senior colleagues to Dublin for talks with FitzGerald and Haughey, he decided to resist moves within his own party to have the SDLP's thirteen members of the Northern Ireland Assembly resign their seats. At a special SDLP meeting at Maghery, on the shores of Lough Neagh, other demands came from the grass roots to take forceful action by means of suspending business in the six councils the SDLP controlled in the province, boycotting the Northern Ireland Office and even organizing street protests. Hume managed to overcome all those calls by wisely arguing that the party could not withdraw from active constitutional politics in such a way because to do so would be tantamount to abdicating responsibility. Mrs Thatcher's response to the report was, he judged, not as grim as many thought. Displaying a remarkable memory for facts and figures, he told me:

> She said 'No, No, No,' to the three proposals. But there was a fourth proposal – Chapter 5 (Paragraph 10) – which nobody had noticed. That's the one she responded to and that was put in the report at our insistence. That, in addition to the three solutions, which gave expression to those principles and realities and showed we would be prepared to look at any other proposals. So talking under that heading didn't commit her to it.

In the New Year, Hume had a useful meeting with Mrs Thatcher in which he encouraged her to continue the dialogue with the Irish government and to construct some machinery which would give expression to the 'legitimate interests' of the Irish government in the affairs of Northern Ireland. Meanwhile, the new Secretary of Stage, Douglas Hurd, had been seeking to encourage the political parties in Ulster to reach a better understanding on practical means of restoring peace and stability. He told the Unionists that the SDLP's continued absence from the Assembly threatened the Assembly's very existence because without Hume's party it was open to allegations that it was nothing more than a powerless talking-shop. He issued an implied threat to close the Assembly when its term of office ended in October 1986 and impose direct rule from London for the next twenty years. Anxious to salvage the last chance of restoring devolved power to Belfast, Paisley issued an invitation for talks to the SDLP. Hume agreed to have discussions with the Unionists, but could see virtually no prospect of reaching the kind of 'internal settlement' Hurd had urged.

The likelihood of Hume's party being willing to participate in such talks was diminishing all the time. Increasingly strident, hard-line Nationalists were making the running. The 'greening' process continued at the party's fourteenth annual conference in January 1985 with a motion calling for the disbanding of the Ulster Defence Regiment. In a speech that reflected the setting of the party's face firmly towards Dublin, Hume told cheering supporters that if the British and Irish governments could sit down and set aside the monumental precondition of sovereignty, a framework for peace could be found. Britain and the Irish Republic, he argued, had already pooled sovereignty in the European Community. The most divisive debate was over the tactics the party should adopt to deal with the new threat from Sinn Fein. The local elections scheduled for May looked certain to pose a serious challenge to the SDLP because of Sinn Fein's determination to contest them on a province-wide basis and its recent decision to abandon the policy of 'abstentionism' and take the seats it won.[7]

Sinn Fein's President, Gerry Adams, had come to realize that if pacts could be formed between Sinn Fein and SDLP councillors it would be possible for the Nationalists to take control of councils where the Unionists did not have an overall majority. He hoped that if pre-election talks could be held between the SDLP and Sinn Fein the distinction between the parties would seem to have blurred, and so on polling day the proportional representation system would enable SDLP voters' second preferences to go to Sinn Fein. As Hume had anticipated, in a BBC Radio Ulster programme Adams publicly invited the SDLP to have talks with Sinn Fein. In the week since the conference, Hume had been preparing for that scenario, talking with contacts in Dublin and colleagues who advised him to 'go for the jugular' and demand talks with the IRA leadership. Accordingly, in the radio studio Hume sought to outflank his opponent, replying that he was only interested in talking to those who took the real decisions – the IRA – so that he could carry out his duty and clearly tell them 'to end their campaign of terror'.

Within forty-eight hours the Provisionals responded with an invitation. When news leaked out that Hume was hoping to meet members of the IRA's seven-strong Army Council there was widespread anger. Garret FitzGerald was furious, considering that the meeting would undermine the Irish government's own policy of having absolutely no contact with the IRA, or Sinn Fein, and damage its efforts in the United States to persuade Americans that the IRA was a purely terrorist organization with no mandate or legitimacy. The discussion looked set to provoke the most serious dispute ever between the SDLP and the Irish government. On RTE radio, FitzGerald tersely pointed out that if there were people 'so soft-headed' as to think that Sinn Fein was a political party distinct from a terrorist front, 'Mr Hume has exposed their delusion.' He read out a warning that the IRA leaders would be immediately arrested if they met in the Republic. Hume was unmoved. On the same programme he insisted: 'I am going to them as the leader of the majority of the Nationalist community in Northern Ireland to ask them to end their campaign of violence and say that violence is destroying the communities both North and South. I am going to confront these people face to face.'

In the Commons at Question Time on 6 February Douglas Hurd paid tribute to Hume, claiming that his 'courage in denouncing and resisting violence is unmatched in this House'. Nevertheless, he appealed to the SDLP leader not to attend the meeting, saying: 'I believe both he and the other elected members of constitutional parties in Northern Ireland have reached a stage when definite practical discussions between them are possible and might be fruitful. I would very much regret it if that were put at risk.' He warned that by having contact with the IRA, and failing to give details of such contacts to the authorities, Hume would be in danger of committing an offence under the Emergency Provisions Act. Announcing that the DUP would be unwilling to have interparty talks with someone who conversed with the bosses of the Brighton bombers, Paisley condemned Hume for 'collaborating with murderers'.

At the other end of the Commons chamber, Hume gave like for like, accusing the DUP of contacts with paramilitaries when the power-sharing Executive was being wrecked in 1974. The

DUP's reaction, he claimed, was 'both dishonest and hypocritical, given that they themselves have openly sat down not to confront violent organizations, but to . . . bring down the power-sharing Executive. It is hypocrisy to criticize me for confronting a violent organization in order to get them to stop.' Paisley jumped to his feet, bellowing that such accusations were 'absolutely false'.

For nearly a fortnight Hume waited in Derry, expecting to hear from the IRA what the arrangements for the secret meeting would be. Everywhere he went he was tracked by an assortment of journalists eager to catch a glimpse of his talks with the terrorists. The security forces, anxious to gather any intelligence on the IRA, also had him under surveillance. When the attention had died down, he was collected from his home one Friday evening and driven blindfold to a rendezvous – believed to be Buncrana in County Donegal. On arrival he was told the meeting would not take place until Saturday because of 'logistical problems'. He remained at the location in virtual custody for twenty-eight hours. At no stage was he informed of any preconditions for the talks. He was finally taken to another location in the Republic late on Saturday evening when he met one person who said he was a spokesman for the IRA. It was Brendan McFarlane, a convicted bomber who had led the 1983 Maze breakout. Also present were two IRA 'witnesses'. The meeting had only just begun when McFarlane announced that the proceedings were to be videoed. Instinctively aware that pictures of the meeting might be used by his enemies – notably Sinn Fein – to brand him as an IRA stooge, Hume refused to allow the filming to take place. 'Then,' said McFarlane, 'the meeting is off.' The discussions had come to an abrupt end after only seven minutes.[8] Hume was disappointed to have been deprived of the opportunity to tell the IRA leadership why he believed they should end their murder campaign. He subsequently became embarrassed that the meeting had taken place at all. When I asked him for details of it, all he would say was: 'In 1985 they'd taken me to meet with the IRA, but the meeting didn't take place.'

At the time, the attempted meeting with the IRA was widely condemned as a folly. Jim Molyneaux, the leader of the Official Unionists, described the incident as a watershed in Ulster politics: the meeting had showed that the SDLP had set its face towards a united Ireland and away from any internal solution. He even dubbed it the most significant event since 1972 when the Stormont parliament was abolished. Hume was isolated and his party vulnerable to accusations of appeasement. On the walls of Derry graffiti appeared – 'SDLP: Stoop Down Low Party'.[9] Nevertheless, Hume could be satisfied that he had exposed Sinn Fein as surrogates of the IRA. Moreover, he had managed to show to the people who mattered – those at the grass roots rather than politicians – that the SDLP would not be cornered into an internal settlement by the British government and the Unionists, and that it was not a puppet of the Irish government.

To Hume's relief the results of the May district council elections confirmed that the decline in support for the SDLP had been reversed. Despite the competition from Sinn Fein, its share of the vote had increased slightly from 17.5 per cent to 17.9 per cent, to give it 101 of the 566 seats at stake. They had been helped by Garret FitzGerald, who in the early stages of the campaign had flown to meet Hume at Eglington Airport and, at a reception at the Derry Guildhall hosted by the SDLP Lord Mayor, John Tierney, had urged people to vote for the SDLP if they 'wanted to keep Sinn Fein out'. In the election Sinn Fein took fifty-nine seats, the slight improvement in its share of the vote to 11.8 per cent coming from voters it had wooed from the Independent Nationalists and the Irish Independence Party.

Despite the bitterness generated by Mrs Thatcher's 'Out, out, out' remarks, Anglo-Irish contact had continued at an official level. Thatcher heartily disapproved of a scheme Hume suggested for introducing a proportional representation system for Westminster elections in Northern Ireland. Nevertheless, it was not lost on her that all the really practical ideas for reform were coming from Hume, rather than from his Unionist opponents. Although she and Hume were as politically unlike as it was possible to be, both were coming to realize that they could be useful to each other. Hume had long foreseen that if there was to be an Anglo-Irish agreement the Protestant boil had to be lanced. To his way of thinking the Irish problem had always been about Unionists threatening British governments. Mrs Thatcher was the right person at the right time and the Unionists, he reckoned, would come to realize that she was not to be broken.[10] Unlike Ted Heath, who had made no proper arrangements to resist the Loyalists' defiance of the Sunningdale agreement and then in the UK general election had effectively been brought down by the miners, she had just achieved the near-impossible and defeated a year-long miners' strike.

Irish civil servants who had been doing the background work for the All-Ireland Forum were brought in to try to find a means of achieving an Anglo-Irish agreement. In Whitehall the new Secretary of State, Tom King, recognized that to refuse to go any way towards meeting the SDLP's requests would be implicitly to state that constitutional Nationalism offered nothing. It was essential to get the SDLP to support an agreement, because they were likely to be the only political party in Northern Ireland that would. Furthermore, the SDLP's endorsement of such a deal would give the green light to the US Congress to approve an estimated $250–500 million aid package for the province. Accordingly, no objections were made when Garret FitzGerald invited Hume and senior SDLP representatives to Dublin to examine the details of the draft agreement.

Unwisely, the British government had made no reciprocal arrangement to take the Unionists into its confidence. Fearing that the (still secret) outline agreement proposed to allow Irish ministers a consultative role in policy formulation on Northern Ireland, in early November Molyneaux and Paisley hastened to Downing Street to warn Mrs Thatcher that such an arrangement would lead to a Loyalist uprising.

The Anglo-Irish Agreement which was unveiled and signed at Hillsborough Castle by Margaret Thatcher and Garret FitzGerald on 15 November 1985 appeared to be an extraordinary achievement for the British Government. Playing on the Republic's fear of terrorism spilling over the border, it had enrolled Dublin's support for its policy. It had regained the initiative in the province, appeased the United States and showed that it was willing to stand up to the Unionists.[11] The Agreement set out Britain's intention to continue with direct rule until power-sharing was forthcoming and to enlist Dublin's active support for that policy.

For Charles Haughey the agreement did not go far enough. Disliking FitzGerald's conciliatory policy towards the North, he condemned the Taoiseach for 'disastrously' acquiring for the Irish government only a nebulous consultative role in Ulster and for locking it into a situation over which it had no real control. Within the SDLP there were also elements who, having hoped for some measure of radical reform, were reluctant to accept the Agreement. Most prominent of those was Hume's own deputy. A close friend of Haughey's, Seamus Mallon had been under enormous pressure from the Irish Opposition leader to denounce the agreement. For refusing to break ranks Hume paid him generous tribute at the SDLP's annual conference, held in Belfast on the eve of the Hillsborough signing. The most rapturous applause during Hume's hour-long speech in the ballroom at the Forum Hotel came when Mallon was described – rather disingenuously – as 'speaking for the entire party'.[12] Reflecting Dr FitzGerald's approach, Hume attempted to assuage the party's disappointment by saying of the fudged Agreement – which even he recognized could only be an interim measure – 'We do not expect a final settlement or an immediate solution. There are no instant solutions, there can only be a healing process. Slogans and aspirations will not suffice.'

Subsequently, Hume took every opportunity to support the Agreement publicly. On 26 November, speaking in the Commons debate on the Hillsborough accord, he noted that:

> The problem in Northern Ireland is a deeply divided society. The framework within which the two governments were working is the first time there has been a framework to address itself to this problem.
>
> There was no road towards a solution to this problem which did not contain risks. The road that had been chosen by the two governments was the road of maximum consensus, and therefore the road of minimum risk, and that was something that should be welcomed.

In a debate in the European Parliament at Strasbourg, he declared that the Agreement offered a unique opportunity to make progress towards peace and conciliation.

Outraged that the Agreement might be the first step on a slippery slope to eventual unification with Eire, Jim Molyneaux and his Official Unionist MPs demonstrated outside the gates of Hillsborough Castle. As the two Prime Ministers arrived by helicopter for the signing ceremony an Irish tricolour was burnt and the MPs denounced the deal, accusing the Northern Ireland Office ministers of being 'quislings' prepared to do Dublin's dirty work. Already they had formed a pact with the Democratic Unionists and were threatening to resign *en masse* from Westminster. Of particular concern to them was the centrepiece of the Agreement concerning cross-border cooperation on security matters. As the terms of the Agreement encouraged the Irish government to 'put forward views on proposals' for major legislation concerning Northern Ireland, the Unionists feared the road had been opened for the Nationalists to exercise influence in the formation of security policy for the province. The first intergovernmental meeting under the terms of the Agreement took place in December between Tom King and the Republic's Minister for Foreign Affairs, Peter Barry, along with the Chief Constable of the RUC and the Commissioner of the Garda. Unionists staged a violent demonstration outside their meeting-place in Belfast.

The British government having rejected Loyalist pleas for a referendum on the Agreement, the Official and Democratic Unionist MPs, who together held fifteen of the province's seventeen parliamentary seats, announced their resignations in the hope of increasing their majorities in the inevitable 'mini-general election'. Reckoning that Whitehall would find it impossible to continue to govern Northern Ireland without the consent of the majority of its citizens, Unionist politicians had begun a process of removing consent by withdrawing members from health boards and starting to adjourn the business of those district councils which they controlled. Hume accused them of leading their people towards a unilateral declaration of independence.

Of the fifteen constituencies where elections had been forced, four were marginal. On a straight Nationalist/Unionist fight it ought to have been possible for the Nationalists to have won Fermanagh and South Tyrone, Mid-Ulster, Newry and Armagh, and South Down. To capitalize on the natural Nationalist majorities in those constituencies, Gerry Adams suggested the formation of a united Nationalist front – never a possibility so far as the SDLP were concerned. Not only was Sinn Fein opposed to the Anglo-Irish Agreement, which it regarded as being far too insubstantial, it was plainly a party with which it would be fatal for the SDLP to be associated. Rebuffing the offer, the SDLP executive met in Belfast and decided that the SDLP would itself contest the four marginal constituencies. As Hume explained: 'We want to take the opportunity to improve our representation and strength at Westminster.' Nevertheless, the party would not contest the other eleven seats because it did not want to give credibility to the notion of a 'mini-general election' referendum on the Agreement.[13]

The most vulnerable seat seemed certain to be South Down, where the Official Unionist, Enoch Powell, was defending a slender majority of 548. But on election night, 23 January 1986, Powell survived. The really sensational news came from Newry and Armagh, where Seamus Mallon had broken the Official Unionists' hold to win a seat alongside Hume's at Westminster. Significantly, Sinn Fein had been routed: Mallon had polled 22,694, compared to his Republican rival's derisory 6,609. Against the odds, Mallon had won the seat through a combination of a energetic house-to-house campaigning, Unionist complacency and an ill-organized electoral operation by Sinn Fein. The share of the poll won by the SDLP in the four seats it contested rose by 6 per cent, mostly at the expense of Sinn Fein, which saw its support tumble by 5 per cent.[14] Tom King expressed delight: 'What must hearten everyone in politics is to see the advance of the SDLP at the expense of Sinn Fein. That is very encouraging.'

In the rest of the province the Unionists ended the day losing a seat and failing to win what they wanted, namely an overwhelming increase in their electoral support. They had polled only 418,230 votes, slightly less than their combined vote in the same seats in the general election, and well short of the 500,000 popular mandate against the accord for which they had hoped. They therefore applied pressure in other ways. The previous November, Paisley and Molyneaux had drawn an estimated 100,000 protesters to a rally outside Belfast City Hall, and in the following few months the Unionists displayed their opposition to the Anglo-Irish Agreement in a series of huge public demonstrations. By a programme of intimidatory tactics – similar to those recently used by the Militant administration in Liverpool – Unionists endeavoured to make the province ungovernable. The Unionists' 'Day of Action' on 3 March was marred by violence and widespread obstruction. As part of an 'Ulster Says No' campaign, shopkeepers were coerced into boycotting goods from the Republic. Even the RUC were branded as representatives of Westminster, and several policemen and their families were driven out of their homes by 'Loyalists'. Such antics prompted Hume again angrily to condemn leading Unionist politicians for appearing in public alongside paramilitaries.

The Unionists' civil disobedience campaign had the effect of bringing Hume closer to mainstream Whitehall thinking than he had ever been. The Thatcher administration was rapidly coming to regard him not just as the architect of the Agreement, but also its linchpin. In April he carefully began drawing a veil over his years of non-cooperation with the RUC and chipping away at the Unionists' image as the sole supporters of law and order in the province. Condemning the Unionist-inspired upsurge in violence towards the police, according to Hansard Hume said in the House of Commons on 9 April:

Those policemen in Northern Ireland, who are so clearly in difficult circumstances, impartially upheld the rule of law in Northern Ireland last week. They deserve not just the support but the appreciation of the entire Northern Ireland community. Those Loyalist members of this House who have consistently come in here to lecture the rest of us on law and order now stand finally exposed as to what they mean by law and order: they mean their law and their order.

He also took the unusual step of publicly heaping praise upon the British government. The Anglo-Irish Agreement, he claimed,

has taken nothing away from the Unionists. It has simply created a framework for equality for the first time. By standing firm behind the Agreement, upholding it and implementing it, the British government will take a major step towards peace and stability in Ireland.

It is only by liberating the Unionist people from the prison into which their leaders have locked them, that they will finally embrace real politics, real dialogue and sit down with the rest of us to begin the long process of breaking down the barriers of prejudice and mistrust which for so long have bedevilled this country.

Increasingly coming to regard Hume as a beacon of hope, at a summit meeting in February 1986 Mrs Thatcher pressed Garret FitzGerald to use his good influence with Hume to get the SDLP to re-enter political life in the province. A week later she had a meeting with Hume in her Commons office and personally urged him to live up to the pledge he had given during the Commons debate in November that he would bring the SDLP into discussions about joining in a devolved government. Along with other ministers, she was concerned that elections for the Assembly would need to be held in October. Assured by Tom King that the British government intended to stand firm on the Agreement, Hume reaffirmed that the SDLP were willing to enter into discussions on devolution at any time without preconditions – other than that they be within the frame of the Anglo-Irish Agreement. However, Paisley and Molyneaux made it clear to Mrs Thatcher that that precondition was totally unacceptable to the Unionists. Hume's fervent wish was that there would be a dialogue after the Protestant marching season was over and that people would realize by then that 'bully boy' tactics, threats and violence would not sway the British government. He also hoped that the Unionists would come to realize that any agreed form of devolution would take over 80 per cent of the functions being performed by the British and Irish governments through the Intergovernmental Council. It was the expectation of reducing the significance of the Anglo-Irish Agreement that Hume reckoned might encourage Unionist leaders to participate in a deal on regional government.[15]

By autumn 1986 Unionist attitudes had hardened so much that even the suspension of the Agreement would not have been enough to get the talks under way. Nevertheless, despite some disappointment at Britain's rejection of the Irish proposal to replace the province's one-judge, no-jury, 'Diplock' courts with three-judge courts, the SDLP were happy that there had been clear movement on other Nationalist grievances concerning the police and discrimination against Catholics in employment.

'The Agreement has led to more progress in Northern Ireland in its first year than had been achieved in the previous sixty,' Hume buoyantly told the party's annual conference at Newcastle, County Down.[16] He challenged the Nationalists 'to cut out the rhetoric' about Irish unity and set about working for the objective of achieving majority consent. The Unionists should have 'the self-confidence to face the rest of us on an equal footing and build structures for the future'. The new star at the conference was Seamus Mallon, who since becoming an MP had proved himself to be a capable party spokesman. Fulfilled by his increased responsibilities, he had drifted apart from his one-time political colleague, Charles Haughey, who had recently called for a renegotiation of the Anglo-Irish Agreement. In a rousing oration Mallon condemned the Unionists for being 'in a state of bondage' to groups like the Orange Order, the Apprentice Boys, the Ulster Defence Association and its paramilitary offshoots. 'Only when Unionists turn their back on the paramilitaries and embrace constitutional politics, as the SDLP did sixteen years ago, will there be any break in the deadlock. I say to the Unionists, and I say it sincerely – get the monkeys off your backs first and then you'll be able to negotiate.'

In Brussels, Hume had told a meeting of British Labour supporters that the Agreement offered all the people of Ireland the same chance of reconciliation as postwar Europe had found through the creation of the European Community. He added: 'It is the search for consensus that is the real search for peace and order in Northern Ireland.' Further afield, the efforts he had been making to secure peace were receiving greater recognition. Hume's links with the United States were being reinforced by his assistant, the SDLP's policy chairman Mark Durkan, who was working on secondment in Senator Edward Kennedy's office. In 1985 the University of Massachusetts awarded Hume an honorary doctorate of letters. In Boston that February he was also presented with the prestigious Harvard Foundation award for public service. Noting that a previous winner had been the United Nations Secretary-General Javier Pérez de Cuellar, some in Irish and American circles even began moves to nominate Hume to succeed him at the United Nations. Strong Congressional backing would certainly have been forthcoming had the Irish government proposed his name.

Somehow Hume found time in his hectic schedule to fly to the Philippines to chair a group of international observers monitoring a general election. The delegation witnessed many cases of intimidation – snatching of ballot boxes and tampering with election returns – during sample monitoring of polling stations. With Senator Richard Lugar, he condemned officials of President Marcos's government for carrying out massive electoral fraud.

The envy such high-profile trips aroused in Unionist leaders – who seldom got invited anywhere – fostered paranoid suspicions that the SDLP was being manipulated from abroad. In June 1986 it was alleged that the SDLP had received a £30,000 grant from the CIA. Paisley triumphantly claimed a 'scandal of enormous proportions' and that the financial link showed the SDLP was on the payroll of the US government. Exasperated by the allegation, Hume explained that the purpose of the donation from the National Endowment for Democracy – a trust recently formed by President Reagan and the US Congress – was merely to establish a research institute to help educate party members and assist in policy formation. Already a dozen SDLP members had visited Washington at the Institute's expense for seminars on campaign organizing and fundraising. Conversely, in November members of the Democratic Party had flown to Northern Ireland to attend the SDLP's conference.

The SDLP's manifesto *Keep Building*, which Hume launched in readiness for the 1987 general election, reaffirmed the party's new-found support for the RUC 'in impartially enforcing the law'. Moreover, it firmly endorsed the Anglo-Irish Agreement and hailed it as the best decision-making structure that had been operated since partition. He claimed the time was right to start to spill sweat rather than blood. 'For the first time all sections of the community are on an equal footing.'

Astonishingly, such sentiments even struck a chord with sections of John McMichael's Ulster Defence Association. The UDA had played a large part in the Ulster workers' strike in 1974, although it had become more of a political organization since then. Their political wing had just produced a discussion document which went further than Molyneaux or Paisley had been prepared to go. In proposing interparty talks to see if agreement could be reached on a power-sharing form of government, they provided the first Unionist recognition that a settlement needed to be based on compromise and include both sides.[17]

Another indication that the province's sympathies were drifting away from those who opposed the Agreement came in May when the Alliance Party leader, John Cushnahan, announced that in the general election his party would not be contesting the West Belfast seat of the Sinn Fein President. He announced: 'We think it is in the interest of Northern Ireland to try to ensure the defeat of Gerry Adams. By staying out we will encourage supporters to vote for the candidate most likely to defeat him.' Effectively, the Alliance were standing aside to give the SDLP a better chance.

Much to the SDLP's liking – and to Sinn Fein's disadvantage –

the campaign in Northern Ireland was dominated by the Anglo-Irish Agreement. In the Irish Republic's general election in February, Sinn Fein had polled only a minuscule 2 per cent of the vote. Its share of the vote fell in Britain's June general election, but not by quite enough to defeat Gerry Adams. Albeit with a halved majority, he managed to retain his seat, doubtless benefiting from the former West Belfast member Gerry Fitt further dishing the SDLP by endorsing the pro-Moscow Workers' Party candidate. Elsewhere the total Unionist vote was found to have declined since the unofficial referendum the previous January. To SDLP delight, Enoch Powell lost his battle for survival at South Down, where he was ousted by the SDLP's Eddie McGrady. Even the majorities of Paisley and Molyneaux slumped. The overall increase in the Alliance vote was interpreted as a consequence of a shift of Unionist opinion in favour of the Agreement. The SDLP failed in its bid to increase its representation at Westminster to four; nevertheless, McGrady's victory had brought a significant gain, and both Mallon and Hume were comfortably returned with increased majorities. In Foyle, Hume widened the gap between himself and the third-placed candidate, Sinn Fein's Martin McGuinness.

'No selfish strategic interest'

While being at the centre of these political developments, Hume had also been busily striving to create jobs in Northern Ireland, and in Derry in particular. After the 1985 Anglo-Irish Agreement the Unionists had refused to meet visiting British ministers or cooperate with them, even on economic matters. In complete contrast, Hume would roll out the red carpet for them. He struck up a close working relationship with the minister with responsibility for economic development, Richard Needham (who became the longest-serving minister under direct rule). Declan O'Hare, who used to represent the Industrial Development Board in the United States, recalls how in 1986, at a trade fair in New York, American investors were greatly impressed by seeing Hume, a Nationalist leader, cooperating closely with Needham, a British minister.

On his own trips to the United States Hume would regularly lobby members of Congress for additional grants for the International Fund for Ireland, which had been established by the British and Irish governments. In 1987, following a series of meetings Hume had with the Mayor of Boston, Raymond Flynn, Derry Boston Ventures was founded with the central purpose of promoting economic development in Derry and the surrounding area. Run by a group of Protestant and Catholic volunteer directors, with O'Hare as its chief executive, it set up offices in Bishop Street, beside the old Derry courthouse. Through this organization, each March and October Hume would take a delegation of small company representatives to American trade festivals and help them market their products, Hume drawing on his extensive network of contacts for their benefit.

While in the United States, too, he would be speaking at every possible function, extolling the advantages of investing in Ulster. He well knew that as his political reputation spread, more and more businesspeople were becoming willing to listen to what he had to offer. As a former businessman and Commerce Minister, he would win their trust by speaking their language. At one such function he impressed senior executives of Seagate Technology, a California-based electronics company specializing in the manu- facture of disc-drive components. Hume put together a pro- gramme for them to visit Derry, meet the City Council, inspect sites and meet all sections of the Derry community. Impressed, they built a multi-million-pound factory there.

In 1989 Derry Boston Ventures played a crucial part in persuad- ing the Boston-based property development company O'Connell Brothers to invest in the £65 million shopping and office develop- ment of Derry's Foyle Street area. Hume had met the company's representatives and introduced them to Needham. Peter Brooke told me: 'The Irish-American money was particularly attractive because, by definition, it was most unlikely that the IRA were ever going to blow up anything which was financed by Irish-American money.' By Hume's efforts Derry Boston Ventures soon obtained for the city $45 million worth of orders and $120 million of inward investment. Derry Boston Ventures became so successful that Hume decided it should widen its catchment area to include other parts of the north-west. Accordingly it was restructured and renamed North West International. Hume became increasingly hopeful that the economic benefits which were resulting from the practical application of his non-sectarian self-help philosophy would help produce political dividends. He told me:

> People grew up in a situation in which there was never any change. Then they see American investment coming in: the big Foyle Street development, the Seagate Company – all brought in directly by our own actions. In other words, politics are working. Part of my argument in getting the IRA to stop was that political means would achieve far more – particularly if harnessed to the enormous international politi- cal strength of the Irish abroad.

Unionist politicians eventually came to look with envy at the investment Hume was attracting to the province. Anxious to

climb on the bandwagon, they too began making investment promotion trips to America. Although many of the representatives
were from Belfast, Hume selflessly encouraged and assisted them
by getting his contacts across the Atlantic to open influential doors
for them. In no sense was Hume consciously seeking any electoral
support for the SDLP from such activities. In East Belfast support
for the SDLP had been so low in some wards that the party did
not even bother to field candidates; yet despite that, Hume had
taken steps to help the shipyards there. Almost continuously
North West International would be getting overseas calls from
potential investors and 'multipliers' – such as investment con-
sultants – wishing to visit Derry. O'Hare claims that while much
is heard of Hume's political work, it is never mentioned that
many evenings when he is in Foyle he is out and about with
businesspeople, showing them the constituency.

The 1987 general election seemed to bring Hume's party no
nearer to solving the political deadlock in the province. Already
the SDLP's position had worsened slightly with the defeat of Dr
Garret FitzGerald's government by Charles Haughey's Fianna Fáil
in the Irish general election. Haughey expressed his displeasure
with the SDLP leadership's stance on the Anglo-Irish Agreement
by not sending the customary message of support to the party's
conference, then by leaving out SDLP members from his list of
nominees for the Republic's Senate.

For once it was the Unionists who took the first step towards
establishing an entente with the Nationalists. In May 1987 Paisley
and Molyneaux met Tom King and indicated that the way might
be clear for talks with the SDLP. The reason for that action became
apparent in a Unionist task force report, *An End to Drift*, which
scathingly stated that the Unionist tactic of sitting back and
doing nothing in the hope that the Anglo-Irish Agreement
would fall apart under the weight of its own contradictions was
the 'ultimate abdication of responsibility'. That September, initial
talks were held at Duisburg, West Germany, between the
SDLP's Austin Currie and representatives of the DUP, OUP
and the Alliance. Still the Unionists demanded the suspension
of the Anglo-Irish Conference and the closure of the secretariat
at Maryfield. No progress could be made because they refused
to accept a scheme which involved setting a date several months
ahead for the next meeting of the joint ministerial conference

in order for it to be said that the conference had been effectively suspended.

Flush with weapons and explosives smuggled in from Libya by the Irish-crewed vessel *Eksund*, the IRA launched a new offensive which they called 'the final phase'. The terror campaign plumbed new depths on Remembrance Sunday, 8 November, when a crowd gathered at the war memorial in the centre of Enniskillen to remember the fallen dead in two world wars, as well as those who had lost their lives in the Troubles. Without warning a bomb exploded, killing eleven people. The atrocity sent shock waves throughout Britain and the Republic and left many with lasting memories of the quiet dignity of Gordon Wilson as he comforted his dying daughter Marie and prayed that her murderers would be forgiven. In the Commons, Hume described the bombing as the greatest act of provocation against the Unionist people in his lifetime. He was cheered when he declared that the lesson for Northern Ireland representatives was that it was past attitudes that had brought them to where they were. 'The first lesson we have to learn is that we need each other. We will only discover how we are going to live together when we sit down to talk to one another.'

Enniskillen marked a new low in the IRA's bombing campaign. It also coincided with a turning-point in Sinn Fein's approach to terrorism. Already, Gerry Adams and a clique of his advisers, including such as the Derry councillor Mitchell McLaughlin, had come to realize that the 'Long War' was incapable of achieving its objective of a British withdrawal. Within a week of the Enniskillen carnage Adams gave an interview to a Dublin magazine in which he declared that another such atrocity would 'undermine the validity of the armed struggle'. Significantly, he added: '*There is no military solution*. Military solutions by either of the two main protagonists only mean more tragedies.' He went on to say that he was now 'prepared to consider an alternative unarmed form of struggle to achieve Irish independence. If someone would outline such a course I would not only be prepared to listen but I would be prepared to work in that direction.' The day before the bombing, Sinn Fein's *Ard Fheis* (annual convention) in Belfast had hotly debated the 'internal contradictions' between violence and political work. Adams outlined in stark terms to that so-called 'glasnost' conference how Sinn Fein had failed to represent the views of ordinary working-class voters in the South and how it had to start from scratch, 'building a political base'. He had become intent on steering the Provisional movement on to a new 'two-track' policy of simultaneously conducting offensive operations and seeking means of negotiating with the British. The question was: how was it to be done?

An ecclesiastical initiative to get all the Northern Ireland parties – other than Sinn Fein – to hold exploratory talks had unsuccessfully been launched in August by the Church of Ireland Primate, Dr Robin Eames. Since the Remembrance Day massacre, Roman Catholic church leaders had similarly called on Ulster politicians to start talking again to try to break the deadlock.

A step in a different direction was taken by Father Alex Reid, a Catholic priest at the Redemptorist monastery at Clonard, near Sinn Fein's offices in West Belfast. In addition to being Adams's confessor, Father Reid had since 1986 been delivering handwritten personal letters from Adams to Charles Haughey. Having written to Tom King to ascertain what would be the Northern Ireland Office's reaction to talks with Sinn Fein, Reid recruited Hume to be the intermediary between Adams and King. Keen to generate a political dialogue, he then contacted Adams and Hume to ask if they would be willing to meet. With the military wing of the IRA still in the ascendant and planning to escalate the terror campaign in 1988, Adams would be taking a considerable personal risk in holding talks with Hume. Having read the magazine article in which Adams had conceded that there was 'no military solution', Hume agreed to commence a dialogue. In a year in which no elections were to be held in the North, he reckoned that to do so would not harm the SDLP electorally. Accordingly, on Monday, 11 January 1988, the leaders secretly met at the Clonard monastery.

Hume outlined the SDLP's viewpoint and what he saw as the flaws in the Sinn Fein stance. Adams did the same. What was discussed was less significant than the fact that the first official contact between the two leaders had taken place. Hume hoped that it might be possible eventually to find a form of words, to which a British government might put its name, that could remove the causes of the conflict.[1] Also hoping that it might be possible to get an IRA ceasefire that autumn, Hume made it clear to Adams that his objective in the talks was to bring the violence to an end and pressed him to reveal what might be the IRA's requirements for a ceasefire. To that effect, on 17 March he sent Adams a highly significant list of questions:

1. Do you accept the right of the Irish people to self-determination?
2. Do you accept that the Irish people are at present deeply divided on the question of how to exercise self-determination?
3. Do you accept that in practice agreement on exercising that right means agreement of both the Unionist and National-ist traditions in Ireland?
4. If you accept 1, 2 and 3, would you then agree the best way forward would be to attempt to create a conference table, convened by the Irish Government, at which all parties in the North with an electoral mandate would attend. The purpose of such a conference would be to try to reach agree-ment on the exercise of self-determination in Ireland and on how the people of our diverse traditions can live together in peace, harmony and agreement. It would be understood that if this conference were to happen the IRA would have ceased its campaign. It would also be understood that if such a con-ference were to reach agreement, it would be endorsed by the British Government.
5. In the event of the representative of the Unionist people refusing to participate in such a conference, would you join the Irish Government and other Nationalist participants in preparing a peaceful and comprehensive approach to achieving agreement on self-determination in Ireland? Would we in fact and in practice take up the challenge laid down by Tone?

On reading the joint statement issued by Adams and Hume after the two-hour meeting, the Workers' Party and the Alliance Party condemned the talks and accused Hume of restoring the credibility of the Republicans, which had been badly tarnished by the Enniskillen bombing. Although Ian Paisley triumphantly cited it as evidence that the SDLP had more in common with Sinn Fein than they had with constitutional parties, the Unionist response was generally rather muted. The talks won the support of the Taoiseach, Charles Haughey, and that of the opposition Fine Gael.

Since that time, Hume has become convinced that those talks which he had with Adams in 1988 were the first real step on the path which eventually led to the August 1994 ceasefire. He told me:

In the published version of the 1988 talks, read my very first letter to Adams and my five questions at the end. You will see the basic principles of the Downing Street Declaration. That was in 1988! My whole approach to them was based on 'What are your reasons for using force?' No one took them seriously. They were traditional Nationalists and their reasons given were that the British presence is the problem. My answer, was 'No, no, that used to be the case. The problem today is that the Irish people are a divided people. Britain no longer has any interest of her own in being here. That was true in the past when Britain went into Ireland because of our links with Spain and France. But today we are in Europe.' Their basic response to me was 'Well, prove that.' On top of that Britain was preventing the Irish people from exercising the right to self-determination. My response to that was that the Irish people were divided on how that was to be exercised. It was the search for agreement that was the real search for a solution. All resources should be devoted to promoting agreement. So we ended up getting the two governments together committing themselves to that and to saying that Britain had no selfish economic or strategic interest in Ireland.

On 19 March, two British soldiers who had become caught up in a funeral cortège of three UDA victims outside Belfast's Milltown Cemetery were hauled out of their car by a Republican lynch mob in full view of television cameras and brutally shot dead on wasteland near the Andersonstown social club. Father Reid, who by chance was passing by, hurried to the scene and gave the corporals the last rites. In the Commons, Hume condemned the murders as 'barbaric', and said the events at Milltown 'underlined for every person the desperate futility of killing human beings in order to unite them'.

Four days later he secretly met with Adams in Belfast for a further round of talks. Accompanied by Seamus Mallon, Austin

Currie and Sean Farren – a former SDLP party chairman – in an attempt to find common ground, Hume exchanged documents with Sinn Fein. In *Scenario for Peace*, which had been issued in 1987, Sinn Fein had stated that Britain would have to set a date for withdrawal before the IRA would lay down its arms. Evidently that position had become less rigid. Flanked by Danny Morrison, Mitchell McLaughlin and Tom Hartley – the Sinn Fein party secretary – Adams told the SDLP delegation that Sinn Fein still wanted the 'demilitarization' of the North, but that *Scenario for Peace* was not necessarily a 'definitive position'.

The position paper Hume presented to Adams catalogued the cost of the violence in Northern Ireland in terms of deaths, imprisonments and the loss of jobs caused by damage to the economy. It pointed out that the main burden fell on the very working-class Catholics Sinn Fein represented. The IRA, through its strategy of a war of attrition against the security forces, was condemning its own supporters to another decade of 'harassment' by those security forces. The document suggested that the Provisionals had not thought through the consequences of their demand for a unilateral British troop withdrawal. 'If the British announce one Monday that they will be withdrawing on that day five years hence, what will happen on Tuesday?' it asked. 'Will the British army be prepared to send its men out to risk their lives for something the government has announced will be abandoned? Mentally at least, they would withdraw to their barracks, leaving a political vacuum.' After a British withdrawal there would be no-go areas, as in Beirut. The 20,000 mainly Protestant RUC and UDR men who would be left would identify with their community and there would be a bloody civil war.[2] The document suggested the IRA should reconsider its methods – unless they were more scared of the consequences of the conflict than its cause.

Subsequently, Hume led an SDLP delegation to Stormont Castle to give an in-depth analysis of the talks to Tom King. The meeting had originally been convened to find out what the SDLP thought of Unionist plans for devolution. Furious that Hume had effectively scuppered a year of Northern Ireland Office effort to get the Unionists to contemplate talks, King stormed out of the meeting.[3] When he had calmed down he agreed with Hume that Adams had probably gone as far as he could for the time being. Both were cautiously optimistic that the SDLP–Sinn Fein talks might accelerate the process of politicization within the Republican movement, leading it away from military action. They knew that it usually took the Provisionals a couple of years to assimilate and adopt new ideas.

The precariousness of Adams's own position within the Republican movement became evident at a rally at Milltown Cemetery, where thousands of Sinn Fein supporters gathered to celebrate the anniversary of the 1916 Easter Uprising. The hawkish Derry Republican, Martin McGuinness, told the crowd that an IRA ceasefire had never been on the agenda: 'The IRA campaign will not stop even for a moment until the British realize that the only progressive action they can take is to set a date for the withdrawal.' Although denying there was a split between himself and Adams about the future direction of the movement, McGuinness poured scorn on those who trusted the SDLP: 'By signing the Hillsborough Treaty, the SDLP has become the linchpin of British government strategy. Our strategy has been to close down every option until the British realize they can do nothing else but leave. The SDLP has contrived to bale out the British by allowing them to believe that an internal solution may be possible.'

From the outset of the discussions with Adams, Hume had purposefully sought to ensure that he had the support of his party. In April, at a central council meeting of the SDLP executive and constituency representatives, approval was given for him to continue with the dialogue 'at his own discretion'. Nevertheless, the party were by no means united on the issue: the proportion of party activists in favour of talks outnumbered opponents only by some 65 to 35 per cent. The most vocal dissident was Eddie McGrady, the SDLP MP who had a sizeable Protestant vote in his South Down constituency. Having stormed out of the meeting, over the next few months he repeatedly and publicly appealed to Hume to end the talks unless a ceasefire was forthcoming. During the summer, as the IRA campaign escalated there was mounting disquiet within the SDLP's ranks, and several SDLP Belfast councillors called for contact to be broken off. Hume's response was to tell them to reserve judgement on the talks until they were over. The talks continued, even though in July a warrant officer became the 400th British soldier to be killed since the Troubles began in 1969. Then an IRA bomb explosion massacred eight off-duty troops travelling in a coach near Omagh.

There were also the Unionist critics to contend with. Jim Molyneaux maintained Hume was merely giving political credibility to
Sinn Fein at a time when – because of the Enniskillen bombing –
public opinion was hardening against Sinn Fein. The decision
Hume and Adams had taken at the start of the process, to make
the substance of the talks a closely guarded secret, had the effect
of increasing Ian Paisley's paranoia. In September 1988 the DUP
leader alleged – with some justification – that the British government had been involved in the talks with 'the apologists for the
IRA'. On Irish radio Hume put him down: 'Mr Paisley has survived on the conspiracy theory too long. It's about time we knew
what he was for. If you took the word "No" out of the English
language, he'd be speechless.'

Despite Hume's perseverance, that month the formal talks
ended. There had been discussions lasting a total of twenty-four
hours at seven meetings. During the seven months of dialogue
the main focus of attention had been on Hume's agenda, which
had identified the three main points as IRA violence; the question
of who had a veto over the future of the province; and the British
government's role since the Anglo-Irish Agreement. On the question of violence, the SDLP stuck to its line that the terror campaign
carried out by the IRA had caused massive unemployment and
deprivation in the Catholic community, and had been directly
responsible for more fatalities in the Catholic community in the
previous ten years than either the security forces or the Loyalist
paramilitaries.

Much of the debate had centred on Britain's motives in Northern Ireland. Hume had argued that Britain would now happily
leave the province if the people of the Unionist and Nationalist
traditions in Ireland could reach agreement on unity and independence. Nevertheless, Sinn Fein clung to the belief that the British
still saw a strategic value in remaining in Ulster. Blinded by what
they regarded as circumstantial historical evidence of 'British
domination' of Ireland, they could not accept the SDLP's assurance that the logic of the Anglo-Irish Agreement was that the
British government had become a neutral party to the conflict.
The real stumbling-block was the question of a ceasefire. Hume
had promoted the concept of military 'de-escalation', but nevertheless insisted that a ceasefire was a prerequisite to further progress. The circumlocution cut no ice with the IRA's hawks,

particularly those who spoke for the rural units. Foreseeing no benefit in ceasing their 'armed struggle', it was effectively they who had forced the abandonment of the talks.

Despite the ending of the formal dialogue, Hume drew some comfort from the belief that the debate which had taken place represented the first real attempt to tackle the *causes* of the unrest rather than the *symptoms* in Northern Ireland. For Sinn Fein's new reformist thinkers such as Mitchell McLaughlin, the process had been about planting seeds for the future.

Hume's peace initiative in 1988 prompted numerous glowing profiles of him in newspapers and magazines. The *Independent* called him 'a practical nationalist'; the *Financial Times*, 'Statesman of the Troubles'; the *Irish Independent* said: 'He has a mission to reconcile the people of Ireland and he believes he can do it'; and the *Economist* claimed that if he were a British politician 'he would by now be a Cabinet minister, if not a contender for party leadership'. Alongside the journalists' plaudits came further honorary degrees from American universities. Already he had received Doctorates of Letters from the Catholic University of Washington and St Joseph's University, Philadelphia; now he was honoured also by Tusculum College, Tennessee, and in 1991 would receive the St Thomas More Award at the University of San Francisco.

Hume used the collapse of the talks with Sinn Fein as an opportunity to distance himself from the IRA, accusing them of dispensing death and destruction with all the hallmarks of 'undiluted fascism'. That November, speaking at the SDLP's annual conference in Belfast, he said that Sinn Fein leaders were correct to say the 'Nationalist nightmare' had not ended, because they and the IRA were the major part of it. Accusing the IRA of moral cowardice, he said they were guilty of killing twice as many Catholics in Northern Ireland as the police and troops. Statistics showed that Republicans had killed six times as many people as the army, thirty times as many as the RUC and 250 times as many as the UDR.[4] Subsequently he called on the people of Northern Ireland to use East European-style 'people power' to urge the terrorists to stop the killing.

Electorally, the SDLP was benefiting from Hume's efforts to keep the Anglo-Irish Agreement alive. In the May 1989 local elections Sinn Fein's share of the vote slumped to a meagre 11 per cent, whereas the SDLP's rose throughout the province to 21 per cent, enabling it to win 121 seats – its best ever total. Hume claimed: 'Everywhere we stood our vote has gone up very well.' The SDLP now had control of two councils and a power-sharing stake in five others. Effectively the SDLP had taken almost 69 per cent of the Nationalist vote in the local government poll. The party had reinforced its position as the power broker of the Nationalist community.

In the June 1989 European elections, in what was similarly seen as an increase in support for a moderate party, the Official Unionists increased their share of the vote to 31 per cent, principally at the expense of Ian Paisley's hitherto towering share of the vote. On the first count, Hume's personal vote of 25.5 per cent had come within four points of Paisley's and was the highest percentage the SDLP had ever achieved. Hume regarded that result as a further vote of confidence in the 'steady building' approach of the SDLP to solving the political stalemate. Significantly, the level of support for Sinn Fein's candidate, Danny Morrison, had fallen to nearly half of that which had been achieved in the 1984 European elections. The 1989 election also further highlighted Hume as the North's pre-eminent non-Unionist politician – prompting John Cushnahan, the former Alliance Party leader, to join Fine Gael and get himself elected MEP for Munster. Another who migrated south was one of the founding members of the SDLP, Austin Currie, who eventually got elected to the Dáil as a Fine Gael member.

The ending of the formal SDLP–Sinn Fein talks in 1988 deprived Hume of one opportunity to get across to the IRA the message that Britain had ceased to have any strategic or economic interest in remaining in Ulster. Another opportunity to do so arose in the autumn of 1989 as a consequence of Peter Brooke succeeding Tom King as Secretary of State. Brooke's switch from the Conservative Party chairmanship to the Northern Ireland Office in 1989 had been a punishment for the Tories' disastrous showing in the European elections; nevertheless, Brooke soon achieved a better understanding than many of his predecessors of the intricacies of Ulster politics. Rather more scholarly than most Secretaries of State, Brooke was a man who was prepared to make an effort to understand the Republican viewpoint. Having become a regular reader of *Republican News,* he had noted the frequent references made in its pages to a 'colonial regime'. It occurred to him that such a stance might be based on a false reading of history. As he saw it, there clearly had been economic reasons for colonial activity on the part of the British over the previous 300 years, as there had clearly been strategic reasons for British policy towards Ireland in the previous 800 years; but neither the economic argument nor the strategic argument was the reason why Britain was there now. Peter Brooke needed to make sure it was understood that the only reason Britain was still there was to protect the validity of the ballot-box. Brooke told me: 'The economic interest is obviously nil since the British government ploughs far more back into Northern Ireland than it takes out in taxes. The strategic argument simply derives from the way in which warfare has gone. In a nuclear world we do not need to have the apprehensions about Ireland that we have had for about the previous six centuries.'

Shortly before Brooke was due to give a series of interviews to mark the end of his first 100 days in office, Hume met him and persuaded him to use a form of words which would make the IRA's hardliners pause for thought. He reminded Brooke that in 1987 Adams had conceded: 'There is no military solution.' Once again Hume put words into the mouth of a British minister – a practice which had begun in 1969, when Callaghan spoke from Grandma Diver's window in the Bogside – when Brooke purpose-fully declared in an interview with the Press Association on 3 November 1989 that it was 'difficult to envisage' a total military defeat of the IRA and that Britain 'no longer has a *selfish strategic or economic interest*' in remaining in Ireland. Brooke then went on to speculate at length on the circumstances in which a British government could feel able to talk to Sinn Fein. In a deliberate overture to the IRA he stated that if a ceasefire were declared the government would be 'flexible and imaginative' in its approach. The remarks caused near-apoplexy among Unionist politicians, but Hume was privately brimming with pleasure. It was not until many months later that in the strictest confidence he felt able to confide to the *Sunday Tribune* journalist Michael Hand that it was he who had told Brooke which words to use. Of that conversation with Hume, Brooke told me: 'He did make clear that he shared my view that there was potential misunderstanding. In other words, they [the IRA] thought that our motivation was something other than what it was.'

Brooke's statement in 1989 was a watershed, and one which

prompted even the IRA's former chief-of-staff, Martin McGuinness, grudgingly to pronounce Brooke to be the 'first British
Secretary of State with some understanding of Irish history'.
Intrigued by the potential of the British government's position,
McGuinness called for 'clarification' – a word which the Provisionals' spokesmen would use increasingly often in the next few
years.[5] For a long time Hume had been insisting that a continuation of violence was futile, as almost all of the IRA's grievances
over prison conditions, emergency laws and censorship of the
media could be removed at a stroke if the terror campaign were
ended. Publicly, Adams denied that Brooke's statement would
have any effect on the armed struggle; but behind the scenes it
had the effect of fuelling an intense debate within the organization,
splitting the terrorists into hawks and doves. The hardliners
believed that any softening of the IRA's position would betray
those who had died or been imprisoned over the last twenty years,
whereas the more pragmatic doves believed that they had been
fought to a standstill and that they had more to gain from political
action than from terrorism.[6] Increasingly the realization was
taking root that no one was going to win the war. Increasingly
Adams was having to move towards finding a political solution.

The failure at a second Duisburg meeting between the Unionist
parties and the SDLP to agree on whether to suspend meetings
of the Anglo-Irish ministerial conference prompted Brooke to take
steps of his own to persuade the Unionists to engage in interparty
talks about talks. Ironically it was Hume who came to be perceived
as being the main obstacle to that 'Brooke initiative' making head-
way. By taking a hard line and insisting that the SDLP supporters
would not accept the Unionist precondition of a suspension of the
Anglo-Irish Agreement, Hume gave the impression that he was
out of step with some of his senior party colleagues. In fact, it
was a stand which proved to be well worth taking.

A crucial step towards resolving the deadlock was taken in
February 1990 when Hume persuaded the Taoiseach, Charles
Haughey, to tone down a policy statement in which he intended
to declare he was prepared to accept a new political deal that
'transcended' the Anglo-Irish Agreement. This was the first time
that any Irish leader had conceded that the Agreement was not
sacrosanct. While keeping the Unionists in play by expressing
a willingness to make limited concessions, Hume achieved the

remarkable feat of persuading Brooke to get the Unionists to give their outline consent to direct talks with representatives of the Irish Republic – none of whom they would have hitherto been seen dead with. Effectively, Brooke had told the Unionists that if they were serious about trying to find a replacement for the detested Anglo-Irish Agreement, then Dublin had to be brought to the negotiating table. The magic formula Hume had suggested involved two proposed sets of talks, the first between the constitutional parties in the province, the second between Britain and Ireland. By June that approach of Hume's had evolved into a 'three-strand' process which comprised talks between the constitutional parties inside Ulster, contacts between North and South, and talks between Dublin and London. Eventually it formed the basis of the historic 1995 Framework Documents.

Within weeks the hope that the so-called 'Brooke initiative' might lead to the first interparty agreement since 1974 was fading. Progress was thwarted by the SDLP's insistence that Dublin be involved at an early stage and that it play more than just a monitoring role in the negotiations. As spring turned to summer there was growing anger within the Unionist community that the question of Dublin's involvement was being allowed to hold back political progress in Northern Ireland. Unionists accused the SDLP – dubbed the 'Martini Party' because of Hume's frequent assertion that he was ready to talk 'to anyone, any time, anywhere' – as being incapable of living up to its promises. Aware that people were taking the view that the SDLP's bluff had been called, to break the deadlock in the negotiations Hume took the novel step of proposing that any agreement would have to be put to the people in a referendum on each side of the border. That notion of offering majority consent in the North and in the South as a safeguard to reassure the Unionist people also became a crucial element of the Framework Documents.

The parliamentary session ended in July, without Brooke having had an opportunity to announce whether interparty talks were going to take place. The original urgency in the plan to get talks under way before the autumn had been due in part to a wish to give a possible future devolved government in Belfast a few months to settle down before the onset of the campaign for the British general election which was expected to take place at some time in 1991. Unionists feared that, in the absence of an agreement, the initiative would unravel during the summer. Hume had rather come to hope that it might, and indeed to think that it should be abandoned in its present form. He had concluded that more was needed than a Mark Two Anglo-Irish Agreement. Along with senior members of the SDLP, such as Seamus Mallon and Eddie McGrady, he now took the view that what the province required was an administration which did not owe its existence to delegated powers from Westminster and which was capable of representing all the people of Northern Ireland.

The murder in July 1990 of the Conservative MP Ian Gow badly shook John Hume. In the House of Commons he said in tribute to one of the few at Westminster who had taken a keen interest in the affairs of Ulster: 'This is an appalling murder of a decent and honourable man. Ian Gow held strong Unionist views, views which he was entitled to hold. It underlines the essential fascism of the IRA that they murder him because he holds different political views.' Then early one morning in October the IRA exploded a 1,000 lb proxy bomb at an army checkpoint at Coshquin on the Derry–Buncrana Road. One of Hume's constituents, Patsy Gillespie, a 42-year-old father of three, died along with five soldiers while driving a van into the search bay at the checkpoint. On hearing that Gillespie's family had been held hostage while the attack was taking place, Hume condemned the bombing as 'total downright cowardice'.

These outrages caused Hume further doubts about his own personal safety and that of his children – even though most of them were living abroad. At this time the IRA were targeting the sons of SDLP members by ordering them to cooperate under the threat of violence and then terrorizing them into joining up with the warning: 'you're now one of us.' Despite the efforts being made by an SDLP councillor, Vincent Currie – Austin Currie's brother – to highlight the problem, teenagers from SDLP homes continued to be regarded by the IRA as prime recruitment targets, not for the active contribution they could make to the armed struggle but because of the propaganda coup of implicating their families in the cause.

For Hume personally there was no challenge in the prospect of being involved in Stormont-level politics again. Moreover, in 1990 he was seriously wondering whether to resign from Westminster at the next general election and lead the SDLP as just an

Jubilant SDLP supporters celebrate Hume's election to Westminster as MP for Foyle on 9 June 1983 (*Belfast Telegraph*)

Instigator of the 'Four Horsemen' initiative, John Hume wielded considerable leverage in Washington. With Speaker Tip O'Neill, President Ronald Reagan and Senator Edward Kennedy

John Hume MEP shows European Commission President Jacques Delors around Derry during a visit to the province, 3 November 1992 (*Pacemaker Press*)

Hume was called to do thirty interviews with journalists from all over the world on the day of the IRA ceasefire – 31 August 1994 (*Willie Carson*)

Seal of approval. Gerry Adams, Albert Reynolds and John Hume meet at Government Buildings in Dublin, 6 September 1994 (*Belfast Telegraph*)

Fêted at the White House, Hume discusses the outcome of the Hume–Adams talks with Vice-President Al Gore and President Bill Clinton, 20 September 1994

During the talks the Labour Party was the only UK political party publicly to place its trust in Hume. In October 1994 he received a rapturous reception when he spoke at their annual conference in Blackpool (*Belfast Telegraph*)

MEP. He had recently been involved in two separate car accidents which had caused him considerable discomfort, and his doctor had told him that for the sake of his health he should stand down. Pat also wanted him to quit the Commons. But his influential and clear-sighted assistant, Mark Durkan, counselled against such a course. In private he argued that people would infer from Hume's resignation that he had lost interest in Derry and in Northern Ireland generally and that what he was really doing was preparing an exit route to a glamorous career in Europe. Moreover, Durkan argued, there was a danger that Hume's departure would create a leadership vacuum in the province. He feared, too, that the discussions Hume was continuing to have with Gerry Adams would carry less weight with Whitehall, because Hume would no longer have the status of being a Member of Parliament; and by standing down as leader of a party in the House of Commons he would forfeit his automatic right to access to the Prime Minister and the Secretary of State. Kevin McNamara, Labour's long-serving front-bench spokesman on Northern Ireland, also advised Hume against resigning. He said the move would only weaken the SDLP, making it as ineffectual in Parliament as the Scottish National Party. Reluctantly Hume heeded the advice and decided to stay on at Westminster.

That winter his spirits were revived by watching BBC television's lavish costume drama series *Parnell and the Englishwoman* in which Charles Stewart Parnell was portrayed as a misunderstood genius. Hume's endeavours to secure a peace were further recognized in the United States, where he was given the prestigious Harvard Foundation award for 'enhancing the quality of common life'; and at the University of San Francisco he was awarded the St Thomas More peace prize, the first Irish person ever to receive that honour.

Hume recognized that Mrs Thatcher's resignation in November 1990 and her replacement as Prime Minister by John Major appeared to provide something of a fresh impetus for change in Northern Ireland. Accordingly, in January he prepared a discussion document which came close to the Unionist position – namely, that there should be five weeks of discussions with local political parties, after which Irish government representatives would become involved in the talks process. After some fourteen months of patient negotiation, in April 1991 Brooke achieved the near-impossible by getting representatives of all Northern Ireland's main parties – with the exception of Sinn Fein – to meet at Stormont. In contrast to William Whitelaw's Darlington conference in 1972, Brooke's initiative offered no precise prescription of how objectives might be met; rather, it merely set the scene in which each party could submit proposals.

Leading the SDLP's ten-strong delegation, with the assistance of Seamus Mallon and Eddie McGrady, Hume hoped that the talks might at least be able to identify and discuss what the problems of Northern Ireland were. He was wise to be sceptical about its prospects for success. A host of petty squabbles soon developed, concerning terms of reference, standing orders, the venue for the discussions and who should be the independent chairman of the second phase, in which the Dublin government was to take part. Fearing that the Unionists might not fulfil their commitment to the second part unless they were fully locked into agreed terms for the process, Hume was adamant that the first strand of talks about an internal settlement should not go ahead until arrangements for the second strand had been finalized. Within minutes of the former Governor-General of Australia, Sir Ninian Stephen, being appointed chairman of phase two on 18 June, Nationalists and Unionists were sitting together at a leather-rimmed mahogany table in the Stormont parliamentary buildings. Position papers were swapped, and politicians were cross-examined on their submissions. As he left, Hume mockingly shouted the Unionists' rallying call 'No surrender' at waiting journalists outside. His suspicion that the Unionists' commitment to discussion was basically superficial was proved justified in July, when the imminent prospect of another Anglo-Irish Intergovernmental Conference prompted Ian Paisley to bring the interparty talks to an abrupt halt, declaring that the Unionist leaders would not be 'sucked into compliancy with the Anglo-Irish Agreement'.

During the next few months a series of tit-for-tat murders and other terrorist outrages alienated all communities from political violence to an unprecedented degree. Public pressure on the political parties to return to the round-table negotiations which Brooke had had to call off in July grew. Despite Hume's perennial claim that the SDLP were willing to participate in talks any time, any place, anywhere, it was not until January 1992 that the Unionists produced four new preconditions for resuming the discussions.

They insisted that all deliberations should be in London; that the number in each party team be reduced from ten to three; that there be no further meetings of the Anglo-Irish Conference before the general election; and that they would pull out of talks on the future of Northern Ireland if Labour won the general election.

It was the last point more than any other which prevented the talks from restarting. A recent statement by Labour's Northern Ireland spokesman, Kevin McNamara, that there should be unity by consent had caused alarm among Unionists and made them fear that a Labour government would give even greater power to Dublin in the North's affairs. Effectively, Brooke had no chance of getting substantive talks resumed before polling day.

Although public talks between Hume and Sinn Fein had ended in 1988, contacts continued in private. Anxious to facilitate that dialogue, in Dublin Charles Haughey selected Martin Mansergh to serve as an intermediary. The scholarly, soft-spoken Mansergh was taken out of the Foreign Ministry and brought into the Taoiseach's 'kitchen Cabinet', where – assisted by Michael Lillis – his job was to advise on Northern Ireland and take notes of meetings between Hume and Haughey.[7] Father Alex Reid was meanwhile continuing with his private shuttle diplomacy. After meeting Adams in Belfast, he would travel down to Dublin, notionally to stay at the Redemptorist order's house there, but with the main purpose of reporting to Haughey at the Prime Minister's palatial Kinsealy mansion north of the capital. Reid would meet Mansergh there, and sometimes Hume would be present too. From those discussions a form of document began to take shape.

At Adam's request the Clonard monastery established another line of communication – to the Unionists. Adams had long believed that the Unionists would come round to the idea of a united Ireland after the British had gone. Now he recognized the need to win the consent of the people who had every reason to fear him and everything he stood for. Prominent among the Protestants who secretly met Adams at a series of regular meetings in 1991 was the Reverend Ken Newell. A year into the dialogue, Newell became sure that Adams had become convinced of the need for a democratic resolution of the conflict and the consequent need to persuade the IRA to call a ceasefire.[8]

In late 1991 Hume and Adams resumed meeting on a regular basis, sometimes at Clonard, but also in Dublin and Donegal. By means of letters, phone calls and personal visits Hume briefed the British and Irish governments on these contacts. Sir John Chilcot, the Permanent Secretary at the Northern Ireland Office, told me:

> Hume was careful – so long as was possible for him – both honourably and sensibly to keep the British government informed about his dialogue with Sinn Fein. What he was doing was sensibly informing both the British and the Irish governments both of his objective and of his purpose. In so far as was possible he was enabling the governments to frame and form an approach to the Irish question. He believed he was bringing about the development of the Sinn Fein position.

Adams was happy that his views were getting through to the British, but elements of the IRA were highly sceptical about where those talks with Hume might be leading. Enlisting the help of Republican sympathizers working for British Telecom, IRA volunteers put a tap on Hume's phone, then established a listening-post in the basement of a terraced house five doors down from Hume's home in West End Park. When the house was searched by the RUC a year later, the police found recording equipment and tapes – at least one of which was of a private conversation between Hume and John Major.

On becoming Prime Minister in November 1990 John Major had decided that Northern Ireland should be one of the top four issues on his agenda. A year later, at a meeting with Haughey in Dublin, the idea of a joint document signed by both governments was agreed upon. His arrival was timely. In the Dáil just two days earlier, the new Leader of the Opposition, John Bruton, had said that Fine Gael would endorse proposals for changes in Articles 2 and 3 of the Republic's constitution. But in February 1992 Haughey was himself toppled by a rebellion within his own party, and Albert Reynolds replaced him as Taoiseach. Haughey briefed his successor on his understanding of the situation in the North and bequeathed him Mansergh.[9] Virtually Reynolds's first act as Taoiseach was to receive a congratulatory phone call from John Major, who proposed that the two former finance ministers should work closely together to achieve a durable peace in Northern Ireland. In contrast to their respective predecessors – Charles

Haughey and Margaret Thatcher – Reynolds and Major instantly established a close working relationship.

Propelled by a new impetus to bring Northern Ireland's political parties together, within five days Major had convened a meeting of Northern Ireland's main political leaders: Jim Molyneaux, Ian Paisley, John Alderdice and John Hume. Incredibly, the occasion was the first time Northern Ireland's political leaders had met in Downing Street since Harold Wilson had called all the main parties together in January 1976. The Unionists were surprised and flattered to see the strength of the team Major had laid on for the ninety-minute meeting. Evidently Major was aiming to revive the stalled Brooke initiative in order to ensure that a political vacuum did not develop in the province before the general election.

Hume was heartened by the forthright talks, which he described as 'positive', but was rather more encouraged by developments which he could sense were taking place across the water, where support for the IRA within the Catholic community was continuing to decline. At Sinn Fein's *Ard Fheis* in Dublin that month, Gerry Adams had indicated that Republican demands might be satisfied by a joint commitment from the British and Irish governments to work towards a united Ireland at some time in the future. The previous August, Adams had written to Cardinal Cahal Daly, the leader of Ireland's Roman Catholic community, proposing discussions. In November, Daly sent him an open letter saying he would not meet him until either he renounced the IRA campaign or the campaign itself was ended.[10] On hearing that meetings aimed at producing a ceasefire were taking place between Presbyterian ministers and the Ulster Defence Association, Hume appealed to the Catholic clergy to come down from their ivory towers and open direct negotiations with the IRA and the Republican splinter group the INLA.

For the SDLP the April 1992 general election campaign was an opportunity to warn against the dangers of the Unionists' unilaterally doing a deal with London. In Belfast at the launch of the SDLP's manifesto, *A New North, A New Ireland, A New Europe*, Hume stated that the Unionists ought to have realized that deal-making in London had never benefited them in the long run: 'It is only when they stand on their own feet and negotiate the future of their people with the rest of us that we are going to get the lasting peace that we need.'

Although over the years Hume had built up a personal rapport with Gerry Adams, during the election campaign he deliberately left the electorate in no doubt that he regarded Sinn Fein as the SDLP's main enemy. The relaxation during the campaign of broadcasting restrictions that had prevented voices of Sinn Fein members being transmitted meant that for the first time in four years Hume could engage in debate publicly with Adams on the subject of achieving peace in Northern Ireland. In a notoriously heated exchange, broadcast from a BBC studio in Belfast, Hume argued that Britain should formally accept that Irish unity was there for the taking if those Irish people who wanted it could persuade those who did not that it was the way forward. He said that Adams should recognize that the talks process offered an historic opportunity. For the first time everyone involved, the two governments, the SDLP and the Unionists, recognized that all aspects of the problem were up for discussion. 'What I would like to see would be a complete cessation of the IRA campaign. Then Sinn Fein can take their place, like any other party that has a democratic mandate, around the table.' While being repeatedly interrupted by Adams, Hume said that there was not a single injustice in Northern Ireland that justified the taking of a single life. Three thousand people had died, and Northern Ireland was being starved of investment, because of the violence. British troops were only on the streets because of violence, which was exacerbating division, not healing it.

As the Member of Parliament for West Belfast, Adams could expect no mercy from the SDLP in the election campaign. For the third time the SDLP's Dr Joe Hendron was attempting to unseat him. In 1992 the local GP was successful. By capitalizing on a damaging split in the Workers' Party – a socialist grouping which had received nearly 2,000 votes at the previous general election – and also targeting former abstainers, he managed to overturn Adams's slender 2,221 majority. It was the only seat that changed hands, although Hendron had managed to increase the SDLP's overall share of the vote in the province from 21.1 per cent to 23.5 per cent. All of the SDLP's MPs increased their majorities. In Foyle, Hume captured a staggering 51 per cent of the vote.

The loss of West Belfast was a blow to the electoral strategy and international standing of Sinn Fein. However, it seemed to have no effect on the military wing of the Republican movement. In a New Year's message the IRA had promised that the terror campaign would be stepped up, especially on the mainland. The day after polling day they showed what they meant by exploding their largest ever bomb in Great Britain, in a van in the City of London, causing some £800 million worth of damage. The IRA warned Britain: 'You haven't seen the half of it.'

Hume–Adams talks

Gerry Adams's authority within the Republican movement had been weakened by Hendron's victory in West Belfast, but knowing that Adams was still struggling to plant in the IRA's mind the idea that Britain's heart was no longer in staying in Ireland, Hume regarded it as prudent that the credibility of the Sinn Fein President should be enhanced. Accordingly, that April he successfully made his influence felt in the United States to get the White House contender Bill Clinton to promise to give Adams a visa. A key player in swinging that decision had been an idealistic Democratic organizer, Nancy Soderberg – a friend of Hume's right-hand man Mark Durkan – who had formerly worked on Senator Ted Kennedy's staff in Boston.

The general election over, Peter Brooke was replaced at the Northern Ireland Office by Sir Patrick Mayhew, an Anglo-Irish lawyer who had wanted the job for some years. Mayhew moved quickly to gather up the threads of the political talks which his predecessor had started in 1991. When the discussions resumed in May it became evident that another of the ideas Hume had been advocating over the years had got through to the Unionists. Now they were demanding that there should be a referendum on Dublin's constitutional claim to the North. James Molyneaux even presented a UUP document proposing new cross-border institutions. Although that represented some movement towards what the SDLP had long been advocating, Hume rejected the proposals, claiming that as a consultative inter-Irish relations committee would have no executive power it would provide no opportunity to expand Nationalist influence in the day-to-day running of Northern Ireland.

Hume's belief that the Troubles could only be solved in a European context manifested itself in a radical and unique SDLP scheme to build both the Irish dimension and the European dimension into the administration of the province. In May 1992 the party proposed that a European-style six-member executive commission be established to cover North–South relations. That body would be made up of three members elected from inside the province and one each appointed by London, Dublin and Brussels.[1] In addition the SDLP plan included a North–South Council of leading politicians and an elected consultative assembly for Belfast. The approach reflected Hume's view that neither majority rule nor power-sharing would produce stability. The scheme was the first detailed proposal for a Northern Ireland Assembly published by the SDLP in ten years. Nevertheless the Unionists viewed it as a device which would weaken links with Britain and therefore rejected it. For their part the SDLP rejected a combined UUP, DUP and Alliance Party proposal to introduce a system of local rule based on an 85-seat assembly and assembly committees. With no agreement possible the talks collapsed in November 1992, Mayhew remarking sadly: 'Things will never be the same again.'

Hume had in any event long regarded the question of interparty talks as something of a sideshow, and as the prospect of such a dialogue disappeared his attention became focused on resuming talks with Gerry Adams. The scene was set by the wave of public revulsion in the UK, Eire and the United States against the IRA for the bombing of a shopping area in Warrington, Cheshire on 20 March. A Semtex anti-personnel bomb exploded in a waste bin, killing two boys – Jonathan Ball and Tim Parry – and injuring fifty-six other people. A week later a meeting took place between two senior IRA representatives and Senator Gordon Wilson, whose daughter had been killed in the 1987 Remembrance Sunday bombing in Enniskillen. Wilson had endeavoured to dissuade the Provisionals from continuing with their armed struggle, but admitted afterwards it had been 'a pointless meeting'.

That encounter having been unproductive, the Clonard monastery's Father Alex Reid and another clergyman then approached Hume and asked him to talk with Adams. They regarded the creation of a joint SDLP–Sinn Fein strategy as essential to the establishment of a peace. On Saturday, 10 April, Adams travelled to Derry for a secret ninety-minute meeting in Hume's house on the edge of the Bogside. The meeting was amicable and centred on the possibility of achieving what Hume called 'a lasting peace'. In these discussions reference was occasionally made to the understanding which had begun to take shape as a consequence of the various talks that had taken place in 1991 between Reid, Albert Reynolds, Martin Mansergh and Hume. To Hume's dismay, no sooner had Adams and the priests slipped out of the front door than the meeting became public knowledge.

Over a pint in a Derry pub that evening, a neighbour mentioned that he had seen Adams entering Hume's house. Overhearing the conversation, Eamonn McCann, now a freelance journalist and a critic of Hume's since the civil rights marches in the 1960s, immediately incorporated the news into a story for the Dublin *Sunday Tribune*.[2] Undeterred by the ensuing publicity, a week later Hume met Adams in Belfast at the Clonard monastery. That evening they issued a joint statement on their talks, saying: 'We see the challenge of reaching agreement on a peaceful and democratic accord for all on this island as our primary challenge.' It insisted that any political settlement in the North had to involve all Ireland. Again the timing was unfortunate. That very morning an IRA bomb exploded in the City of London's Bishopsgate district, causing £350 million worth of devastation.

Cardinal Cahal Daly, the Roman Catholic Primate of Ireland, was nevertheless swift to praise Hume for taking a political risk in the cause of peace. On BBC radio he said: 'I admire the risks John Hume has taken, not for the first time, for peace. I think that is a good sign. Thousands of people out there will welcome that.' Archbishop Dr Robin Eames, Primate of the Church of Ireland, was more cautious: 'Time alone will tell, but we have got to remember as Christians on his day of Resurrection that hope is the name of the game.' The Democratic Unionist leadership, however, were becoming increasingly bitter and angry. Ian Paisley claimed the meetings were part of a conspiracy by the British and Irish governments, the Roman Catholic hierarchy, Sinn Fein and the SDLP to outflank the DUP. Other Unionists responded by mounting a campaign to discredit Hume. Regardless of that intimidation, to show he was prepared to be even-handed Hume declared in an interview on BBC Radio Ulster that he was willing to meet Loyalist paramilitaries on the same basis. Later he explained to me the background to those discussions with Adams:

When our talks in 1988 failed we put out a statement saying that we would continue the debate in private, and we did that. That eventually led to the approach to the Downing Street Declaration. When I resumed talks with Gerry Adams in the early 1990s I kept both governments fully informed throughout, and he knew that. It was a very intense and difficult period. But it became really difficult when it became public that we were talking. The pressures that created were quite enormous – because of the abuse and because of the threats. People tend to forget that I have opposed violence all my life.

At Hume's suggestion, and with the Northern Ireland Office's encouragement, Major took a step towards establishing a favourable climate with the IRA. In late December 1992 he acknowledged that grave mistakes had been made by paratroopers on 'Bloody Sunday' some twenty-one years previously when, in a published letter to Hume, he made the first ever official acknowledgement that the thirteen people gunned down by soldiers on the streets of Derry that day had been 'innocent'. Major added that he was aware of the depth of feeling that remained in Derry about the massacre but that he 'hoped the families of the dead would accept this assurance'.

Meanwhile the British government's views on the prospects for peace had steadily begun to undergo a sea-change. One Wednesday evening in February 1993, while doing some paperwork in the Cabinet Room at 10 Downing Street, Major was interrupted by an aide who rushed in with a note received from the IRA via an intermediary. It announced: 'The conflict is over, but we need your advice on how to bring it to a close.' The message said no public assurance could be given at that stage 'because the Volunteers would be confused', but a ceasefire could be guaranteed privately. The unsigned note was believed to have come from the vice-president of Sinn Fein, Martin McGuinness. When the note was made public many months later Sinn Fein denied it had ever been sent, and have continued to do so ever since; but in early 1993 Major's advisers believed it might be genuine and began to consider means by which channels of communication with the Provisionals might be opened. Sir John Chilcot told me: 'That message certainly was received. It clearly was genuine. It represented a historical comment on the particular phase of the Republican struggle. It was a recognition that the position of the British government and the British people was different from what they thought it was.'

The two-track system that had been developed meant that on 22 March, the day when an apparently enraged John Major was telling the House of Commons that the Warrington bombers would be 'hounded for the rest of their lives', a British civil servant met face-to-face with McGuinness in Derry, even exchanged key position papers with him, and said: 'Eventually the island of Ireland will be one.' Whitehall spelt out in its paper that substantive talks would have to be accompanied by an IRA ceasefire. In May, Hume – having been sworn to confidentiality – was informed of those secret contacts between London and Sinn Fein. He too, although he did not hand over any documents, kept Chilcot continuously informed on the progress he was making in his own talks with Adams.

Even so, others in Whitehall were wary of Hume. That autumn he would be shocked to find that British Intelligence had been constantly bugging the Hume–Adams talks – not only at the Clonard monastery, but also at his home in West End Park. Although the Northern Ireland Office unofficially approved of the initiative Hume was taking, publicly it said nothing. For fear of antagonizing the Unionists it had no choice but to leave him to flap in the wind.

At the time most commentators saw little prospect of a ceasefire and suspected Hume of Machiavellian motives. They saw a Nationalist leader, fearing that the government was becoming more sympathetic to a Unionist analysis of the scope for a new settlement, trying to strengthen his position by adding another dissenting voice to the Nationalist side of the argument. Many observers believed that Adams was no longer as influential with the Sinn Fein leadership as he had been. Even senior figures within the SDLP were privately expressing reservations about the talks, particularly about the decision to issue a joint statement.[3] By the late summer, reports were circulating that Hume was becoming increasingly isolated within his own party. Evidently the SDLP was undergoing its worst unity crisis since the hunger strikes in the early 1980s. A surge in IRA attacks caused the new MP for West Belfast, Dr Joe Hendron, publicly to question the wisdom of talking to Adams. Referring to the recent killing of Adrian McGovern, a Roman Catholic contractor, in front of his young children, on the television programme *Inside Politics*, Hendron said the Republican movement could not keep on murdering and killing and then start talking about a joint strategy with the SDLP or the Irish government. 'You begin to wonder, are these people using John Hume?' Sinn Fein alighted on those words to show that the SDLP leadership were divided. Hendron subsequently told me that, in fact, he was 'five hundred per cent supportive of John Hume' and that his comments had been deliberately taken out of context by Sinn Fein. However, Hume's deputy, Seamus Mallon, also believed the talks were giving Adams an undeserved importance, and expressed impatience with the Republican movement: 'Patience is not finite. The IRA must make a clear declaration of their intent and that declaration must come in the form of a cessation of violence.' A new phase of attacks on SDLP members added to the tension: that autumn the Ulster Freedom Fighters planted fire bombs at the homes of more than a dozen SDLP councillors. Hume's own house was also fire-bombed.

Undeterred by such intimidation, in early September Hume met Major and discussed the prospects of the IRA calling a cease-fire. He argued that his talks with Adams offered the most hopeful sign of bringing an end to the violence that had been seen in the previous twenty years. Emerging from Downing Street, Hume expressed his determination to continue to talk with Sinn Fein: 'I don't give two balls of roasted snow what anyone advises me, I will continue the meetings.'

Having given their formal approval to the Hume–Adams talks, as a reminder that they remained ready to continue the 'Long War', on 1 October the IRA detonated a car bomb in the High Court area of Belfast, then, on 2 October, further bombs in North London. Five days later, Hume met the Irish Prime Minister, Albert Reynolds, and Foreign Minister, Dick Spring, in Dublin, where he presented them with a document which contained the broad principles on the basis of which he and Adams had agreed a peace could be established.[4] Those principles were:

The Irish people have the right to self-determination.
An internal settlement is not a solution.
Unionists cannot have a veto over British policy.

The consent and allegiance of the Unionists is crucial to any agreement.
The British government must join the persuaders to such an end.

Implicit in this list was the understanding that Sinn Fein and the IRA Army Council would agree to a full ceasefire if the British government declared that the Irish people had the right to decide their own future. For the sake of appearances, at that stage the British government were not shown the document – although they already had a rough idea of its contents from their bugging of the Hume–Adams talks. Publicly, Major pretended to be uninterested in the Hume–Adams initiative. Although he was not in such a weak position electorally as Harold Wilson had been at the time of the Loyalist workers' strike, his room for manoeuvre was limited: he was desperate to get the Ulster Unionists to support the government in the forthcoming Commons vote on the Maastricht agreement. Major cemented a new accord with the Unionists at the Tories' annual conference in Blackpool in October 1993, telling delegates that the only message he wanted to hear from the IRA was 'that it had finished with violence for good'. As if to confirm the rumour that in July the Conservatives had done a deal with the UUP in return for support on Maastricht, Jim Molyneaux, the Official Unionists' leader, responded by saying his party would keep the Tories in office for as long as Major remained Prime Minister.

Annoyed that foot-dragging by London and Dublin might cause a window of opportunity for peace to be missed, Hume issued a statement complaining that the two governments were ignoring his agreement with Adams.[5] Having flown to Washington, where he briefed Irish American politicians on the Hume–Adams initiative, he commenced a ten-day mission lobbying members of Congress and seeking to encourage inward investment. In Europe, too, he was building on his success earlier in the year, when he had persuaded the European Parliament to send a team of investigators to Northern Ireland to assess how the European Union could contribute to the resolution of the conflict. On his return from the United States he went to Strasbourg to lobby for more economic development funds for the province.

The Hume–Adams peace initiative was nearly blown to pieces

on 23 October 1993 when an IRA bomb exploded in the heart of Protestant Belfast. Believing that an upstairs room of Frizzell's fish-shop was being used as a meeting place by members of the paramilitary Ulster Freedom Fighters, that Saturday afternoon two IRA active service members, Sean Kelly and Thomas Begley, attacked the building. Just as Begley was about to hang the 5 lb bomb on a meat hook at the back of the shop the device exploded, devastating the tiny building. Begley died in the blast with nine innocent civilians, among them two children from a local school. Fifty-eight passers-by were injured. The atrocity united the people of Belfast in revulsion. To demonstrate their disgust more than 5,000 Catholics and Protestants from the Harland and Wolff ship-yard and Shorts aircraft factory marched side by side up the Shankhill Road to a Methodist church next to Frizzell's. As boiler-suited workers led the singing of 'The Lord's My Shepherd' in an open-air service, relatives hugged each other and wept.[6]

The bombing was one of the IRA's worst blunders. The bridges Gerry Adams had been secretly building to the Protestants now threatened to collapse. Trying to limit the damage, the Sinn Fein President said that what had happened in the Shankhill was 'wrong and inexcusable'. Adams made sure he was photographed helping to carry the coffin outside Begley's house in the Ardoyne. It was an act which he knew would cause widespread offence but his priority was to move the IRA forward with him. To have dis-tanced himself from the funeral might have destroyed the peace process.

Hume was swift to condemn the bombing publicly, but Adams's performance at the funeral made a mockery of the Hume–Adams peace initiative and inevitably tarred Hume with the brush of collaboration with Sinn Fein. In the Commons, John Taylor sarcastically referred to the SDLP 'and its friends the IRA'. Robert McCrea, the DUP member for Mid-Ulster, claimed Hume had 'soiled himself' by meeting Gerry Adams: 'If you lie down with dogs, you rise with fleas. John Hume has lain down with the dogs.' Hume was unrepentant, saying he made 'no apologies to anyone for entering into dialogue with Mr Adams for the objec-tive of bringing about a total cessation of violence'. Later he pointed out: 'While De Klerk and Mandela were talking the atroci-ties continued, but at the end of the day the dialogue produced results. I believe I have a duty to try that talks process.' The analogy was tenuous, and also offensive to many Unionists because, unlike Hume and Adams, Mandela represented the majority of people in his country. Even within the SDLP there was an increasing number of people saying of the apparently fruitless Hume–Adams initiative 'I told you so.'

On the eve of Hallowe'en the bar of the Rising Sun pub at Greysteel, just nine miles east of Derry, was crowded with drinkers watching a football match on television. Suddenly the door burst open and two armed Ulster Freedom Fighters wearing ski-masks entered shouting: 'Trick or treat?' Opening fire with automatic weapons they wounded eleven people and killed seven, including the 81-year-old Jim Moore. Six of the dead were Catholics. That widely condemned reprisal for the Shankhill bombing a week earlier made October the worst month for deaths since 1976. Nevertheless, at the Star of the Sea church, where the funerals of the Catholic victims were held, dozens of mourners came up to Hume and urged him not to abandon the Hume–Adams initiative. When he greeted the victims' relatives, he broke down in tears.

More than 500 letters of support for the initiative had been delivered to Hume's home in Derry, but the stress involved in putting the deal together, the threats he had received to himself and his family, and the flood of vitriol poured on him by his critics had put severe strain on his health. The peacemaking effort also meant the Humes had few opportunities to enjoy the bungalow they had built as a weekend retreat near Greencastle on the Donegal shore of Lough Foyle. The 56-year-old party leader was paying the price for a lifetime of boozy late nights, too many Dunhills and an addiction to Crunchie bars. Within days of the Greysteel funerals he was admitted to Derry's Altnagelvin Hospital, where several of the people injured in the pub massacre were still being treated. Suffering from a high fever, he was given tests and kept in for observation for the rest of the week.

Despite Hume's urgings, the Irish government were still a long way off from devising their own response to the Hume–Adams proposals. A start was only made in July 1993 when Dublin began pressing for a joint authority in the run-up to an Anglo-Irish Intergovernmental Conference meeting. A proposed framework for a solution – which contained elements of what eventually came to be the Downing Street Declaration – was handed to the British governments. Additionally, in an interview with the *Guardian*, the Irish Foreign Minister Dick Spring advocated an appeal directly to the public over the heads of objecting politicians.

In October, alarmed that the Shankhill bombing might totally destroy the peace process, Spring instructed his Ulster specialist, Fergus Finlay, to devise a few more proposals. For two nights the lights in the Ministry of Foreign Affairs on St Stephen's Green burned late as Finlay worked on a formula which incorporated key elements of the secret Hume–Adams document. With Finlay's draft in his hand, Spring rose in the Dáil on 27 October to deliver what he declared were 'six democratic principles' for a sustainable peace. He claimed that these principles all derived from the principle in Article 1 of the Anglo-Irish Agreement – namely, that consent should 'underpin the peace process'. They were, first, that people living in Ireland – North and South – should be free to determine their own future, which should 'ideally lead to the possibility, ultimately, of unity on this island'; second, that that freedom should be expressed in the building of new structures for the development of relations between North and South; third, that no agreement could be reached in respect of any change in the present status of Northern Ireland without the freely expressed consent of a majority of the people of Northern Ireland; fourth, that consent would include the recognition of the freedom of Unionists to withhold their consent to change; fifth, that the Irish government would be prepared to express its commitment to consent in fundamental law; and sixth, that the Irish government would have to be prepared to say to the men of violence that they could come to the negotiating table if they stopped the killing, the maiming and the hurting.[7]

Significantly, those declared principles acknowledged both that the Irish people as a whole had the right to self-determination, and that the consent of the Unionists was crucial to any agreement – concepts which had been integral to the Hume–Adams agreement. Seamus Mallon – one of the very few SDLP figures to have seen the Hume–Adams document – claimed that the six Spring principles incorporated three from Hume–Adams. Acknowledging Hume's spirit in the formation of the 'six principles', Spring spoke in the Dáil of them as 'a complement to, rather than a substitution for, the peace-loving efforts of John Hume'.

Anxious that the Unionists should understand that it was the

British and Irish governments, and not John Hume and Gerry Adams, who were driving the negotiations, on 29 October Major and Reynolds met at the European Union summit in Brussels, and at a subsequent press conference issued in a joint statement a set of six key principles which were a refinement on the peace formula Spring had recently announced:

> Negotiations on a settlement can take place only between democratic governments and parties committed exclusively to constitutional methods, and consequently there can be no talks or negotiations between those who use, threaten or support violence for political ends.
>
> Any settlement must depend on consent, freely given in the absence of force or intimidation.
>
> The situation in Northern Ireland should never be changed by violence or the threat of violence.
>
> There should be no secret agreements or understandings between governments and organizations supporting violence as a price for its cessation.
>
> All those claiming serious interest in peace in Ireland should renounce for good the use of, or support for, violence.
>
> If and when such a renunciation has been made and sufficiently demonstrated, doors could open.

Major had become convinced that Ulster urgently needed a political process that could lead to a permanent settlement of the problems that had defied governments for decades. At the press conference, for the first time he held out the prospect that the IRA could eventually join in negotiations with Britain if it announced an unconditional ceasefire. 'We want to hear from the Provisional IRA that they are going to repudiate violence – not a simple and straightforward ceasefire casually tossed away, but the clearest indication that they are going to give up violence and give it up for good. That has to be evidently demonstrated over a period of time. Then it would be possible for them to take a proper part in the discussion.' Publicly, at least, Major and Reynolds sought to distance themselves from the Hume–Adams document. Declining to endorse it, they insisted instead that initiatives were for the two governments to take. Were those measures to lead to the removal of violence, they pledged that 'new doors would open' and would 'open imaginatively'.

Although it had become expedient for the government to adopt a dismissive attitude towards the Hume–Adams initiative, ministers were happy to lavish personal praise upon John Hume. In the Commons, Sir Patrick Mayhew saluted his courage for spearheading the nationalist peace initiative; the Foreign Secretary, Douglas Hurd, claimed he had shown himself to be 'brave and persistent'; even Major acknowledged his 'courageous and imaginative efforts'.

Unconcerned that he should have received no official recognition for the Hume–Adams initiative forming the basis of the six principles, Hume was nevertheless determined that the momentum towards peace should not be lost. He left hospital intent on capitalizing on the public pressure which was forcing Major to agree to meet him to hear details of the initiative. Having already spoken to Reynolds – who was beginning to hope that there might be peace by Christmas – in a meeting with Major in Downing Street on 4 November Hume repeatedly told the Prime Minister that the Hume–Adams initiative would lead not just to a ceasefire but to a cessation of violence; indeed, the initiative represented the best opportunity for peace for twenty years. Despite Hume's insistence that Sinn Fein had moved away from the IRA's demand for a united Ireland and a British withdrawal, Major was adamant that the British government could not be seen to be following a Nationalist blueprint. Undaunted by such intransigence, Hume emerged from the unexpectedly long ninety-minute discussion determined to increase the high level of public and political interest in the Hume–Adams initiative. Talking to journalists and television news crews outside Number 10, he declared with a flourish that if the initiative were accepted there would be peace in Northern Ireland 'within the week'.

Major's self-righteous declaration in the House of Commons on 1 November that 'sitting down and talking to Mr Adams would turn my stomach over' was soon proved to be hypocritical. Later that month the *Observer* revealed that a channel of communication had existed between the British government and the Provisionals for years. The next day Sinn Fein released documents proving beyond question that Whitehall had been in contact with the Republicans. Reacting furiously to these revelations, Ian

Paisley accused Mayhew of lying to Parliament – an outburst that caused the Speaker to suspend him from the Commons. Hume had for some weeks been angered by Major's denial that he had ever read the Hume–Adams document. I was later told by Kevin McNamara that he had been so livid that he had taken the document to the Leader of the Opposition's room and privately read it out to John Smith and McNamara.

Continuing with his own efforts to bring about a ceasefire, in late November Hume met Adams and reported on what Major had said to him at the Downing Street meeting. They agreed that despite all the difficulties a process could be designed which could provide a basis for lasting peace. Hume told the SDLP's annual conference at Cookstown that the Republicans' case was historically correct when the British–Irish conflict had been about sovereignty, but that those arguments were no longer valid. 'Their challenge is simple and obvious – prove it. I cannot prove that alone. The major role in proving it rests with the British government, which is what Mr Adams and I are asking them to do.' The Hume–Adams document remained unpublished but Hume insisted that the statements issued alongside those talks should reassure sceptics that the achievement of peace had been the principal objective of the discussions. He told me:

> If you get copies of all the statements that Gerry Adams and I made you'll find that we were very consistent and very truthful in what we were saying. There was nothing hidden about the talks. We said that our first objective was a total cessation of violence, followed by dialogue involving both governments and all parties whose objective was agreement among our divided people. Virtually every statement that we put out emphasized all of that. When you look back over it, that was all it was about. That's what the Downing Street Declaration says.

Incessantly trying every means he could to influence the British establishment, in early December Hume hosted a visit to Derry by the Leader of the Opposition, John Smith. During the visit, knowing that the Smith family regularly took holidays on the Scottish island of Iona, the burial place of St Columb, he said to the Labour leader: 'John, do you know that Derry was founded by Columb in the sixth century? He left Ireland to go to Iona. He returned from exile to settle a quarrel and he sailed away again in 547 AD.' Hume told him that the anniversary of that voyage was coming up in a few years, and suggested that to commemorate it they take a sailing ship from Derry to Iona. Smith promised: 'I'll be there, John.' But it was not to be. The following summer the Labour leader died of a heart attack.

At a summit in Dublin Castle in early December 1993, Major had been persuaded by Reynolds to formulate a joint declaration on the future or Northern Ireland. The hope was that it might serve as the foundation stone for a political settlement. To facilitate the reaching of such an agreement Reynolds offered to give a written guarantee that the territorial claim to the North in Articles 2 and 3 of the Irish constitution could be put to a referendum. Some twenty drafts having passed between London and Dublin, on 15 December the two Prime Ministers launched their historic document at a joint press conference on the steps of Downing Street against a backdrop of Christmas decorations.

This was the most comprehensive declaration in seventy years by both governments concerning their relationships with the province. The carefully worded seven-page agreement they had just signed contained the clearest statement so far that the British government would not stand in the way of a united Ireland if that were the wish of the majority in the province. It stated: 'The British government agree that it is for the people of the island of Ireland *alone*, by agreement between the two parts respectively to exercise their *right to self-determination* on the basis of consent, *freely* and concurrently given, North and South, to bring about a united Ireland if that is their wish.' That commitment was balanced by Dublin's acceptance that it would be wrong to impose a united Ireland in the absence of the 'freely given consent of a majority of the people of Northern Ireland'. Significantly, the use of the phrase 'united Ireland' represented a move by Major towards recognizing the aspirations of the Nationalist community and thus an attempt to draw the IRA into the democratic process. If the Provisionals declared a permanent end to violence, the document said, three months after that event preparatory talks between their leadership and the British government could start on how to involve Sinn Fein.

The Downing Street Declaration, like the Anglo-Irish

Agreement and the 'six principles' before it, had Hume's finger-prints all over it – nowhere more than in its grandiloquent reference to a 'European dimension'. The officials who composed the text of the Declaration nevertheless mentioned this aspect only in one line, to avoid turning Major's Tory Euro-rebels into critics of the Declaration.

The Prime Minister was cheered by Tory backbenchers when he arrived at the Commons. Opposition parties also praised the Declaration, which John Smith fervently hoped would be 'an important first step in a peace process'.[8] The UUP supported the document. Although their leader, Jim Molyneaux – who had been closely informed of the progress of the negotiations – sought further assurances from Major, it was significant that he did not condemn the deal. Showing some metal at last against Ian Paisley, Major emphasized that he personally wanted to make sure that no more coffins were carried away week by week in Ulster 'because politicians haven't the courage to sit down and find a way through'.

For a while the Declaration exacerbated divisions within the Republican movement. Most IRA members were far younger than the Republican leadership in West Belfast and had less immediate incentive to seek an end to the violence. Hardline rural areas like South Armagh and East Tyrone were inclined to reject it out of hand. Derry was said to be divided. Although tantalized by the Declaration, many Provisionals viewed it as being a peace treaty which they had not negotiated: to have accepted it would therefore have been a form of surrender. Even in 1992 the IRA's Army Council had voted 3–2 against a lengthy Christmas ceasefire. There was anger, too, that the Declaration had made no mention of 'political prisoners', and pressure was put on the Republican leaders to demand an amnesty for all such inmates. Gerry Adams and Martin McGuinness could see some merit in the peace process and therefore stopped short of outright rejection of the Declar-ation. Nevertheless, they had to try to reassure hardline Republi-cans that there would be no 'sell-out'. Firing off the only shot he could muster from his locker, Adams called for 'clarification' of certain aspects of the Declaration – notably, what was meant by 'self-determination'. At the same time he told a Belfast newspaper that he was not prepared to ask the IRA to end its campaign of violence on the basis of the Declaration. 'If the Republican struggle needs to continue for another twenty-five years, then so be it, we continue for the next twenty-five years.'

Unfamiliar with the practice of negotiating with terrorists, Major feared that Adams might be seeking clarification as a ploy to get Sinn Fein involved in talks without the IRA ending its campaign of violence. Irritated by the Provisionals' unenthusiastic response, he publicly used inflammatory phrases and words, such as: 'take it or leave it', 'decontamination periods', 'crackdown' and 'gauntlets'. He had good reason to be sceptical. That year the traditional Christmas ceasefire ended with an IRA mortar attack which destroyed an empty police station in County Tyrone sixteen minutes after the three days were up.

Hume was heartened by the Declaration because essentially it addressed the stated reasons for armed struggle given by the IRA – as his path-clearing dialogue with Sinn Fein had first done in 1988. Having returned from a short holiday, on 4 January he issued a carefully considered response to the Declaration in the form of a typed statement. Magisterially he argued that it needed to be recognized that the most important response would be that of the Republican movement and that, given the nature of their organization, that response would take time to emerge. Equally, the language used by the Republicans had not been helpful, since their immediate reaction had been based on a view of the Declaration as a settlement of the North's problems, which it was not.

He maintained that the Declaration underlined that, while past reasons given by the Republican movement for armed struggle no longer existed, the legacy of that past remained and 'what is today's problem is the divided people of our island.' Generously giving others the credit for his own idea for an organized political alternative to tackle the problem, he stated:

> That initiative has been clearly offered by the Taoiseach in his offer of a permanent Forum for Peace and Reconciliation to face up to the challenges that face us if we are to peacefully resolve the problem of our divided people in a manner that threatens no section of our people.
>
> There can be no doubt of the powerful impact that such an institution would have. Given that there would be a permanent Northern representation together with the South for the first time since 1920, that representation would ensure

that all problems would be consistently and positively addressed.

Alluding to the need to assure the Unionists that any peace settlement would respect their democratic dignity, he reminded the Republican movement that distrust lay at the heart of the Irish problem, which could be resolved peacefully only by means of a healing process.

It is an enormous challenge and it is a major challenge to all of us. It is a challenge that will require from the Republican movement – given the experience that its members have been through – one of the greatest acts of moral courage of this century. But at the end of the day it is moral courage that gives real leadership and that creates truly historic opportunity.

As we face the twenty-first century, surely the time has come to leave the past behind us. Our present has been created by that past and it is not all that pleasant. The time has come to leave it behind and to look to the future so that the next century will be the first in our island history that has not been scarred by the gun and the bomb and in which we will have at last created an island where institutions have the allegiance of all our traditions and respect our diversity so that together we can use all our energies to build a new Ireland in the new Europe of which we are already a part. Let us commit ourselves to spilling our sweat and not our blood.

A week after issuing that statement, Hume received an invitation from John Major to attend a private discussion in Downing Street. Disconsolate that the Declaration appeared to have been so emphatically dismissed by Sinn Fein, the Prime Minister wanted to sound out Hume's views on Nationalist opinion. He knew that if the IRA did not agree to a protracted ceasefire, neither would the Loyalist paramilitaries. Hume told him that Sinn Fein's leadership was committed to the peace process and that Adams's call for clarification was, in effect, a request for negotiation – an opportunity to which Major would do well to respond. Indeed, the gap between Sinn Fein and the British government was actually fairly marginal. Major, however, was unconvinced and suspected Sinn Fein of playing for time – merely seeking ways of rejecting the Declaration without incurring political penalties. Insisting that the Declaration was not an invitation to negotiation, he rejected Hume's recommendation that the government provide the additional information required by Sinn Fein.

The arrival of a letter from Gerry Adams made Major wonder if Sinn Fein were not playing a devious and divisive game to acquire entry into negotiations without conceding a ceasefire. In that lengthy communication – in which Major was addressed as 'a *Chara*' (friend) – Adams had listed twenty questions covering the key issues on which he said clarification was required. These were textual matters arising from the Declaration; contradictory commentary and interpretation by both Prime Ministers and related commentary from British ministers; and how the Declaration fitted into the peace process – in other words, what mechanisms or measures were envisaged to move the situation towards a 'lasting peace'. The questions had been compiled by Sinn Fein's chief strategist, Mitchel McLaughlin, in consultation with the organization's thinkers in Derry. The official British response was dismissively to lump the questions into groups and reply using words from the Declaration. But in fact the Adams letter was an invaluable communication, for in it Sinn Fein had raised all the issues that might cause future peace talks to collapse.[9]

Publicly, Hume continued to play the part of honest broker, urging the IRA to suspend its campaign of violence while at the same time calling for clarification of the Declaration. On 31 January he did one of the things he did best: provided an overview of what needed to be done. In 'Towards a New Ireland, Towards a New Century', an article he wrote for the *Irish Times* – aimed as much at the Unionists as the Republicans – he enthusiastically lent his support to the British government's commitment to the Joint Declaration. He insisted: 'Their primary interest is "to see peace, stability and reconciliation established by agreement among all the people who inhabit this island". If we do not want them to impose a solution, which is not self-determination, what more can they do?' 'The basic divisions among our people,' he went on to argue, 'go back far beyond partition and the challenge of facing up to them by reaching agreement has never been faced up to by either of our traditions. Surely the time has come to be positive and to

seek and work for agreement, the challenge of which is to persuade
one another that neither side wants victory but wants an agreement which represents our different heritages and identities.'
There was, he claimed, 'not a single stable society in the world
that is not based on respect for diversity'.

> The challenge to both traditions is clear. To the Unionist
> tradition, who have a genuinely different heritage from the
> rest of us in this island, and who have every right to protect
> that heritage, the challenge is to recognize for the first time
> that their real strength rests in their own numbers and their
> own geography and the problem cannot be solved without
> them.
>   The challenge to the Nationalist tradition is equally clear.
> It is people who have rights and not territory. It is a particular
> challenge to Sinn Fein and the IRA. Have they the self-
> confidence in their own convictions to come to the table
> armed only with those convictions and their powers of per-
> suasion? Is all this not totally in keeping with the peace pro-
> cess defined in my joint statements with Mr Adams?
>   We have reached a historic moment in our island history
> and my hope is that the moral courage will be there on all
> sides to seize it. It is to me self-evident that no instant package
> will end our differences forever. But whatever form our
> agreement takes, once our quarrel is over and all the talents
> of our diverse people are committed to working together to
> build our country North and South, the healing process will
> have begun and the old prejudices and distrusts will be pro-
> gressively eroded. Down the road in the future, out of that
> process will emerge a New Ireland, built on respect for our
> diversity, whose model will probably be very different from
> any of our past traditional models.

Slowly a trickle of public figures were coming round to Hume's
way of thinking. In January Labour's veteran Northern Ireland
spokesman, Kevin McNamara, began calling for a 'clarification'.
The Catholic Primate, Cardinal Cahal Daly, followed suit, as did
Albert Reynolds, who urged Major to give Sinn Fein more time
to consider the Declaration and to stop using inflammatory
expressions such as 'running out of time'. Despite Sir Patrick

Mayhew's statement of willingness to clarify the Declaration once violence had ended, in February Sinn Fein's *Ard Fheis* (annual convention) voted to reject the Declaration. Like the Republicans, Major became resigned to a stand-off which could last for several months.

Convinced that Adams's position within the Republican movement needed to be strengthened, in February 1994 Hume was influential in getting the White House to arrange for a visa to be granted to the Sinn Fein President. A few weeks earlier, at Tip O'Neill's funeral, Hume had dined privately with Edward Kennedy and had used the opportunity to emphasize the need to allow Adams in. Kennedy, who had been on a private visit to Ireland in December, did what he could. As long ago as April 1992, when only a presidential contender, Bill Clinton had told Hume that he would support the granting of a visa for Adams, and as it had not been forgotten in the White House that Conservative Party operatives had advised George Bush's Republicans in the 1992 election campaign, persuading him to honour that undertaking was not a difficult task.[10] With Edward Kennedy and Daniel Moynihan leading the charge, three dozen mostly Irish American legislators – some of them taking their cue from Hume – lobbied for the visa. Despite the best efforts of the Foreign Office, Warren Christopher, the Secretary of State, and Nancy Soderberg, the staff director on the National Security Council, ensured that the visa was issued.

The ostensible purpose of Adams's 48-hour trip was to attend a conference of the National Committee on American Foreign Policy, a non-profitmaking group whose honorary chairman was the former Secretary of State, Henry Kissinger. Adams was restricted to visiting only New York City, but that did not prevent him from being lionized on all the main television news programmes. Congressmen who spoke out in support of Adams included the New York politicians Pete King, Carolyn Maloney and Bob Menendez – a member of the House Foreign Affairs Committee. They were joined at the conference by other leading Irish Americans. The United Irish Societies even offered him an invitation to attend a St Patrick's Day parade. Backbench Tory MPs fumed, and ministers and officials in Whitehall gritted their teeth in frustration at Adams's publicity success; his triumph in the Big Apple caused even Hume to wonder if it might have been a mistake to have granted the visa. The Sinn Fein President now seemed poised to eclipse Hume as Northern Ireland's most internationally renowned statesman. Moreover, Adams's refusal to make any sort of peace gesture during the visit had made Hume seem rather gullible.

In the absence of any clarification of the Joint Declaration by the British government, in March the IRA launched a spectacular mortar attack on Heathrow airport. Hume nevertheless remained convinced that the Provisionals were trying to end the violence, and so continued to press the British government to clarify the Declaration. On BBC television's *The Frost Programme* he argued that there would be no point in Sinn Fein accepting the Declaration if a large majority of the IRA continued the terrorist campaign; and he told the London Weekend Television *Walden* programme: 'My reading is that they are still giving it detailed study, which is what I expected, given the nature of that organization. Their immediate reaction is suspicion and that is what I expect.' That call for the Provisionals to be given more time coupled with a claim by Hume that the Heathrow mortars were only 'powder puffs' which had not been designed to detonate, merely to warn of the IRA's potential, infuriated the Ulster Unionist MP, David Trimble. On *Channel Four News* he clashed with Hume, accusing him of 'either being Adams's dupe or accomplice'. Hume, who at the time was in Washington with Albert Reynolds for talks at the White House with President Clinton, retorted over the satellite link: 'I have never, unlike certain Unionists, advocated violence in any shape form or fashion.' The next day he was appalled to read a headline in the *Boston Globe*: 'Ulster leader, backing IRA, prods British.' Protesting that such a gross distortion could 'get my people killed', he won a printed clarification. But the damage was done.

In the Maze prison the Ulster Defence Association's deputy commanding officer, Addie Bird, confirmed to reporters that 'the Catholic SDLP led by John Hume is now a legitimate target. They are part of the Republican war machine, without doubt. They are negotiating with Sinn Fein so they are now viewed as Republicans who can be targeted for assassination.'[11] Subsequently the Ulster Freedom Fighters admitted that they too had targeted John Hume for assassination. Their commander, a former British army soldier, said:

At the minute within working-class areas, John Hume has brought the SDLP almost to the point where they are inseparable from Sinn Fein. No matter what Mr Hume calls his peace process, we don't see it as a peace process. We see it as a Dublin process. We couldn't do business with Hume. He will never be able to recover and gain the confidence of Unionists. He's part of the pan-Nationalist front and he's a target.

Hume's response was typically courageous, even saintly – he again offered to have talks with the Loyalist paramilitaries.

Despite the efforts Hume was making to help Sinn Fein, the IRA were still attacking SDLP politicians. In late March, John Fee, a prominent SDLP councillor and nephew of the late Cardinal Tomás Ó'Fiaich, condemned the IRA for firing on an army helicopter in his village of Crossmaglen. For that 'crime', just hours before he was due to meet Mary Robinson, the Irish President, he was set up by a renegade IRA gang and beaten so badly with baseball bats that Newry hospital had to cut his clothes from his bloodied body.[12]

Although the SDLP's faith in John Hume's leadership remained unshaken, the prospect of further attacks on SDLP members created tensions within the party. Seamus Mallon expressed his colleagues' impatience with Sinn Fein by alleging in the Commons that Adams had rejected 'the principle of self-determination based on consent'. He argued that the level of tension would be lessened if the text of the Hume–Adams document were published; that, he reckoned, would show there was little substantial difference between the agreement to which Adams had put his name and the Downing Street Declaration. Hume, however, continued to keep it secret. He was wise to do so: a recent poll for the BBC's *On the Record* programme confirmed that very few people in the province would wish to endorse any plan that appeared to come from Sinn Fein. In early April 1994 Adams went on *Channel Four News* to declare that clarification of the text of the Declaration and conflicting interpretations of it could be done 'in less than an hour' as there were only three main areas of doubt: 'tactical matters in the declaration, conflicts in interpretation, and the processes envisaged in it'.

While in the United States that March, Hume was presented

with the Order of Thomas More at the Saint Louis University
School of Law. As usual, he used the opportunity of his acceptance
speech to put forward to an influential audience his remedy for
the Troubles.

The violence of the quarrel today is such that it is necessary
in the city of Belfast – which is the highest church-going city
in western Europe – on both sides of the religious divide to
build no not one, but thirteen walls to separate and protect
one section of a Christian people from another.

Those walls are something that I use very strongly as a
political leader to try and make people think about how we
can solve this problem. Those walls are an indictment of
every one of us. They are an indictment of the Unionist
people, the Nationalist people, and the British government
who ruled Northern Ireland throughout this century. What
those walls mean, if you stop and think, is our past attitudes
have built those walls and, therefore, they are an indictment
of us all. When you have a divided people, you count the
victory when one side is victorious over the other. That is
not the way to really solve the problem. Will the Greek
Cypriots ever defeat the Turkish Cypriots or vice versa, and
if they try what will they do but only deepen the problem?
Will the Serbs ever beat the Croats, or vice versa? Of course
they will not, at least not with guns and bombs. They will
only drive themselves further apart.

The Unionist people's objective is to protect their Protestant heritage in Ireland. I totally support that objective
because I think every society is diverse and has differences,
and the essence of democracy must be respect for difference.
There is no peaceful society or stable society anywhere in the
world which is based on uniformity where everybody has
to toe the line for one section of the people. Diversity is
essential.

My quarrel with the Unionist people is not in their objective of protecting the Protestant heritage, it is the method
which they use to do so. That method has been very simple
and it reflects a mind-set that exists everywhere in the world
with this sort of conflict. I call it the Afrikaner mind-set,
which says that the only way we protect our people is to

hold all power in our hands and exclude everyone else. That mind-set led to fifty years of discrimination in Northern Ireland. It is bound to lead to conflict in the end. In any society in the world, if one section based on colour, creed, or class holds all the power and leaves everyone else out, it is bound to lead to conflict in the end.

What I say is very simple, but I think quite defined: it is people who have rights, not territories. Without people, any piece of earth is only a jungle. It is the people who made Ireland what it is – Protestants, Catholics and the dissenters. The people of Ireland are divided, and therefore, we cannot be brought together by any form or force on the earth. Anywhere you have a divided people and you try to unite them by force, it is a contradiction; you only drive them further apart. So that mind-set has to change, and we must recognize that if the people of Ireland are ever to come together, they can only do so by agreement. Therefore, those of us who want them to come together should be working together to get all parties, particularly the British government, committed to promoting agreement among the divided people of the island, because there never has been agreement on how we should live together.

The British government has to rethink its position as well. Its basic position was: 'That's them over there, let them look after themselves.' For fifty years they did not lift a finger when Northern Ireland, as part of that kingdom, exercised all the discrimination that I am talking about. What I say to the British government today is that they have a responsibility to promote agreement among the divided people of Ireland. Whatever that agreement takes, they should legislate for it.

With Hume's encouragement, prominent Irish Americans who were disappointed by Adams's failure in America to announce any concessions but pressure on the Sinn Fein President to secure a ceasefire. Bill Flynn, the New York businessman who had invited Adams to America, had in recent weeks been voicing increasing impatience with Sinn Fein.[13] The publicity coup in America was at risk of turning sour. The IRA had originally intended to call a ceasefire in June, but now, under pressure, they decided to announce an unconditional and unilateral 72-hour ceasefire. As Easter was normally a time for IRA shows of strength and orations over the graves of fallen volunteers, the announcement of a ceasefire at this season was as great a departure from tradition as could be expected. Adams went on a propaganda offensive, writing an article for the *Guardian* headlined 'Bridge over troubled doubters', in which he claimed: 'All of us who are concerned or involved with the peace process are committed to bringing about a total and *permanent* end of armed actions by all armed groups.' And in an interview with the *Observer* he said: 'None of us is interested in four months' suspension or three days' suspensions or two years' suspensions; we're interested in a peaceful Ireland, and all those knee-jerkers who are responding almost on a weekly basis to all the twists and turns – if they have some better strategy, they should spell it out.'

Wanting a complete cessation of violence, Hume was disappointed that the Easter ceasefire was so short. But, determined to capitalize on it, he suggested that John Major send a senior backbencher – possibly the co-chairman of the British–Irish Parliamentary Body, Peter Temple-Morris – to meet representatives of Sinn Fein and ask them to put in writing what they wanted clarifying. The backbencher would then return with the government's response in writing. That way there could be no allegations that secret deals were done and Sinn Fein's request would have been met. Adams agreed that this plan to break the impasse was a sensible suggestion which he would readily accept. It also won the support of Kevin McNamara, the shadow Northern Ireland Secretary, who called for the government to re-establish contacts with Sinn Fein. 'Nobody should be given an opportunity to say that, but for the positioning of a comma or a full stop they would have been at the peace table.' Dismissing the pleas of Hume and Cardinal Cahal Daly to leave no stone unturned, Major dismissed the ceasefire as a 'cynical self-serving exercise'.

Bowing to the wishes of the Ulster Unionists, Major continued to insist that there could be no talks until the violence was brought to a permanent end. The Official Unionist leader, Jim Molyneaux, agreed. Furious with Hume for suggesting that the truce offered a chance for peace, he accused the SDLP leader of being 'the actor's voice of Gerry Adams'. Hume was unflustered. He knew from conversations with the MP for West Belfast, Dr Joe Hendron, that Protestant businessmen in the province's capital were privately saying that there should be talks with Sinn Fein. On GMTV's *Sunday Best* programme he said even British soldiers patrolling Ulster's streets supported his peace plan. 'The young soldiers in the streets knew more about our problems than those right-wing backbenchers.'

Unperturbed by the lack of public figures in the North who were prepared to speak out publicly in favour of the peace process, on 12 April Hume issued a statement in favour of the Downing Street Declaration, entitled 'A Challenge to All, a Threat to None', the key section of which read:

In my first election in 1969 my central point in challenging traditional Nationalism was that it was the people of Ireland who were divided, not the territory, and that such division could only be healed by agreement. Our party – the SDLP – was the first party to put the word 'consent' into its original constitution. That word is now central to the approach of all parties in the Dáil, and indeed Sinn Fein in the very flexible language that they have used throughout the public debate on the peace process have also moved in that direction given that they have publicly agreed that any final solution must involve the agreement of our divided people, an agreement which must earn the allegiance and agreement of all our traditions.

It is worth pointing out that the change in the historic British position is not just a matter of direct clarification by the British government. They are now committed to it in international agreements with other governments. The European Union commits all twelve countries to an 'ever closer union' between the peoples of Europe. That clearly means an ever closer union among the peoples of Ireland as well as between Britain and Ireland and ten other countries. Borders are gone all over Europe. The real world in Ireland then will be that there is no border, there is free movement of goods, people and services and the activity that would arise from that will consistently break down the real border in Ireland, which is in the hearts and minds of our people.

The challenge to the IRA and Sinn Fein is clear. There is no justification of any description for the taking of a single human life. Let them lay down their arms and join everyone else in the real task of breaking down those barriers in our hearts and minds and in tackling the real human problems of economic deprivation, which is what politics is really about – the right to a decent existence for all our people in their own land.

Since the Downing Street Declaration had been made, although London had had virtually no contact with Sinn Fein, there had been an exchange of several letters between Reynolds and Adams, in which Reynolds had willingly replied to questions about the Declaration. However, having gone out of his way to provide some measure of clarification, he was profoundly disappointed that the best Adams could reciprocate with was a 72-hour cease-fire. Now, backing Major's rejection of Republican pleas for direct talks more firmly than ever, he set his officials the task of drawing up a joint document with London on the future government of the province. Hume's preachings and initiatives of the previous thirty years were eventually to form the dominant part of that Framework Document.

Aware of Hume's contribution to the peace process, Major took every opportunity to consult with him. One Friday in May, Hume was walking away from the church after John Smith's funeral in Edinburgh when a car drew up beside him and the Prime Minister got out. Major wanted to know what Hume thought of the government's response to Sinn Fein's latest demands for clarification of the Declaration, and how he rated its chances of persuading the IRA to end the violence. 'I want very much to make this peace process work,' the Prime Minister told him quietly.[14] Hume nodded in agreement.

Determined to use the 1994 European elections as an opportunity to demonstrate the growth in the province of support for the peace process and the Downing Street Declaration, Hume began campaigning early. In a speech to a conference in Tralee on 8 April, while speaking in favour of greater European regionalism, he could not resist alluding to his stock theme that humanity transcends nationality: 'The essence of unity is the acceptance of diversity.'

While the SDLP pinpointed the need to create jobs as the key issue in the election, on the hustings Sinn Fein campaigned with a list of traditional Republican demands, including the speedy release of long-term prisoners. The DUP's Ian Paisley tried to turn the election into a referendum on the Declaration. Of Hume, Paisley claimed: 'He is delivering Ulster into the hands of our enemy and giving hope to the minority that they can trample over the majority, but they will never be able to do that.'

The result of the June election was a strong endorsement of Hume's peace efforts. Increasing his share of the vote by 25,000, he captured 28.9 per cent of the poll – the highest ever percentage in the history of the SDLP. With 161,992 votes, Hume had sensationally come within just 1,254 votes of pushing Paisley into second place. Sinn Fein's share of the vote remained low at a mere 9.9 per cent. Hume's score had been an ambiguous one because some of his voters were anti-Sinn Fein, while others had voted for him because of his talks with Gerry Adams; nevertheless, he was right to claim that the election results were proof of growing support for the peace process and indeed for the Downing Street Declaration.

All the while the debate on the Declaration between IRA volunteers and Sinn Fein thinkers was continuing. Meeting in the Clan Ree motel near St Eunan's cathedral in Letterkenny, Co. Donegal, they were excited by the progress British and Irish officials were making in drawing up a framework agreement. Sinn Fein were being informed by Irish officials of the developing terms, which included the prospect of Britain amending the 1920 Government of Ireland Act in return for the Irish government holding a referendum on ending its constitutional claim to the North.[15]

In August the IRA secretly decided to call another short ceasefire. On hearing that, Reynolds decided it was time to be firm. He sent a private message to Adams which said: 'I'm not interested in three months or six months. I've invested a lot of initiative and effort in this and it's either an indefinite ceasefire or nothing.' For Adams, proposing an indefinite ceasefire so far short of achievement of the IRA's goal of a united Ireland was going to be a monumental gamble. He told a friend: 'Some frightening decisions will have to be taken soon.'[16]

Recent developments abroad – the reunification of Germany, a tentative peace in Palestine, and the attainment of black majority rule in South Africa – although not directly relevant to the Troubles in Northern Ireland, cumulatively contributed to a sense that even apparently intractable conflicts could eventually be resolved peacefully. The broadcasting of a spate of television programmes in August 1994 marking the twenty-fifth anniversary of the outbreak of the Troubles gave rise to a groundswell of feeling in the province that the time had come to give peace a chance. By late August, having consulted with Hume – who had just returned from holiday in France and attended the dinner at the reopening of the Parnell Summer School – Adams decided that the ceasefire was a risk worth taking. Reynolds knew the right decision had been made when the Irish government received a handwritten note from the IRA saying that a ceasefire had been agreed. When the Taoiseach relayed that to Major a few days before the actual announcement the British Prime Minister was extremely surprised. Saying 'I sincerely hope you are right in your view,' Major initially did not believe him.

On 31 August 1994 the IRA sent a fax to Sinn Fein declaring that an indefinite cessation of military operations would commence at midnight. Making the announcement on the IRA's behalf, Sinn Fein expressed a wish to be involved in negotiations which could in due course transform the ceasefire into a durable peace settlement. Hume's response was to appeal to the Unionist community not to reject the ceasefire. Unionists, he said, had nothing to fear: 'Our primary challenge is to reach agreement among our divided people. This problem cannot be solved without the Unionist people.' In gratitude to a stalwart political ally who had supported him through thick and thin, on the day the ceasefire was declared Hume telephoned Labour's Northern Ireland spokesman, Kevin McNamara.

Reynolds was confident that he had a deal and that it was going to stick – so confident that within the first week of the ceasefire, on 6 September, he brought Gerry Adams into the political process by inviting him, along with Hume, to his office in Dublin. Earlier he had made a promise to Adams: 'If you take the right decision you will be into the process within one week.' The ending of a boycott which had lasted a quarter of century effectively meant that Sinn Fein was being brought in from the cold; Reynolds's invitation was a gesture which was vital for Adams's credibility with the IRA.

An hour before they gathered for a photocall they met privately over a cup of tea. They talked about Republican history and the point at which it had arrived. Adams was very nervous. He well knew that Irish history was littered with reformers who had been attacked from behind. Even the Sinn Fein leader, Michael Collins, had been assassinated for doing a deal with the British. Reynolds reassured Adams, congratulated him on his courage and the vision he had shown, and said that history would be very kind to him in that respect. Hume, Adams and Reynolds went downstairs for the historic handshake, to show to the world explicitly that the Nationalists had come together. Afterwards Reynolds, Hume and Adams signed a joint statement.

A few months prior to the ceasefire declaration there had been speculation that Peter Temple-Morris, the vice-chairman of the Conservative backbench Northern Ireland Committee, might be preparing to have talks with Gerry Adams. Many MPs at Westminster were putting pressure on Temple-Morris to do no such thing. Hume trusted Temple-Morris so much he even showed him the secret three-page Hume–Adams agreement. Late one night in the Smoking Room at the House of Commons, Temple-Morris, Hume and a few other MPs were chatting when someone cracked a joke, saying that if Temple-Morris saw Adams and a political breakthrough resulted he would be known as the 'Peacemaker'. 'Oh no,' protested Temple-Morris, 'the only person who deserves that honour is John.' Then, in what Temple-Morris and the MPs present instantly recognized as an illustration of Hume's essential humility, John quietly and firmly growled: 'I don't give a damn who goes down as the "Peacemaker" so long as we have peace.'

— 10 —
Nobel candidate

The IRA's indefinite ceasefire brought an unexpected reward for John Hume in the form of a nomination for the Nobel Peace Price. As the wife of a Labour Party leader, over the years Glenys Kinnock had heard gruesome stories of how John and his family had been publicly vilified, how their cars had been destroyed, how their home had been fire-bombed. In her capacity as an MEP Glenys persuaded the leader of the European Socialists, Pauline Green, to urge their group to nominate Hume to the Nobel Committee. In late September the European Parliament, meeting in Strasbourg, agreed by 384 votes to 5 to welcome the ceasefire. It also called for a rapid injection of extra EU funding for Northern Ireland. Green used that opportunity to acknowledge Hume's work in bringing about the cessation of violence. Shyly listening in the chamber, Hume heard her pay tribute to his 'courage, vision and fortitude'. In the United States, Edward Kennedy and three other Senators subsequently also nominated him for the Prize. In a letter to the Nobel Committee they described him as 'one of the greatest apostles of non-violence of our time'.

Many citizens of Northern Ireland were totally surprised by the ceasefire. Still more could scarcely believe it. For months, indeed years, Hume had been regarded as an absurd optimist for claiming that a permanent ceasefire could be achieved, and criticized, both within and beyond his own party, for even having contacts with the Republicans. The declaration of the ceasefire had changed all that and totally vindicated his actions. A Gallup poll for the *Daily Telegraph* showed that the public gave him far more credit for the halt to hostilities than they gave to either the British or the Irish Prime Minister: his 27 per cent rating on this point outscored Reynolds's 18 per cent and Major's 12 per cent, and towered above Paisley's derisory 2 per cent.

Now that Major and Reynolds had taken centre state in the peace process, to consolidate the ceasefire they accelerated work on the drafting of the Framework Document. For the two premiers the main political task now was to determine how to ease the peace process along without upsetting the delicate balance so far achieved. On the one hand, the Republicans were bound to be impatient to get substantive talks going, whereas on the other the Unionists were already indicating they would be furious at any such 'indecent haste'.

In these circumstances it seemed that Hume in his role as a power-broker and visionary would probably be less prominent. Nevertheless, aware that the ceasefire was fragile, he issued a statement, 'A new era for Ireland opens at last', which he hoped would focus all minds on the benefits of the ceasefire.

> Now we must move on to our next major challenge: to reach agreement on how we share our piece of the earth together. The challenge is to find common ground between two fundamentally different mind-sets – the Unionist and the Nationalist . . .
>
> Unionists and Nationalists can only give their allegiance to a dispensation which is legitimate according to their respective traditions. Therefore the means of validating any agreement emerging from talks involving both governments and all parties must recognize and recruit the legitimacy of each tradition. We cannot embrace or express the equal validity of each tradition if we do not allow for dual validation of a new agreed political dispensation. The SDLP's proposal for a dual referendum would meet this requirement in a way that diminishes no tradition or any assurances it has or needs.

Having made a detailed risk assessment in the first days of the ceasefire, British security chiefs decided it was safe to take a series of measures to lower the army's profile if the ceasefire held. Accordingly, Whitehall ordered troops patrolling the streets of Northern Ireland to wear regimental berets rather than helmets, and to stop using camouflage cream. Flak jackets were also discarded. Although Sinn Fein was not satisfied and called for an immediate withdrawal of British troops from Catholic areas, some Nationalists in the SDLP were apprehensive and wanted them to remain as continued protection against Loyalist violence.

In mid-September the Cabinet's Northern Ireland Committee decided that if the ceasefire continued to hold, the clock could start ticking towards exploratory talks with Sinn Fein in three months. Accordingly, on 18 September, in another measure designed to placate the nationalists, Sir Patrick Mayhew announced that a number of cross-border roads would be reopened. On the same day, while visiting Belfast, Major announced the immediate lifting of the six-year-old broadcasting restrictions on Sinn Fein. It would serve, he said, as a new challenge to Sinn Fein's leaders to spell out clearly and unequivocally whether the IRA had abandoned violence for good. 'All paramilitaries now have an opportunity to tell us directly, not under the cover of an actor's voice, that they are truly committed to peaceful methods only. Let them tell the people of the United Kingdom, loud and clear, face to face, that their commitment to ending violence is lasting and genuine.' For some members of the theatrical profession the lifting of the ban was a financial blow: the rota of half a dozen actors who had for years been overdubbing the Adams voice for £30 an hour apiece suddenly found their services were no longer required.

Peace was becoming infectious. On the afternoon on which Hume, Adams and Reynolds met for their symbolic handshake in Dublin, Major had Ian Paisley thrown out of 10 Downing Street for refusing to accept his word that he had made no secret concessions to the IRA. Despite Paisley's histrionics, the DUP hardliner John Taylor was publicly remarking that his gut belief was that the IRA ceasefire was 'for real'. Paisley subsequently assisted the peace process by demanding a referendum on whether or not there should be talks with Sinn Fein.

Fittingly, Hume was the first Ulster politician to go abroad to generate international pressure to keep the peace process going. On 19 September he flew to Washington, met Vice-President Al Gore and invited him to Northern Ireland. During their discussion in the White House, President Clinton dropped by for another symbolic handshake, along with an exchange of pleasantries and good wishes. After talking with Senator Edward Kennedy, Hume addressed members of the Senate Foreign Relations Committee, encouraging them to support initiatives for investment in Northern Ireland. He received no firm promises of aid, but was left in no doubt whatsoever of the administration's commitment to assisting in the peace process and in the economic challenges that would follow.

Hume's most useful discussion in Washington had been with Nancy Soderberg's boss at the National Security Council, Tony Lake. Capitalizing on his reputation as the most respected Northern Irish politician in the United States, Hume had impressed upon Lake the need to reassure the Unionists that the British government had made no secret deal with the IRA to secure the ceasefire. Consequently the Ulster Unionist delegation headed by David Trimble, who arrived the next day in Washington, received red-carpet treatment. Making every effort to appear even-handed, the Clinton administration made sure that the Unionist team also met Gore, plus Lake and other senior officials. Al Gore purposefully flattered them, praising their response to the developing political situation in Northern Ireland following the IRA ceasefire. Trimble had told the White House representatives that they should say to Sinn Fein: 'If you are sincere, hand in your guns and explosives.' News of that conversation heartened Hume as it indicated that at least the Unionists were now prepared to have their views conveyed to Sinn Fein, if only via intermediaries.

Another purpose of Hume's Washington trip had been to ensure that for the second time in 1994 Gerry Adams was granted a visa to enter the United States. With one eye on the 42 million Irish-American votes in November's congressional elections, Clinton ignored the British government's protestations, and gave a green light for the sixteen-day trip. Accompanied by his aides, Richard McAuley and Aiden McAteer (both of whom had been imprisoned), on 24 September Adams arrived at Boston airport, where he was greeted by Edward Kennedy. The longest-serving Senator in the history of Massachusetts was ailing in the opinion polls and desperately needed the support of Irish-American voters in the forthcoming elections. At a press conference on the tarmac Kennedy warmly described Adams as a 'courageous leader in advancing the cause of peace in Northern Ireland'.

The purpose of Adams's coast-to-coast tour was to present his

case to every important constituency in the country: from auto
workers in the midwest to the politicians in Washington, the
Jewish lobby in New York, the business community and the
American press.[1] He was also concerned to make a favourable
impact in the nine US cities which had the largest Irish popu-
lations. Everywhere he went in Boston – where Kennedy hosted
a reception for him – he was announced by fanfares from an Irish
pipe band. Happy to play the role of Arafat, Adams spoke in the
Detroit City Council chamber; charmed television audiences and
attended a Catholic Mass and rally in Cleveland; lectured to the
National Press Club in Washington: saw New York's Empire
State Building bathed in green in his honour; was presented with
the key to San Francisco; and on his forty-sixth birthday drank
champagne with movie stars in Hollywood. Nevertheless, despite
Kennedy's lobbying on his behalf, in Washington he was unable to
see anyone more senior than Tony Lake and a few administration
officials; under intense pressure from the British Embassy, the
White House agreed that Al Gore should not break the long-
standing embargo on public meetings with Sinn Fein. The best
Adams could get was a brief telephone conversation with the
Vice-President. The prized photo-opportunity at the White House
never materialized.

Adams's hopes that Sinn Fein would be perceived as having
assumed the mantle of the American civil rights movement, and
that he himself would be regarded as some sort of Irish Nelson
Mandela, were disappointed. Unlike the barnstorming visit in
February, this tour had generated scarce media interest in the
United States. Outside of the Irish strongholds on the east coast
he was not front-page news. Now that the press had become
aware that Sinn Fein had polled a mere 10 per cent at the last
general election they regarded him with some scepticism.
Unaccustomed to being asked in interviews to turn his nebulous
generalizations and cutting one-liners into specific peace proposals, he floundered in the face of hostile questioning.

To ensure that Adams did not have the free run of the television
studios, as he had done in February, the Foreign Office dispatched
the former Northern Ireland minister Michael Mates to the United
States to articulate vigorously the British government's point of
view. Hours before Adams arrived in Boston, Mates was
embarking on a hectic round of television interviews. The inevi-

table showdown came during a debate recorded in New York for BBC Television's *Newsnight*. It was the first meeting between Adams and a leading member of the British Parliament since the IRA ceasefire. The two shook hands before the programme began, but once the cameras were rolling they repeatedly interrupted each other angrily. In trying to impress the volunteers back home Adams made himself ridiculous by saying of the envoy: 'You are a person who has served in the British army in my country and you are a person who defended the killing of Irish citizens.' Undoubtedly it was Mates who won the contest, sagely noting: 'This is what democratic debate is about, it is about disagreeing. Mr Adams isn't used to it. I hope he will become used to it. I hope he will understand that other people have a different point of view which must be settled by argument, by the wishes of the majority, and never by the use of force.'

Next it was Ken Maginnis's turn. Having regarded Adams's encounter with Mates as symptomatic of the 'bully-boy' tactics that Sinn Fein and the IRA used every day against their opponents, the Ulster Unionists' security spokesman hurried to Washington to confront Adams. In an electrifying live debate on CNN's *Larry King Live* he accused the Sinn Fein president of 'trying to negotiate with the barrel of a gun'. 'If someone is sitting on over one thousand tons of weapons, how can you trust them?' Maginnis thundered as King sought to control the debate.

Embarrassed by his own past, Adams insisted he had repudiated terrorism: 'Ken, I'm prepared to take a chance for peace. You're making excuses.'

So far that autumn it had been Adams, Major and Reynolds who had been getting all the credit for the ceasefire. Somehow, Hume had been virtually ignored. However, within the Labour Party – the sister party of the SDLP – moves were taking place to change all that. Since the ceasefire they had come to regard him as something of a hero. Glenys Kinnock had already caught their mood by nominating him for the Nobel Peace Prize. In his first annual conference speech as Labour leader, Tony Blair paid tribute to John Hume, and for that kindness was rewarded with a prolonged round of applause. Hume had accepted an invitation to attend and speak at the Labour conference in Blackpool, partly because of his deep sense of gratitude to Kevin McNamara, partly too because he shrewdly anticipated that the televised event would be a unique opportunity to convey his ideas to a wider British audience. He knew he could expect a favourable reception when he arrived that Wednesday afternoon. In fact it was ecstatic. As he took to the rostrum the delegates rose to their feet applauding as did the entire platform. Unbeknown to the audience, the speech he brought with him had been cobbled together by Mark Durkan from various statements Hume had issued that year. Even so, as the following extract illustrates, it provided an illuminating snapshot of Hume's view at that moment and provided a compelling argument for his philosophy of an agreed Ireland.

> If you study conflict – as I have done – looking for answers, you find that it's about the same everywhere. It's why people see difference as a threat. Difference is an accident of birth. An accident of birth what you are born, and where you are born. Whether your accident of birth is colour, creed or nationality. Humanity transcends nationality. There is no greater socialist principle than that. And there is no greater principle of peace in the world than that. The acceptance of difference, the acceptance of diversity. Humanity! There's not two human beings in the whole human race who are the same. Humanity is richer for its diversity. So the answer to difference is to respect it and accommodate it, and that's what the peoples of Europe did. They set up institutions which respected their differences but allowed them to work the common ground, the real economics – bread on your table, a roof over your head, the right to existence. Not just the right to life, but the right to a decent standard of living, to a home, to a job, to education, to health. And in doing that, in working the common ground together, as I often say, in spilling their sweat and not their blood they broke down the prejudices of centuries to make the healing process take place.
>
> My message is let's do the same in Ireland – the last remaining quarrel within that European Union. Let us now build institutions in Ireland which respect the diversity of our people, and earn the allegiance of all our traditions. Because if we can develop institutions which do respect our diversity and allow us to work together in our common interest, if we spill our sweat and not our blood we will begin the healing process and down the road will evolve a new Ireland, a

place that respects diversity, whose morals will probably be very different to any traditional morals but will have this allegiance of all its people. In this hall we believe totally that people matter most. Without people this world is only a jungle. It's people who are the real wealth of this world. We have to all recognize the right of people to physical well-being, to material dignity, and to the integrity of their own identity. We can't dehumanize people in any way. All of us might resent people being units of cost, attack them as uniforms, or abandon them as an underclass. But we have never and will never compromise or sacrifice anybody's human dignity in the name of economic expediency, social indulgence, ideological certitude, market imperatives or territorial ambitions.

As he finished, the conference, deeply moved by his words, leapt to its feet. Tony Blair stepped forward to shake him warmly by the hand and present him with a special award. During the two-minute ovation, Hume gave a thumbs-up sign to Neil Kinnock and shyly waved to the audience. In the debate that followed, speaker after speaker praised his courageous vision. Moving the NEC's statement on Northern Ireland, Kevin McNamara described him as 'the man who, more than any other, brought the IRA to its complete cessation of military operations. We salute you as a man of honour, who has fought a peaceful and democratic fight. But above all a man who has helped to create the prospect of an agreed Ireland.' Having spoken at a fringe meeting and had private talks with Tony Blair, Hume emphasized in a BBC interview that the Labour Party's policy on a united Ireland in terms of majority consent was the same as the SDLP's. He summarized: 'If unity is going to come about in Ireland – it is the people of Ireland who are divided, not the territory – it can only come about by agreement and consent.' Out of the halls and studios the bonhomie continued, with Hume in fine voice at one late-night party singing a song about Derry; but still the grim reminders of the Troubles resurfaced. Outside the conference centre, Hume was stopped by a couple who had been maimed in the 1974 Birmingham pub bombing. They said to him: 'We wish you well, because we don't want it to happen to anyone else, what has happened to us and our family.'

As Hume had long predicted, a lengthy ceasefire seemed likely
to be rewarded with economic development funds. He knew they
were going to be needed. Some 20,000 jobs in the province were
reckoned to be dependent on the security forces. If the British did
eventually withdraw their military presence from the province,
alternative forms of employment would need to be found. In
September, within three weeks of the ceasefire being declared, the
European Commission announced that the grant paid annually by
Brussels to the International Fund for Ireland would rise by £12
million to £40 million over the next three years and that a task
force was being established to investigate new projects on both
sides of the border. Encouraged by Dick Spring, European ministers met in Luxembourg to consider providing EU funds for the
regeneration of Derry and Belfast and the tearing down of the
'peace line', the barrier which had been built between the Falls
and the Shankill by British troops in 1969. All the while Hume
had been busy devising his own scheme, a 'Fund for Peace in
Ireland'. Presented to the President of the Commission, Jacques
Delors, on 14 October at a meeting in Brussels attended by MEPs
Ian Paisley and Jim Nicholson, the £800 million scheme for industrial revival aroused immediate enthusiasm. With tremendous skill
Hume had put together a plan of which even Ian Paisley could
approve. Distinctively, it was not a fund for all of Ireland – neither
Dublin nor London would be allowed to have any influence over
how it was spent. Paisley was delighted and described the talks
as 'the best meeting I have had in my fifteen years in Europe'. He
even took the unique step of accompanying Hume to the BBC
studios in Brussels to eulogize the plan.

Part of the scenario envisaged by the architects of the Downing
Street Declaration had been – as Reynolds had continually said –
that if the IRA stopped its terror campaign a Loyalist cessation of
violence would be hoped for as well. Indeed, since the IRA ceasefire Loyalist violence had been relatively muted, with a car-bomb
outside the Sinn Fein press centre in the Falls Road and the murder
of one Catholic. In the period immediately following the ceasefire
there had been a great deal of fear and suspicion on the Loyalist
side, with people talking about deals having been hatched between
the government and the IRA;[2] but over a period of time the loyalists had been reassured. Having spoken to eminent individuals in
their own community, such as Jim Molyneaux, Archbishop Robin

Eames and the Reverend Roy Magee, they came to accept that Northern Ireland's position within the UK was more secure than they had first believed. A decisive catalyst in this process was a speech John Major had made in Belfast, pledging that any agreement which might emerge at some time in the future would be put to the people of Northern Ireland in a referendum. Acceptance of this position constituted a remarkable climbdown: hitherto, the Loyalist paramilitaries had insisted they would not stop their terror campaign until they had seen the Framework Document.

Relentlessly the peace in Northern Ireland was gathering a momentum of its own. Increasingly it was coming to be realized that there was no turning back. At the weekends people were voting with their feet on the streets of Belfast, flocking into shopping centres as they had not done for many years. These throngs symbolized the hope and growing expectation that the longer the ceasefire lasted, the longer it was likely to last.

In expectation of a ceasefire as a consequence of the Hume–Adams dialogue, in 1993 the Loyalist paramilitaries (the Ulster Volunteer Force, Ulster Defence Association and Red Hand Commando) had combined to form an umbrella group, the Joint Loyalist Military Command. Now public opinion was requiring them to re-form it for the purposes of laying down their weapons. In early October 1994 Sir Patrick Mayhew decided that 'hopeful days demanded hopeful measures' and took the usual step of sanctioning a meeting in the Maze prison between influential Loyalists and Loyalist paramilitary prisoners. He knew that the hard men inside needed to be consulted, otherwise there would be a risk that they might resume their campaign when eventually released. Their agreement having been given, on 13 October the umbrella group convened a press conference in a Loyalist community centre in north Belfast. Gusty Spence, a convicted terrorist who had founded the modern UVF, spoke for them all when he read out a statement declaring the commencement of a universal Loyalist ceasefire. 'We are on the threshold of a new and exciting beginning with our new battles being political battles fought on the side of honesty, decency and democracy.' Astonishingly for someone making an announcement of that magnitude, Spence publicly apologized to the loved ones of all the innocent victims who had been murdered by the Loyalists over the previous twenty-five years: 'In all sincerity we offer abject and true remorse.'

Hume's response to the Loyalists' declaration was to hail it as:

A good day for Northern Ireland. It takes us well forward because now we have a situation where human life is not at risk in Northern Ireland. That's a very valuable situation. It's very definitely a new beginning in view of the terrible tragedies of the past twenty-five years. Today being a new beginning is a day we should remember all of those people who have lost their lives and their families. Let us hope they will be the last people on our island to do so, because this has being going on for centuries. If we are going to begin a new era we should all leave the past behind us, because we've all got things to complain about in the past about other people. All that does is keep the problem alive. Let's now look to the future and reach a new agreement.

Soon he was on the phone to his American contacts, pulling strings to secure visas for Spence and the Progressive Unionist Party leader, David Ervine, to enable them to visit the United States. That in itself was an act of remarkable Christian forgiveness, considering that only a few months earlier Hume had been high on the Loyalist paramilitaries' list of assassination targets.

That formal stand-down was almost as significant as the IRA declaration just forty-three days earlier. Accepting the Loyalist ceasefire as also being permanent, Albert Reynolds described the announcement is marking the 'closing of a tragic chapter in our history. It is the dawn of a new era.' To cement it he invited Spence and other paramilitary leaders to Dublin for talks. On receiving the news of the ceasefire, relayed to him at the Conservative Party conference, John Major commented: 'Another piece of the jigsaw has fallen into place.' Knowing the announcement had brought the previously unimaginable one step nearer, when making his set-piece speech to the party faithful he generously praised the efforts being made by Paddy Mayhew and Albert Reynolds. For John Hume there was not a single word of thanks.

The Loyalist ceasefire declaration nudged events forward a further step. Immediately it was announced, ministers began to talk publicly of the prospects for there being a 'working assumption' that the IRA ceasefire was permanent. Significantly, they had also begun to speak of a 'talks process', not just a 'peace process'. The Downing Street Declaration had given the first sign to the paramilitaries that if they gave up violence they could get into the political process within three months; at the outset of the IRA ceasefire Major had reaffirmed that offer, saying that if the Republicans made clear they had given up violence for good, 'We could be talking at or around Christmas time.'

The IRA's reluctance to advance from a position of 'indefinite' to 'permanent' ceasefire had left an obstacle in the way of a date being set for the start of that dialogue. Now, however, with the Loyalist terror gangs no longer posing a threat to the Provisionals, it had become prudent for the Cabinet to assume that the IRA were unlikely to return to a campaign of violence. Accordingly, on 21 October Major visited Belfast to declare in a wide-ranging speech to businessmen in the Europa Hotel that he was willing to make a 'working assumption' that the IRA ceasefire was intended to be permanent. Having backdated the necessary three-month quarantine period to the announcement of 31 August, he was able to pledge that preliminary talks with Sinn Fein could commence before Christmas. Additionally he announced the lifting of the eleven-year exclusion orders banning Gerry Adams and Martin McGuinness from mainland Britain, and the opening of all border roads. Delighted at the news, Hume told journalists: 'This is the first day on which I can say that the entire Northern Ireland situation, both political and economic, is centre stage. Now we should all use our energies to take advantage of it. Particularly in the economic sense.'

An opportunity for Hume to help take the peace process a stage further came in Dublin at the Forum for Peace and Reconciliation. Very much Hume's brainchild, the Forum had its origins in the Council of Ireland which Hume had first mooted in 1972. Officially foreshadowed in paragraph 11 of the Downing Street Declaration, the Peace Forum was to be run along the lines of his New Ireland Forum, which had begun deliberating in 1983. Even so, there was no real sense of *déjà vu* for the 300 diplomats, church leaders and politicians present at the opening ceremony in Dublin Castle on 28 October who heard Hume speak of 'working for peace'; for whereas the task of the New Ireland Forum had been to devise economic plans and constitutional options, the principal purpose of the Peace Forum was to bind Sinn Fein ever more tightly into the political process and thereby to help that party's transition into normal political life. Hosted by the Irish government, the Forum was an open-ended undertaking which was expected to go on for months, if not years.

Hume threw himself into the deliberations, diligently flying to Dublin every Friday from wherever he was in the world in order to participate in the Forum's weekly meetings. Not wishing to be seen to be having contact with Sinn Fein, the British government refused to send any representatives to the Forum. Similarly, the Ulster Unionists would not participate. Despite their absence the Forum included most of the parties in the island of Ireland – including the Workers' Party and the Alliance Party – and they could not stop Sinn Fein and the Republic's political parties from exchanging ideas.

In the first plenary session of the Peace Forum, Hume spelt out his own philosophy:

> It seems incredible that we have taken so long to get to this point, of actually talking to each other about our differences. It would be even more incredible if we were to leave this table prematurely, without resolving those differences. I believe that however long it takes, however difficult the issues, whatever hiccups there may be along the way, we must not leave this table until our differences are resolved.
>
> If we are to succeed in resolving our differences, then we must face those differences honestly and directly. There is little point in either of us saying to the other, 'We cannot change, so you must.' Neither of us can change what we are. What we can, and must, change are our attitudes, our intolerance of difference, our repeated pushing of difference to the point of division. We must begin by accepting each other for what we are, accepting that we each have an absolute right to be what we are and that we cannot, either of us, change what we are.

All the while steps were being made towards reconciliation. On the anniversary of the Greysteel massacre several hundred people stood solemnly in the rain outside the Rising Sun bar, some in tears, as a memorial plaque was unveiled and the names of the eight people murdered there were read out. A Protestant dele-

gation from the Shankhill service consoled those Catholics who
earlier had been at a service in memory of those who had died in
the Frizzell's fish shop explosion. In a moving speech, Hume
praised the people of the Shankhill and Greysteel: 'The people of
Greysteel and the people of the Shankhill have shown a great
example to everyone. Given the terrible suffering that they have
been through, they have shown great forgiveness and great willingness to leave the past behind them. That is the attitude that
everybody has to learn in this society.'

Anxious that the momentum towards a lasting peace should
not be lost, in early November 1994 the Irish government
announced that as a goodwill gesture several IRA prisoners would
be released before Christmas. But almost immediately the Justice
Minister, Maire Geoghegan-Quinn, had to rescind that conciliatory decision as a consequence of a maverick IRA gang raiding
a Newry post office. The embarrassing volte-face was itself overwhelmed by the consequences of a scandal involving a priest
accused of child abuse. On 17 November Albert Reynolds was
forced to resign as Taoiseach when an Ulster TV programme
Suffer the Little Children disclosed that a law officer Reynolds
had just appointed as President of the Supreme Court had been
slow in processing extradition warrants against a Catholic priest
who had been accused of abusing children. In protest against
Reynolds's error of judgement, Dick Spring led the Labour
Party out of the coalition government. The public having no
enthusiasm for a general election, for a while Fianna Fáil were
able to stagger on in office with Bertie Ahern as their leader.
However, this could only be a temporary measure, and the prospect of a government being formed by Fine Gael with John Bruton
as Taoiseach initially caused much concern to the Sinn Fein
leadership.

Whereas Reynolds had been a good ally to the Republicans and
had been putting pressure on London to speed the talks process
along, Fine Gael were known to be closer to the Unionist position.
Unlike Fianna Fáil, they had historically been absolutely committed to the concept of Unionist consent; they had persistently
opposed the early release of prisoners, maintaining that prisoners
should be released only when arms and explosives were surren-
dered; and for some ten years they had been recommending the
removal or amendment of Articles 2 and 3 of the Irish constitution.

For twenty-five years Bruton had been denouncing Republican violence; indeed, his attacks on Sinn Fein had been such that he had gained the name 'John Unionist'. Hume hastened to reassure Adams and McGuinness that the change of governing party might actually be beneficial to the talks process because it would reassure the Unionists. If anything, the change of government which did take place gave the process a fresh impetus. Encouraged by Hume, practically Bruton's first act on taking office on 16 December was to bury the hatchet and meet Adams at the Peace Forum, where he declared that the search for a durable peace settlement would be at the top of his agenda.

Hume's influence continued to make itself felt in London, too, where he had been urging the government to accelerate their response to the IRA ceasefire and commence talks with Sinn Fein without a delay. On 1 December, departing from tradition, John Major concentrated much of his speech at the Lord Mayor's banquet at the Guildhall on domestic rather than foreign affairs, and announced that those talks would begin before Christmas.[3] Accordingly he instructed his private secretary, Roderic Lyne, to send a letter of invitation to Gerry Adams. So it was that on 8 December – exactly 100 days since the IRA ceasefire had begun – a Sinn Fein delegation led by Martin McGuinness boarded a battered black taxi in the Falls Road and headed off to Stormont. Symbolically, as it approached the parliament building, it swept past the statute of the statesman so revered by Unionists – Lord Carson.

Outside the premises which had for so long been associated with the Protestant ascendancy, McGuinness claimed: 'We are entering these discussions on the basis of our electoral mandate.' Nothing, in fact, could have been further from the truth. Even at the height of its influence in 1983 Sinn Fein had polled only 13.4 per cent of the vote. It had got to the negotiating table on the back of its support for the IRA's terror campaign, and its sympathies with that organization were easily identifiable from the fact that of the five persons on its delegation, three (including McGuinness himself) had at one time or another been members of the IRA.

As with the Peace Forum deliberations, the exploratory talks at Stormont were intended to familiarize Sinn Fein with the workings of democratic government. The atmosphere was tense and the discussions were 'careful'. Neither side wished to declare too many of its own cards – certainly not the British delegation, led by the deputy secretary at the Northern Ireland Office, Quentin Thomas, who was head of the British section of the Joint Liaison Group of officials who were drafting the Framework Document. It soon became apparent that the main issues which would have to be addressed in the weeks ahead were the release of 'political prisoners' and the decommissioning of illegally held weapons. That the meeting was taking place at all was a demonstration of the barely credible pace of events during the previous few months.

Hume was overjoyed that these historic deliberations at Stormont had begun. On the phone from the United States he gleefully told the BBC's *World at One* programme:

> Well, I'm very pleased because it's a very important step in the peace process. I am hoping that now that we will move swiftly into dialogue involving both governments and all parties because that is the real dialogue at the end of the day which faces us with the real challenge which is reaching agreement. We all recognize that reaching agreement is not going to be easy. Because you don't wipe out in a week the prejudices and distrusts that have gone on for centuries. But while we are working at that – and that will require what I have described as a 'healing process' – we can work together on the common ground which is economics. From that we will break down the barriers and make the difficult process of political agreement easier. A year ago no one would have forecast that we could be where we are today. I think that minds will keep concentrated on the ultimate objective of reaching a lasting agreement for the first time this century.

Since the ceasefire had been announced there had been a powerful lobby at work in the United States. Irish American businesspeople were getting together, in much the same way as the Jews in America had traditionally organized themselves to pour investment into Israeli. To coordinate efforts to promote American investment in Ireland, the President appointed the retiring Democratic leader in the Senate, George Mitchell, as his special adviser for economic initiatives. Meanwhile, in addition to his personal crusade to bring lasting peace to Northern Ireland, John Major was also endeavouring to put himself at the forefront of efforts to attract foreign investment to the province. To that end he had ordered a large international investment conference to be convened in mid-December in Belfast's Europa hotel. His intention was that the two-day event would not only help consolidate the peace but would also change perceptions of Northern Ireland.

Major would be hosting the conference himself, but as the time was not quite ripe for British ministers to meet with Sinn Fein representatives it had been decided to ban Sinn Fein from attending. American involvement was considered to be crucial to the conference's success, yet it was steadily becoming apparent that the event might become something of an embarrassment because angry US business executives were hinting that they would not bother to cross the Atlantic unless Sinn Fein was invited. They regarded the snubbing of Sinn Fein as proof that discrimination in Northern Ireland was still continuing. To prevent such absenteeism, Hume contacted the White House, while Gerry Adams phoned Jean Kennedy Smith in Dublin, both acting with the intention of putting pressure on the British government. It worked. The decision to exclude Sinn Fein was rapidly scaled down. Six elected Sinn Fein councillors from Derry and Belfast would be allowed to attend – although only for a few hours when Major was not present.

To Sinn Fein that was unacceptable. In the absence of a full and open invitation they organized a demonstration against the conference, complaining that its delegates were being treated as 'second-class citizens'. Despite the Sinn Fein boycott the conference saw the signing of a significant Anglo-American agreement to link businesses in the province with US research and development projects. This deal followed hard on the heels of a pledge by Washington to increase its annual contribution to the International Fund for Ireland. Furthermore, the European Parliament had just approved the aid package for the province which Hume had outlined to Jacques Delors in October – although the Eurocrats had slashed the total funding from £800 million to £240 million.

The Europa had been the ideal venue for the international investment conference. Bombed dozens of times during the Troubles, now recently lavishly refurbished with gleaming glass and marble it was a potent reminder of the change that peace had brought to Belfast. On the Lagan waterfront a multi-million-pound concern hall was taking shape. House prices were rising. The province as a whole was benefiting from a tourist boom. Cross-border air routes were being expanded. Already the opening of a cross-border link between the Shannon and the County Fermanagh waterways had increased river traffic. In Derry and Belfast taxi drivers told me that an initial wave of French and German 'white-knuckle riders' who had come to observe the immediate aftermath of the Troubles was being succeeded by a broader range of tourists. Increasing numbers of people from the South were making the journey North. For the first time in twenty-five years Dubliners went to Belfast to do their Christmas shopping.

With every week and month that had passed since the declaration of the ceasefire the roots of the peace had grown stronger and there had been less danger of the plant withering. Belfast had become a city reborn. In its pubs the security cameras and grilles were being taken down. Between the Falls Road and the Shankhill, the gates of the peace line which had once constituted an unbridgeable divide had now come to be a crossing-point. On New Year's Eve there was a tremendous atmosphere of hope and celebration. With torchlight processions and singing the two divided communities took their first steps towards each other. They prayed the New Year would be the start or a new era.

As a first tentative step towards the eventual withdrawal of all the 18,500 troops from Northern Ireland, British soldiers had stopped patrolling the streets of Derry just three weeks after the IRA ceasefire had been declared. Another milestone was reached on 15 January 1995 when for the first time in twenty-five years troops ceased to patrol the streets of Belfast in daylight hours.

In his speech to the Lord Mayor's banquet in November 1994, John Major had also announced that the British government would be having talks with the political representatives of the Loyalist paramilitaries with the intention of drawing them out of violence and into the democratic mainstream. On the very next day, the anniversary of the Downing Street Declaration, that meeting with the Loyalists took place. To the Republicans it seemed unfair that Whitehall was happy to talk to the Loyalists, whereas its attitude to any dealings with Sinn Fein remained reticent and unenthusiastic. The Loyalist paramilitaries had only a few locally elected councillors; not only did Sinn Fein have many more, in terms of having an electoral mandate it was unique in so far as it was an all-Ireland party. Annoyed by this imbalance,

Hume and Adams issued a joint statement just before Christmas in which they tackled the issues on which they considered the British government was stalling. They noted that fewer Republican prisoners had been released this Christmas than last. Declaring that throughout Nationalist Ireland there was a belief that London was being 'begrudging' about the entire peace process, they said there was a sense of frustration that British officials were not yet prepared to meet socially with Sinn Fein representatives.

In fact at the Northern Ireland Office there had long been an admiration for Gerry Adams's political skills. That judgement was made public on 30 January 1995 when BBC television broadcast a *Panorama* programme on the Sinn Fein leader. In it the former Secretary of State, Peter Brooke, praised him for his 'bravery' in persuading the IRA to lay down their weapons and seek a political settlement: 'That was a crucial step. He led them across that Rubicon. It was like many great acts of leadership, it was a courageous step.' The remarks angered many Unionist MPs, who interpreted them as evidence that the British establishment was taking an increasingly Nationalist position.

Those fears seemed to be confirmed a couple of days later when *The Times* published what it claimed to be a leaked draft of the much-delayed Framework Document. Written by Matthew d'Ancona, an assistant editor sympathetic to the Unionist cause, the front-page article, headlined 'Anglo-Irish plan for powerful joint body', claimed the British and Irish governments had drawn up a document 'that brings the prospect of a united Ireland closer than it has been at any time since partition in 1920'. It further claimed that London and Dublin were proposing a joint North–South authority with radical executive powers; a 'harmonization' of agriculture, trade, education and health policies; and a declaration of the right of everyone born in either jurisdiction to be part of the Irish nation. In inflammatory terms, the article stated: 'Crucially, the extent of the body's eventual responsibility is left open-ended. The new cross-border institution will be seen by many on both sides as the engine for the reunification of Ireland. The remit of the body will be dynamic, enabling progressive extension of its functions to new areas.'

The Unionists reacted furiously to what they considered the British government's 'betrayal'. Only the previous week John Major had promised them that the draft would contain 'no proposals' for joint authority. The phraseology of the draft – words such as 'expansion' and phrases like 'bodies growing' – confirmed their suspicions that the British government was preparing to put the province on the slippery slope to reunification. At Westminster there was a definite mood of crisis. Instantly the Unionists were beginning to threaten to vote against the government and force a general election. To steady nerves at Westminster, Major immediately convened a meeting of some eighty Tory MPs in his room, then took the unusual step of asking for a prime ministerial broadcast. In his televised address to the nation he declared that the 'prize of lasting peace must not be thrown away by fears that are unreal and accusations that are unreal' – a plea endorsed in subsequent broadcasts by opposition leaders Tony Blair and Paddy Ashdown.

This crisis was just the sort of political bombshell Hume had long feared might derail the peace process. He never said 'I told you so,' but its occurrence amply justified the demands he had been making over the previous few weeks for the Framework Document to be completed and published as soon as possible. Early on the morning *The Times* article appeared he was on the BBC radio *Today* programme using all his skills of dissection and analysis to discredit its claims:

At this sensitive period speculation is not only wrong, it's also very irresponsible. Let's stick to the facts which are that both governments have agreed that the ultimate objective has got to be an *agreement* among our divided people. Therefore, rather than having all this speculation, why don't both governments – particularly the British government – as speedily as possible now get all elected representatives around the table to begin the discussion process. Let's not forget either that my party has proposed, and the British government have proposed, that any agreement reached at the end of the day should be put to the people of the North and the people of the South for approval on the one day requiring a 'Yes' from each side. That reassures the Unionists' people. Let's not forget that. Let's stop all this and get to the table.

That day, and indeed for much of the rest of the week, he repeatedly appeared in television and radio studios, calming fears and restoring faith in the Framework Document – which even he had not yet seen. As the mood of crisis abated he still battled on, realizing that his efforts to reinforce the peace were providing him also with an opportunity to spread the gospel of his own philosophy. In a live debate with Ken Maginnis on Jonathan Dimbleby's television programme he reminded the audience that the SDLP was challenging the territorial mind-set and that the quarrel in Ireland was the last territorial quarrel in the European Union. It was only somewhat belatedly that he called on the IRA and Loyalist paramilitaries to give up their explosives as a first step towards total disarmament.

Fearing that the wheels might fall off the peace process if the efforts to reassure the Unionists failed, the British and Irish governments urged their Joint Liaison Group of officials to get the Framework Document ready for release. By Wednesday, 22 February the government publicists had made their arrangements. In a carefully choreographed press conference at Hillsborough Castle, John Major and John Bruton unveiled *Frameworks for the Future*. In two parts it outlined how a new democratically elected assembly could take far more control over the way Northern Ireland was governed, and showed how cooperative links between North and South might be to the mutual advantage of all. While Bruton pitched his introductory speech towards a wide Nationalist audience, Major sought to reassure the Unionists by emphasizing that what the discussion document contained were proposals, not plans. Safeguarding the Unionists against unwanted change would be a 'triple lock' mechanism of all-party agreement, parliamentary approval and a referendum on both sides of the border. He pleaded: 'Read it, study it, think about it, discuss it, talk about it, let it mature. Think of the overall prize that lies at the end.'

Their ardour dampened by the bitter sleeting rain that lashed the city, the Unionists' response to the consultation paper was subdued. Despite the basic Nationalist dynamic of the document, their anxieties were deflected by the Irish government's formal readiness to end the Republic's territorial claim to Ulster. They were even cheered by paragraph 33 of the document, which at last clarified that the two governments meant by cross-border 'harmonization' of policy. At variance with what *The Times* leak had predicted, that proposed harmonization was to be pragmatic rather than ideological, limited to certain aspects of policy in areas such as education and health. In the Commons that afternoon the document received a warm all-party welcome. Most of the Unionists stayed away from the chamber, but their muted response was very different from the outcry with which they had greeted the signing of the Anglo-Irish Agreement some ten years previously.[4]

The historic significance of the occasion did nothing to improve Hume's abilities as a parliamentary debater; indeed, his perform-ance that afternoon was dull and unoriginal. He seemed almost like a shy schoolmaster upstaged by his brightest pupils. In selfless support at Major, he told the House: 'This problem cannot be resolved without the participation and agreement of the Unionist people because of their geography and their numbers.'

The initial print run of *Frameworks for the Future* was 600,000. But although Hume had undoubtedly been the main architect of the historic understanding, he only received his copy a few minutes before the Belfast press conference began. The discourtesy did nothing to take the shine off his delight at reading its contents. So much of what he had devised and preached over the past thirty years was contained in those thirty-seven pages: the three strands, commitment to proportional representation, the cross-border bodies, all-Ireland referenda, and the allusions to Europe. But his greatest pleasure came from knowing that his basic philosophy had become common currency to the people of Northern Ireland. That evening, to gauge reaction to the document, *Newsnight* con-ducted a series of 'vox pop' interviews in a Belfast pub. One of those asked for his opinion was a Unionist. Using words he might never have thought of uttering a few months previously, the drinker told the film crew: 'Discussion harms nobody. What we need is an agreement.'

Within five days of the launch of the Framework Documents a European Commissioner had met Hume and agreed to provide Northern Ireland with an additional £126 million worth of devel-opment funding. North West International, the development agency which Hume had evolved from Derry Boston Ventures, had detected a tremendous new surge of interest in Northern Ire-land. To see what progress was being made, President Clinton's special economic adviser, George Mitchell, visited the province and with Hume's help met political and business leaders.

Determined to lock Sinn Fein ever more firmly into the peace process, Hume set about helping them to improve their links with Washington. In March 1995, Adams was due to fly across the Atlantic, notionally to open Sinn Fein's first office in the United States. Early that month, at Hume's request, Edward Kennedy had pleaded with Clinton to lift the ban on Sinn Fein's activities in the US. In Dublin, meanwhile, his sister – the US Ambassador, Jean Kennedy Smith – was putting pressure on the Irish government to exert some similar leverage. When, on the advice of Nancy Soderberg, Adams issued a statement announcing Sinn Fein's willingness to discuss decommissioning of weapons during future talks with the British government, Clinton immediately removed the ban.

The road was now clear for Hume to engineer a meeting between Adams and Clinton, and thereby confer a mantle of international respectability on Sinn Fein. The opportunity came on 16 March at a lunch in Congress hosted by Newt Gingrich, the House Speaker, and attended by Hume, Kennedy Smith, the Alliance Party leader John Alderdice, and seventy-five other guests. The US President approached Adams, shook his hand and had an animated five-minute discussion with him while a harpist played Irish folk songs.[5] At a St Patrick's Day dinner at the White House the following evening they met again. Adams gave the President a copy of his book, *Falls Memories*. Later Adams and Hume got up on stage for a rendition of 'A Town I Love so Well' – to the enthusiastic cheers of the 350 other guests, including Paul Newman.

In an astonishingly short period Adams had gained an entrée into American political society. For the best part of twenty years Hume had been going to the United States, often several times a year, making contacts and diligently developing them. Now he had selflessly given Gerry Adams the benefit of all those contacts. Officials at the Northern Ireland Office and Dr John Alderdice both told me that there was no greater example of Hume's selfless altruism than this.

A battalion at a time, British troops were now being withdrawn from Northern Ireland. It was a pattern which was inching the province even further along the path towards political normality. However, the question of decommissioning weapons remained unresolved. As far as the government were concerned, there could be no direct talks between British ministers and Sinn Fein until that matter had been resolved. Hume had apparently never given much thought to decommissioning, and indeed had rather fudged the question. Only in mid-April, when Sinn Fein and the IRA were becoming frustrated that no progress was being made towards direct talks, did he make a comment. Anxious as ever to get all parties around the negotiating table, he angrily called for the British government to set the issue aside, arguing that never in Irish history had there been a tradition of surrendering arms: instead, terrorist groups had let themselves wither on the vine and then – like Fine Gael – become respectable political parties. It was an impressive historical argument, but one which demonstrated how Hume could sometimes be so concerned with the tactics of encouraging peace that he overlooked the considerations of which the British government need to take account to maintain it.

Conclusion

John Hume's greatest achievement has been to end what could well be the last armed conflict between the British and Irish peoples. During his thirty years of involvement in public life he has transformed the political scene in Northern Ireland. His remarkably visionary outlook has influenced government thinking in Dublin and London, and has thus variously been incorporated into the Anglo-Irish Agreement, the Downing Street Declaration and subsequently the Framework Document. The Peace Forum concept which he pioneered is now taking a central role in the so-called 'healing process'. Such has been his influence that even Unionists have gradually come to accept his concepts and use his vocabulary. For example, by the late 1980s he had got Unionists to talk in terms of any agreement reached between themselves and the SDLP 'transcending' the Anglo-Irish Agreement.

Throughout the Troubles it was the working class – Catholic and Protestant – who suffered the most. By means of the contacts he has established in Europe and the United States, Hume has been able to garner valuable development funds for the province, and thereby helped alleviate hardship by creating jobs. To date he has been responsible for attracting some £500 million worth of investment to Northern Ireland.

His real strength during the Troubles was his personal integrity. It has served him well. During his talks with Gerry Adams in 1993–4 when many, even within his own party, doubted his political judgement he was trusted because he was straightforward and honest. Hume also deserves a medal for his courage. During the 1980s he had been on the IRA's death list. Then, while he was engaged in the Hume–Adams talks, Loyalists named him as an assassination target. It would be naïve to assume that as time goes on the risk of his being assassinated will totally disappear. The future danger will come not from mainstream Loyalist groups but from factions and mavericks who might resent the consequences of political change. Even more at risk is Gerry Adams. The celebrity status which he now enjoys as a 'war poet' – clutching a yuppie Filofax, appearing on television, making glamorous trips abroad and travelling by chauffeur-driven Mercedes – is undoubtedly causing resentment in Republican ranks. If he fails where his predecessor as Sinn Fein leader, Michael Collins, failed – in the attempt to remove British jurisdiction from Ireland for good – he might be assassinated as a traitor to the Republican cause.

During the Troubles, Hume battled against seemingly impossible odds. But, like every successful politician, he was lucky. He was fortunate that the Unionists were unable to produce a leader as visionary, talented and resourceful as himself. He was also fortunate that one by one the SDLP's founder members had left the party and thereby deprived it of any heavyweight leadership challengers.

His political career has by no means been error-free. Ian Paisley was not the only 'wrecker' during the Troubles. In the early 1970s Hume had been at the forefront of the SDLP's attempts to bring down Stormont. It should be remembered, too, that, under Hume's leadership, in 1982 the SDLP boycotted the Assembly. Ten years later a crucial interparty agreement might well have been reached had it not been for Hume's refusal to allow the SDLP to participate. As for the SDLP, although Hume had continuously preached a gospel of non-sectarianism, he had failed to detach the party from its image of a Catholic Nationalist organization. He has done nothing to encourage Catholics to join the RUC. Nor, observes the Alliance Party leader John Alderdice, has he managed to win the trust of a significant section of the Protestant community.

Despite being well travelled and carrying scarcely any ideological baggage which would cloud his political judgement, Hume could be painfully provincial in outlook – especially in his dealings with the British government. He was apt to forget that Whitehall had wider considerations with which it had to contend. Being a Derry man was also sometimes a handicap. Archbishop Robin

Eames told me: 'At times I have felt he has lacked definite knowledge of feelings and experiences beyond his city. As bishop there for some years I too was conscious that what worked in the northwest did not automatically apply elsewhere. There have been times when John has made the mistake of assuming that the rest of the province would feel precisely the same as his city.' Other sceptics, such as Reverend Martin Smyth MP, have told me that although they are full of praise for the ceasefire Hume has brought about, they doubt whether he has worked out in his mind what the constitutional future of Northern Ireland should be.

By the time of the next general election, John Hume will be aged sixty. Although he has never liked Westminster, he has stayed on there as an MP in order to achieve a permanent ceasefire. Now that peace has been attained he has disclosed to his closest advisers that he intends to stand down as MP for Foyle, but to continue to lead the SDLP as an MEP – just as he did between 1979 and 1983. The battle to decide who shall succeed him as MP has already commenced. Hume's preferred successor is the party chairman, Mark Durkan; however, there are some within the SDLP who believe Denis Haughey, Hume's long-serving European researcher, has a fairer claim.

Freedom from constituency duties will enable Hume to concentrate more on his efforts on strengthening Northern Ireland's links with Europe and the United States. Of stories that he has been offered lucrative jobs at the United Nations and in Europe, Hume said to me: 'I have had it suggested to me but not in any clearly formulated sense. What I have been getting is a lot of international awards. The International League of Human Rights gave me the peace award at the United Nations. I've had offers of doctorates from American universities. I already have five, but I've been offered another four. After what I've been through recently it takes a lot out of one.'

As a reward for his public service, on retiring from the Commons, Hume might even be elevated to the House of Lords, as Gerry Fitt was. John Hume has selflessly said that the only reward he wants for his years of struggle is peace. That now having been achieved, he deserves to win the Nobel Peace Prize for his great acts of Christian leadership.

Notes

Chapter 1   Citizen John

1 *Commonweal*, 14 December 1984 and 21 October 1994.
2 Bradley, et al, *Rosemount*, pp. 125–7.
3 *The Times*, 10 February 1995.

Chapter 2   Civil rights leader

1 B. White, *John Hume: Statesman of the Troubles*, Blackstaff, 1984, p. 31.
2 Ibid., p. 37.
3 Ibid., p. 38.
4 L. de Paor, *Divided Ulster*, Penguin, 1970, pp. 156–7.
5 White, *John Hume*, p. 69.
6 *Daily Express*, 12 September 1969.

Chapter 3   Stormont

1 *Daily Mirror*, 17 January 1969.
2 *Irish Press*, 25 August 1970.
3 *Daily Telegraph*, 21 April 1969.
4 Ibid.
5 *The Times*, 22 July 1969; *Daily Express*, 23 July 1969.
6 H. Wilson, *The Labour Government, 1964–70*, Penguin, 1971, pp. 870–8.
7 *The Times*, 31 October 1970.
8 *Evening Standard*, 20 October 1971.

9 *The Times*, 19 August, 7 September, 20 November 1971.
10 Quoted in *Guardian*, 7 November 1971.

Chapter 4   Labours of Sisyphus

1 *Daily Telegraph*, 31 July 1972. *Sunday Tribune*, 4 September 1994.
2 J. Haines, *The Politics of Power*, Coronet, 1977, pp. 124–31.
3 C. Keena, *Gerry Adams*, Mercier Press, 1990, p. 1.
4 *Guardian*, 11 September 1972.
5 White, *John Hume*, p. 158; *Sunday Times*, 20 January 1974.
6 S. Wichert, *Northern Ireland since 1945*, Longman, 1991, pp. 165–6.
7 J. Bowyer Bell, *The Irish Troubles*, Gill & Macmillan, 1993, pp. 411–18; *Guardian*, 27 May 1974.
8 *Guardian*, 12 November 1974, 21 January 1975; *Daily Telegraph*, 2 November 1974.
9 *Daily Telegraph*, 3 February 1976.

Chapter 5   Martini politician

1 *Daily Telegraph*, 19 April 1974.
2 White, *John Hume*, pp. 183–5.
3 *Guardian*, 4 July 1978.

4   *Cork Examiner*, 9 June 1990; White, *John Hume*, p. 194.
5   *Financial Times*, 24 June 1977.
6   *Guardian*, 30 November 1970.

Chapter 6   Humespeak

1   *Guardian*, 9 September 1976.
2   *The Times*, 21 September 1977.
3   *Daily Telegraph*, 22 June 1978; *The Times*, 22 June 1978.
4   *Daily Telegraph*, 1 December 1979.
5   *Sunday Times*, 10 December 1979, 6 January 1980.
6   Wichert, *Northern Ireland*, p. 187.
7   *Financial Times*, 19 June 1981.
8   *Guardian*, 11 December 1981.
9   Ibid., 12 August 1982.
10   Ibid., 2 October 1982.
11   *The Times*, 30 May 1983.
12   Ibid., 16 March 1983.
13   Ibid., 6 June 1983.

Chapter 7   Squaring the circle

1   *Guardian*, 18 July 1984.
2   *Daily Telegraph*, 19 August 1983; White, *John Hume*, pp. 253–7.
3   *Guardian*, 30 January 1984; *Daily Telegraph*, 30 January 1984; *Guardian*, 20 June 1984; *The Times*, 20 June 1984.
4   *Financial Times*, 25 June 1984; *Daily Telegraph*, 25 June 1984.
5   *The Times*, 24 May 1984.
6   *Guardian*, 26 November 1984.
7   Ibid., 28 January 1985; *Sunday Times*, 10 February 1985; *Financial Times*, 12 February 1985.
8   *Daily Mail*, 26 February 1985.
9   *Guardian*, 26 February 1985.

10   *Observer*, 27 April 1986.
11   Wichert, *Northern Ireland*, pp. 194–5.
12   *The Times*, 14, 16 November 1985.
13   Ibid., 30 November 1985.
14   *Daily Telegraph*, 25 January 1986.
15   *Observer*, 27 April 1986.
16   *Financial Times*, 24 November 1986; *Guardian*, 24 November 1986.
17   *Financial Times*, 30 January 1987; *Guardian*, 30 March 1987, 13 June 1987.

Chapter 8   'No selfish strategic interest'

1   *The Times*, 13 January 1988; *Sunday Times*, 4 December 1994.
2   *The Times*, 18 July 1988.
3   *Guardian*, 29 March 1988, 22 August 1988.
4   *Financial Times*, 28 November 1988.
5   *Sunday Times*, 4 December 1994.
6   *Daily Telegraph*, 23 March 1990.
7   *Sunday Times*, 4 December 1994.
8   BBC1, *Panorama*, 30 January 1995.
9   *Sunday Times*, 4 December 1994.
10   Ibid., 1 March 1992.

Chapter 9   Hume–Adams talks

1   *The Times*, 12 October 1992; W. D. Flackes and S. Elliott, *Northern Ireland: A Political*

Directory 1968–1993, Blackstaff, 1994, p. 106.
2 *Sunday Times*, 4 December 1994.
3 *The Times*, 26 April 1993; *Guardian*, 20 September 1993.
4 *Guardian*, 14 January 1994.
5 *Sunday Times*, 4 December 1994.
6 *The Times*, 26 October 1993, 28 October 1985; BBC1, *Panorama*, 30 January 1995.
7 Flackes and Elliott, *Sunday Times Magazine*, 6 March 1994.
8 *Daily Telegraph*, 16 December 1993.
9 *Sunday Times*, 4 December 1994.
10 *Guardian*, 2 February 1994; *Observer*, 6 February 1994; *Sunday Times*, 18 December 1994.
11 *Guardian*, 21 February 1994; *Observer*, 17 March 1994.
12 *Sunday Times*, 27 March 1994.
13 Ibid., 3 April 1994; *Guardian*, 31 March 1994.
14 *Observer*, 22 May 1994.
15 *The Times*, 31 August 1994.
16 BBC1, *Panorama*, 30 January 1995.

Chapter 10 *Nobel candidate*

1 *The Times*, 26 September 1994.
2 BBC Radio Four, *The World Tonight*, 12 October 1994.
3 *The Times*, 15 November 1994.
4 Ibid., 23 February 1995.
5 Ibid., 17 March 1995; *Sunday Times*, 19 March 1995.

Bibliography

Newspapers and journals

Belfast Telegraph
Boston Herald
Commonweal
Cork Examiner
Daily Express
Daily Mail
Daily Mirror
Daily Telegraph
Evening Standard
Financial Times
Fortnight
Guardian

Independent
Irish Independent
Irish Press
Irish Times
Observer
Sunday Business Post
Sunday Republican
Sunday Times
Sunday Tribune
The Times
Washington Post

Books

K. Bloomfield, *Stormont in Crisis*, Blackstaff, 1994

J. Bowyer Bell, *The Irish Troubles*, Gill & Macmillan, 1993

J. Bradley, H. Gallagher and B. Canning, *Rosemount: The Village and the School 1891–1991*, Cityprint, 1991

J. Callaghan, *A House Divided*, Collins, 1973

A. T. Culloty, *Nora Herlihy*, Irish League of Credit Unions, 1990

L. de Paor, *Divided Ulster*, Penguin, 1970

P. Devlin, *Straight Left*, Blackstaff, 1993

G. FitzGerald, *All in a Life*, Macmillan, 1991

W. D. Flackes and S. Elliott, *Northern Ireland: A Political Directory 1968–1993*, Blackstaff, 1994

J. Haines, *The Politics of Power*, Coronet, 1977

HMSO, *Northern Ireland*, 1992

J. Holland, *The American Connection*, Viking, 1987

C. Keena, *Gerry Adams*, Mercier Press, 1990

B. Lacy, *The Siege of Derry*, Eason, 1989

I. McAllister, *The Northern Ireland Social Democratic and Labour Party*, Macmillan, 1979

D. McKitterick, *Endgame*, Blackstaff, 1994

E. Maloney and A. Pollak, *Paisley*, Poolbeg, 1986

Maynooth College, *Celebrating 200 Years*, Maynooth College, 1995

T. Ryle Dwyer, *Charlie: The Political Biography of Charles J. Haughey*, Gill & Macmillan, 1987

B. White, *John Hume: Statesman of the Troubles*, Blackstaff, 1984

W. Whitelaw, *The Whitelaw Memoirs*, Aurum, 1989

S. Wichert, *Northern Ireland since 1945*, Longman, 1991

H. Wilson, *The Labour Government, 1964–70*, Penguin, 1971

Index